Publisher information

Rob Rich

ebook@ob.net.au

Contributions by Hannah Moore & Lisa Tyree

Edited by Dr Bob Rich

Cover by Heidi Jenkins

Date 20th September 2020

To order a copy of Exploring Your Intelligent Body go to www.eyib.com.au

This book is designed to assist a person to explore how their body works and help them change limiting patterns. If what you are doing creates pain, stop and seek help from a medical professional.

ISBN: 978-0-6450080-1-2

CONTENTS

	Page
Acknowledgements	7
Introduction	9
Introduction to Ortho-Bionomy	11
Chapter 1 - Your ability to self-correct	19
Chapter 2 - Working with your stress response	31
Chapter 3 - Sleep	49
Chapter 4 - How pain works	61
Chapter 5 - Working with the mind	73
Chapter 6 - Emotional self-care	91
Chapter 7 - Soul wisdom arrives in the space when we listen	109
Chapter 8 - Exploring your ability to self-correct	127
Chapter 9 - Diet and the self-corrective process	145
Chapter 10 - Bringing it all together	169
Chapter 11 - Personal development	175
Recommended Talks	187
References	188

ACKNOWLEDGEMENTS

If I see further it is because I am a dwarf standing on the shoulders of giants
Isaac Newton

This book is the end result of the work of many people, each contributing their time, wisdom and willingness to explore how things work, and sharing that knowledge.

These include A. T, Still, the father of Osteopathy in the late 1800s, Arthur Pauls, who discovered what he termed Ortho-Bionomy in the mid 1970s, to my instructors Bruce Stark, Luann Overmyer, Eileen Jeboult and Lois Logan who have put up with me during my learning process.

Harry Palmer, who developed the Avatar course that greatly increased the pace of my personal development.

The thousands of clients who taught me so much during sessions over the last 20 years.

And Colleen, Luci, Nyree, Bodan and Jarvis who contributed in many ways over the last 20+ years.

I would also like to thank my father, Bob Rich, whose editing work massively improved the quality of this book, Lisa Tyree and Hannah Moore for their help and the chapters they have contributed, and Lani Paxton for a number of drawings throughout the book.

There are many others who have influenced how I think and have inspired me, two of whom are my sisters Anina and Natalie.

I would also like to thank Jessica Alhert, James, Chantel, and a special mention to Urban for the live music during the photo shoot for chapter 8.

Thanks Heidi from The Creative Frog for making the book look great.

This book is really a snapshot of how we can work with the body's amazing ability to self-correct. There is so much more to learn about how this process works and I hope this contributes to more people being interested in finding new ways to work in alignment with the natural laws of life.

Rob Rich
Sunshine Coast Qld 2020

INTRODUCTION

My life changed in January, 2000. For a couple of decades, I had had ongoing lower back pain, which ranged from a constant nagging ache to savage pain that would stop me doing anything. I had tried many things to find relief including chiropractic, massage, physiotherapy, and acupuncture, and got mostly short-term relief but nothing seemed to really change how my lower back functioned. Then on the recommendation of my sister, I had a session of Ortho-Bionomy. I was sceptical that something that I couldn't pronounce could produce a different result from everything else I had tried.

I was lying on a massage table fully clothed and Alison, the therapist, started pushing on points, then slightly bent me to one side and compressed my foot toward my hip.

The relief was incredible. My lower back softened and relaxed, for what felt like the first time in my life.

It made no sense that something so gentle could create such a big effect. How did this work and why, if this worked, wasn't everyone doing things this way?

The session continued and when I stood up my whole back felt different. I felt taller and was able to stand more comfortably. It occurred to me that I had to learn this modality even if it was only to know how to work with my own body.

Shortly after I attended my first class in Brisbane, and on learning about the principles, I recognised some similarities between the underlying principles of aikido, which I had trained in and Ortho-Bionomy.

That first session has led me to study Ortho-Bionomy for the last 20 years, and today I am learning more about how the body self-corrects than when I started.

This book is really a summary of what I have learnt about how the body self-corrects, some of the science that supports the ideas I have presented, and most importantly tools for you to play with, to help you discover things about yourself.

Your body is amazing. It performs miracles on a daily basis. It converts everything you eat into energy to keep you going, deals with all the microbes that want to use you as a food source, and it organises itself so you can move, lift and carry things under the constant force of gravity. When something goes wrong, it heals itself.

Take a moment to appreciate that last sentence. Imagine if your car or phone could heal itself. How cool would you think that was? Well, your body can and does with many things and with the right information we can extend how well the body can self-correct to include chronic musculoskeletal pain as well as physical and emotional traumas.

The ability to self-heal is incredible. The body is designed to return to a functional state, adapting to whatever illness or injury we have had.

This system relies on having the right information in order to resolve chronic pain and dysfunction. When this information isn't available, the body will struggle to return to a fully functioning state. Over time, our adaptions to past injuries accumulate, and this creates rigidity in the system. Ortho-Bionomy works by putting information into the nervous system that helps the body to recognise the dysfunction and how to unwind the tension patterns and become functional again.

In this book, you will find what factors inhibit the self-corrective process and what you can do to work with them.

Natural forces within us are the true healers of disease.
Hippocrates

My main focus in this book is on musculoskeletal pain, and the relationship between the emotions, the physical body and pain. There is a growing body of evidence supporting this holistic view of working with the body. Working only physically or only emotionally limits the success of a treatment modality. You might get some relief, but the condition may reoccur though time, like my periodic lower back pain 20 years ago.

We are a whole system, from our bones to our thought processes. We need to be able to put information into the nervous system in a way that connects to the level of the dysfunction and enables the mind/body to understand that dysfunction and stimulate the body to self-correct.

This book has many different exercises that offer you the opportunity to explore how your system functions. Some of these will work well for you and others won't. This is not because the exercise is ineffective, but because it is not what your nervous system needs at present.

Because there is so much research happening in multiple different fields, there will always be more to learn and discover, so I consider this to be an ongoing exploration. In the reference section, I have included some great talks by different researchers who look at different aspects I have examined as well as the numerous papers that support some of the ideas presented here.

A dysfunction can be physical, mental, emotional, or in a movement pattern, and therefore is not limited to a particular level of structure. For instance, lower back pain can be due to a physical dysfunction such as a rotated vertebra, which creates the sense of the lower back being unstable. The body then recruits the muscles around the joint to brace the area.

Alternatively, lower back pain could be associated with an emotional or mental dysfunction such as feeling fearful, feeling like a victim, or from a worry such as experiencing financial hardship, all of these cause stress hormones to be released in your body, this causes the psoas muscle in the lower back to contract, increasing the tension in the lower back.

So, this approach is really about being able to find what level to work on to assist the body/mind to reorganise itself to a more efficient way of functioning.

When we talk about the self-corrective process, we are looking at how we can stimulate the body to work in the way it is designed to. The body's ability to self-correct is what enables us to respond to the changing environment we live in. If that innate ability of the body is stuck, then something is inhibiting the process. To help the body, we need to identify what the dysfunction is and help the body become aware of what is happening. This is very different from trying to "fix" the dysfunction.

The value of working this way is that the body is an intelligent system and it learns how to become more efficient at self-correcting a certain dysfunction. In effect, it up-skills in that area.

With my clients, one of the milestones I look for is when someone, who has had chronic pain for quite a while, has become pain free and then feeling better, they overdo some activity they haven't been able to do for years. This will aggravate the original area and some pain will return, but after a night's sleep, it disappears. This means their system has enough information to self-correct the presenting dysfunction. We then move onto working with the posture, so the system becomes more stable under gravity when loaded. Postural work makes the body far more resilient.

If you don't want your clients to get better, then don't do postural work with them.
Arthur Pauls

Arthur Pauls, the Osteopath who developed Ortho-bionomy in the 1970s, used to say, "if you don't want your clients to get better don't do postural work with them."

So, with Ortho-Bionomy, we work with the posture right from the first session, but once a person is pain-free, the ability of the body to change posture increases as there is less fear of change within the system.

Even after 20 years I still find the ability of the body to self-correct to be amazing. It doesn't matter how long a dysfunction has been present, when the right information is put into the nervous system, the body can change incredibly quickly.

One of the most useful things about this approach is to stay curious about what is happening. Curiosity invites you to notice new things, and this new information may be the piece you need to unwind a dysfunction. So, as you read this book, stay curious, experiment with the exercises and see what you notice. Fine tune them to suit your mind/body.

AN INTRODUCTION TO ORTHO-BIONOMY

Ortho-Bionomy is a hidden treasure, a form of bodywork that has been around since the mid-1970s, yet few people have heard of it. Ortho-Bionomy is great for working with both acute and chronic painful conditions.

Ortho-Bionomy developed out of Osteopathy. As I mentioned before, the primary focus of Ortho-Bionomy is to stimulate the body's ability to self-correct.

There are no forced manipulations or painful techniques in Ortho-Bionomy, because we don't need them to assist the body to change. When you apply force or cause pain, the body is quite likely to treat this as a threat. This turns on the protective mechanism and focuses the awareness on minimising the likelihood of being injured. While this is happening, the nervous system is not paying attention to what it can learn about the dysfunction. Without the system learning how to self-correct the dysfunction, there is greater likelihood of the body returning to the same pattern and the painful condition recurring. When no force or pain is used in the treatment, the body can relax and feel safe. This is when the nervous system shifts into the right mode to notice new information, which is the internal version of being curious.

Ortho-Bionomy is non-invasive. You remain clothed during sessions. It is wholistic in that we work with the whole of the physical body, including the alignments of bones, tension in the muscles and fascia, the ligaments and the movement of fluids, and the interaction of suppressed emotions with the physical body. Ortho-Bionomy also works on the reflexive responses of the body, helping to balance the fight/flee response with the rest/digest response. It also works energetically on the patterns that you have built up in response to past experiences, injuries or negative beliefs.

This is done by working with your nervous system in order to increase awareness of the dysfunction(s), so your innate ability to self-correct can function. The Ortho-Bionomy practitioner's role is one of facilitating change by putting information about the dysfunction into the nervous system in a form that the body can understand.

This is a quite different approach from trying to "fix" the body. The body is complex systems within a complex system, so the likelihood of an external person having all the necessary information to actually fix you is fairly low. This is why it often takes so long for a dysfunction to change and remain stable long term using forced manipulations or painful techniques. The greater the complexity of the dysfunction, the more precise a forced manipulation needs to be in order to stimulate the system to change and the more likely the protective mechanism will lock down preventing change from occurring.

Of course, there are a few issues with attempting to impose change. Force or painful techniques can cause further injury. Also, the body can become more rigid after the session as it tries to prevent further pain. There is also an increased risk with conditions like osteopenia or osteoporosis that force can cause damage to the weakened bones.

In reality, what fixes the body is the body itself. Just as the band aid or stitches don't heal the wound, the forced manipulation doesn't fix your skeletal alignment. The change that occurs with a forced manipulation is that the skeletal system around the mobilised joint has to adapt to the force and this can stimulate the body to self-correct. This can also trigger the body's fear response, especially in the upper back, where a spike in stress hormones often occurs with a forced manipulation. The best approach I have found to working with skeletal misalignments is to put information into the nervous system and then get out of the way and let the amazing ability of the body to heal itself to do the rest.

This distinction means that the Ortho-Bionomy practitioner is not an expert on your body. It is more like having a conversation, exploring the dysfunction together, than being told the solution. This process of discovery means that when the body unwinds a dysfunction, it has learnt something and is therefore empowered to take a more active role in maintaining the more functional way of operating.

Ortho-Bionomy is principle-based, rather than technique based. This means, the practitioner adapts the techniques to meet your body. This is what is going to make the most sense to your nervous system. Like in a conversation, it can sometimes take time to work out what is the most effective way to present information. Some people like traction, others compression, some joints need information about the alignment of the bones, other joints need work on the ligaments to create more support for the joint before information about alignment can be used. Sometimes the trauma of an injury reduces the range of movement, so releasing that clears the physical limitation more effectively than working with the bones or muscles.

Ortho-Bionomy principles are useful for working with more than just your body. How we deal with conflict, how we organise ourselves within our relationships, how we work with other people, can all be influenced by incorporating the principles, and this will lead to increased awareness and improved interactions with others, or alternatively a way to approach things when something goes wrong.

The majority of people who choose to learn Ortho-Bionomy are from one of two groups: first, therapists who seek a way of working that is gentle on their own body, extending their working career, and giving better results for a broad range of painful musculoskeletal conditions they see in their clinic.

Second are people who, like myself, have had incredible results with Ortho-Bionomy and are keen to learn how it works. Ortho-Bionomy training is really a self-development process that increases your awareness from a structural level right through to the energetic level.

A change happens on a psychological level when you feel chronic pain or rigidity in your body dissolve effortlessly after years of trying many things. This change leads you to ask the question: if a long-term chronic condition can release without force, what else can I change by getting a better understanding of what the dysfunction really is?

How can I increase my awareness to find the information my system needs in order to self-correct?

HERE IS A QUICK SUMMARY OF THE ORTHO-BIONOMY PRINCIPLES

Structure Governs Function

From a bodywork perspective, we work with the skeletal structure, and your relationship with gravity. Getting your bones in alignment so they support your weight enables your body to move more efficiently.

A muscle spasm, for instance, is part of a compensation pattern for an unstable joint. The body recruits the muscles to create more stability. Working with the joints allows the body to become more stable and therefore the tension in the muscles is no longer required.

From a practitioner's perspective, understanding the structure of the body is the starting point, so we can explore how this current situation is the same or different from what we have noticed/experienced before in other clients, and in the same client previously.

As most of us have fairly similar things we do — walking, sitting, lying down — we will have some similar patterns, but as we do these things quite differently, there will be some patterns that we all have in common and some that are our personal adaptions to our experience, emotions, injuries, and lifestyle.

Function also affects the structure – if you repeatedly do the same action your body will try and become more efficient at that movement. This builds up functional patterns that can then interfere with movements that require a different range of motion. Ortho-Bionomy uses movement-based techniques to shift these patterns. This can be really important for athletes as training can create imbalances within the body that if left can lead to overuse injuries.

In a broader life perspective, if you create a structure that works for you, then you become more functional.

If there is dysfunction in an area of your life, assess its structure. In most cases, when things naturally evolve without a plan, there is little structure, which is fine unless it becomes dysfunctional. Taking some time to put a structure into place simplifies the situation and makes it more functional.

Structures do not have to be rigid or curtail creativity. Creating a framework so the repetitive parts of what you are doing can be done with minimal effort leaves the fine tuning or variations from the norm to be focused on. This creates greater stability and enables you to achieve more with less effort

The Rule of the Artery is Supreme

This idea dates back to A. T. Still, the father of Osteopathy in the late 1800s, and refers to the stagnation of fluids being a cause of disease. Fluids, especially lymph, require movement to flow efficiently. The modern take on this is, "Motion is Lotion."

In bodywork, fluids refer to air, blood flow, lymph, and life force.
Fluids are far more important to health than most people think — right up until they have a dysfunction of the system that moves fluid around the body.

In Ortho-Bionomy, we make the connection from the fluids to the fascial tension patterns that restrict fluid movements.

> *Fascia is a band or sheet of connective tissue, primarily collagen, which lies beneath the skin. It attaches, stabilises, encloses, and separates muscles, bones and other internal organs.*

We then look at why the fascia tension patterns are there. Often this relates to posture, which is how you use your bones to support your body weight under the constant force of gravity. Therefore, we take a wholistic approach and work at assisting the posture to become more efficient in order to help the fascia to relax and the fluids to move. There are also other causes for fluid retention that require different ways of working.

If you would like to test the idea that fluid movement matters, hold your breath. At a guess, within a couple of minutes you will have experiential clarity on the value of fluid movement to life.

The Body Has the Inherent Capacity to Heal and Balance Itself

The ability of the body to self-correct is also known as homeostasis and is fundamental to life. We simply do not have the capacity to understand what is happening in someone else's body in fine enough detail in order to fix it.
An example of this is that there is no such thing as standard anatomy. Just as we look different on the outside, we look different on the inside as well.

For example, you grow your bones in relationship to gravity, but your age, diet, ability to digest and absorb the nutrients you eat, the emotional environment you grew up in and currently live in, the impact of the activity you do and genetics all play a role in your skeletal development.

It takes anywhere from 15 to 25 years for the pelvis to fully ossify (turn to bone). If you are a couch potato it might take 25 years, while if you play sport, the impacts will speed up the process.

Each of us also constantly remodels our bones as we age: the angles of things like the neck of the femur change.
So, with all these variables, how can a practitioner really know with enough confidence that a forced movement will not cause injury?

It is really a testament to the resilience of the human body that there aren't more injuries from forced techniques and that when injuries do occur the body can often recover from them — unless the person is one of the really unlucky ones.

By working with the body's ability to self-correct, we avoid having to know. Since we don't use force, there is no risk of injury and the worst that can happen is no change to the underlying dysfunction. This shows that the information provided to the nervous system is not the information it needed to change the dysfunction.

One of the findings of pain research is that when the body feels safe, the intensity of pain reduces[32]. With Ortho-Bionomy, we find that when the body feels safe, the ability of the body to change dysfunctional patterns improves dramatically. Often a chronic condition that has been present for years can unwind quite quickly if the body feels safe and the right information is presented to the nervous system for it to make sense of the dysfunction.

Follow or join another person's energy while maintaining your own balance

From a bodywork perspective, this refers to holding your own space, both physically and energetically, while noticing what is happening for someone else. In a broader context, this refers to trying see things from another's perspective while remaining true to yourself, like experiencing how another person sees the world without losing your own inner perspective.

If you can see another person's perspective, you can then find where/how you can meet them. What do you have in common? People from opposing political parties often want the same end goals, for instance making the country a safe place to live, but they see that the only way to get to that goal is by very different means. Finding common ground allows you to connect and change dysfunction elegantly without losing yourself in the process.

Flow With Force, Do Not Resist It

In a bodywork sense, if you try and force the body to change, you have to overcome the body's protective mechanism by applying more force. The other approach is to understand that the body is functioning in the most efficient way it can at this time with the information it has.

So, for instance, a muscle that is tight is being recruited by the nervous system to create more support for the body. Pounding the muscle into submission is one way to work with this. A more efficient way is to recognise that the body is actively choosing to recruit that muscle, then investigate why this is necessary. When you change the underlying driver of the pattern, the muscle will no longer need to be recruited, and so the tension will release.

In a broader context, the same principle can make potential conflicts become fertile ground for personal growth. When you resist, you take a fixed position opposing all other options. This usually requires limiting your thinking about how to deal with the situation. If you study the situation without a fixed viewpoint, opportunities to change the situation on a much deeper level can often be found.

No problem can be solved from the same level of consciousness that created it.
Einstein

Soften Around the Tender Spot

One of the simple ways of demonstrating the way the self-corrective process works is to release muscle tension in the mid-neck (or other areas of the body) by softening around the sore point.

Find a sore point in the mid neck.
Bend your head toward the sore point using a combination of moving your ear to shoulder (lateral flexion) and nose to shoulder (rotation) and if the point is on the back area of the neck, you will need to add some chin to ceiling (extension). This movement should feel comfortable and soften the muscle under your finger.

Hang out there for 10 - 30 seconds, then straighten up and recheck the sore point. Has the level of pain or tension changed?

As we will see in the chapter on pain, a sense of safety reduces the intensity of pain. By softening around the tender spot, we take the load off the area, make it feel safe, and give information to the nervous system about the alignment of the bones underneath the contracted muscles. This allows the body to reorganise itself and releases the tension and pain.

Exaggerate the Preferred Position

When we talk about exaggerating the dysfunction, we are taking the load off the area by meeting the body as it is and then shifting it in the same direction a small amount, the size of which will vary depending on the body. However, this is comfortable and feels safe for the body to relax the muscular holding patterns around the joint. In the absence of the muscular tension, the opposing tension patterns in the ligaments that have been wound up by the misalignment are then able to pull the bone back into alignment.

In a broader context, exploring the dysfunction to enable a better understanding of what is happening is important in order to avoid recreating the situation. If we fail to fully understand the dysfunction, we will miss the subtler signs that the imbalance is still there and it will be more likely to recur. By taking the time to explore the dysfunction, we can learn from it. This greater awareness is the first step in allowing mental and emotional patterns to unwind as well.

Less is More

With Ortho-Bionomy, we work by putting specific information into the nervous system. We want the body to pay attention to feedback from the joint we are working with.

To do this, we apply a light compression into the joint once we have found the position that may help the body understand the dysfunction.

So, this is like dropping a pebble in a pond: the ripples are the information. If you throw a handful of pebbles in to the pond, the ripples become chaotic, and meaning is lost.

Since many ways of working with the body are aimed at changing what the muscles are doing, when you shift to working with the nervous system, the actual amount of work you need to do is greatly reduced.

The nervous system is sensitive, and too much information all at one time can overload it. Particularly if there is acute pain or trauma in the system, this causes the body to feel unsafe. The system then holds tension through the muscles to slow down the rate of change in order to protect itself.

So, we aim to give the right amount of stimulus, then allow the body to have time to integrate it. The body will have an initial change during the session, and this will continue for 2-3 days as the body reorganises itself.

For most people, a one-hour session of Ortho-Bionomy will be well within the body's capacity to deal with change without being overwhelmed.

No Pain to Release Pain

There is a difference between a "good" pain such as when we have feedback from an area in our body that has relaxed and is starting to move again after months or years of tension, and a "bad" pain when the body perceives a threat to it due to an external force being applied such as a stretch that is applied too fast, or sustained pressure on an area of tissue damage.

Often the use of painful techniques is aimed at creating an endorphin release, which initiates a healing response in the body. This may change some localised patterns but is unlikely to change the underlying conditions that are creating the painful dysfunctional or postural patterns in the body. For instance, having a massage therapist work with an elbow into the Iliotibial band (ITB) (the tough connective tissue band down the outside of the thigh), which is usually a very painful technique, may reduce tension short term but will need to be repeated often because that is a compensation pattern. The underlying driver of that pattern is distorted hip ligaments. If the hip ligaments are worked with and assisted to recoil, the tension through the ITB disappears within seconds.

Pain releases stress hormones into the body, which can make the body feel unsafe, particularly if there is a lot of pain already and therefore the body focuses on avoiding more pain or further injury. The protective mechanism turns on and the body prepares to resist. The opposite occurs when we avoid painful techniques in a session.

An added benefit of not using painful techniques is that the parasympathetic nervous system (the rest/digest response) is stimulated, which makes deeper sleep more likely, improves digestion and allows the body to recover from the stresses of everyday life.

In a broader perspective, if people feel safe, they will make far better decisions and be able to integrate socially in a far more harmonious way than when they are scared.

In chapter 3, we will look at the connection between fear and pain in a much more complete way.

No Attachment to an Outcome

As the human being is a complex system, there is no real way to predict how an individual is going to respond to a particular treatment. This is why a doctor may try multiple drugs to see which creates the least adverse responses. The complexity of the system means it is always an experiment.

The same holds true for bodywork in general and Ortho-Bionomy in particular, because we work by putting information into the system and we can't be sure how the system will respond until we do something and feel for the body's response.

So, in Ortho-Bionomy, we see it more like a conversation. How your body responds teaches us how to interact with your nervous system, this then informs us on how to fine tune what we are doing to meet your body more effectively. Of course, there are similarities between how your body responds and how other bodies respond, but keeping it as an exploration enables the practitioner to be more present and attentive to how you respond during the session.

The aim is to find what is driving the dysfunction and to work with that. The body changes quickly and effortlessly when we work with the driver of the dysfunction, and it is highly likely that the system will be stable and more efficient once it releases. This is why long-term chronic conditions can change quickly when working in this way.

If the body needs a particular piece of information, it doesn't matter how many years it has lacked it. Once you have created complex compensation patterns, these can remain fairly constant through time, although further impacts such as falls or car accidents can complicate things even more. The nervous system is always looking for how to reorganise itself to become more efficient. When this information is available, the body changes.

However, since we don't have complete knowledge of everything that is happening in someone else's mind/body, we are not sure what information the body needs until it starts to respond. So, for instance, if the symptom is a sore shoulder, several things could be creating that pain. By working in a structured way, we can use a process of elimination to offer the body different information, and feel for how it responds. This response may be muscles releasing, a rebound (the body pushing out against the gentle compression), a recoil (the body pulling in against gentle traction), changes in temperature, a pulsing, fascial unwinding (movement that originates in the body).

The key attitude is to not get attached to a particular outcome, but remain curious about the body's response.

In a broader context, if we are attached to a particular outcome, we are more likely to use force, and experience tunnel vision. This means we are more likely to miss more subtle information that would help us fine tune what we are doing to meet the body in a way that would stimulate the self-corrective process.

We can best stimulate the self-corrective response by approaching the dysfunction holistically, and acknowledging that we do not know how a person's healing journey is going to proceed.

All Levels of the Work Embody the Principles

This means we approach the dysfunction in a coherent way.

In Ortho-Bionomy, we are focused on what level the dysfunction is at and how we can interact with it. So, when nothing works, we ask questions such as:

- What level is the dysfunction at, e.g., is it in the muscle? Joint capsule? An emotional holding pattern? A functional pattern associated with repetitive use?
- How does this dysfunction fit in with the rest of the body?
- What are the compensation patterns?
- What is driving this dysfunctional pattern?
- How can we work with these patterns to introduce new information in order to stimulate change?

The answer to these questions is in how your body responds. If your system responds really well to traction, then the practitioner will pay more attention to your ligaments and fascia before working with joint alignment.

With Ortho-Bionomy, when what we are doing is not working – there is no response from the body, we lighten our contact, look for where the body has the capacity to change, and build trust so the body feels safe enough that it can release the protective mechanism. Paying attention to what information other areas of the body respond to can also give us more information about what the nervous system likes, we can then offer this form of information to the area of dysfunction.

In challenging cases, it is a bit like finding the right language to communicate in. This might start off with information about skeletal alignment, keeping in mind that repressed emotion, particularly trauma, can make all change feel unsafe. If this is the case, then creating safety becomes the priority before physical change is possible.

A great example of this is working with a whiplash injury.

The protective mechanism in a whiplash is really important and techniques that cause pain will make the body feel unsafe, so holding the muscular tension makes sense for it. This in turn reduces movement. Often when I work with someone with whiplash I will start in the pelvis so the body has a chance to experience that it is alright to release and move without it threatening the system.

By the time we get to the neck (within the first session) the body trusts it is OK to relax. We then support the neck in the shape it is in because the exaggeration of rigidity is stillness. This support takes the load off the neck and slowly as the body feels safe (usually 30-45 seconds), the nervous system starts to try and work out what the underlying dysfunction is. Often, with whiplash, the 6th cervical vertebra (C6) is jammed in a forward position, which changes how the rest of the neck functions. This creates a head position that is forward of the body, with tension up the neck. Once the neck feels safe and the neck is placed in a position to take the load off the C6 vertebra, the body can reorganise the alignment of the vertebra and the whole neck relaxes back into a more functional position.

In a broader context, being consistent with your approach to life creates a sense of safety for people who are in some sort of relationship with you. This creates a life where you create trust and are dependable.

CHAPTER 1.
YOUR ABILITY TO SELF-CORRECT

YOUR ABILITY TO SELF-CORRECT

Have you ever had the experience that you have overdone it with physical exertion and gone to bed with pain, yet woke up the next day to find that the body has reorganised itself and the pain is gone?

That is how the body is meant to work. When pain stays around, the body needs help to understand how to reorganise itself. In this book, we look at what can get in the way of the self-corrective process, and we will explore ways of working with these things so your body can reorganise itself in a more efficient way. Try the different exercises and see how your body responds.

How Your Body Works

Your body/mind is an amazing, complex system made up of different components. It has an innate intelligence that coordinates and controls your internal environment to enable you to survive and hopefully thrive under challenging conditions. The constant force of gravity, the constant presence of microbes, stresses from mental, emotional and physical challenges — all need to be countered by your system. In general, it does this incredibly well.

Your self-corrective process is part of how your body deals with these challenges.

Another name for the self-corrective process is homeostasis. All the systems in your body have sensors and feedback mechanisms in place to allow your body to maintain itself within a narrow band, which enables you to survive. For instance, your body temperature is on average 37 degrees C. However, variations of 0.5 degrees are normal on a daily basis, with a low at 4 am and a high at 6 pm.[2] This range allows all the biological functions in the body to continue to function. Your survival relies on your ability to maintain this normal range.

Your body also has the capacity to self-correct on a musculoskeletal level, as well as on a mental and emotional level. We are designed for this to happen, and it is an anomaly when it doesn't.

As a species, humans in general really suck at dealing with emotional pain, and there is an evolutionary reason for this. If you are walking through a forest and your best mate gets eaten by a bear, you don't stop to grieve for him then and there. Your flight response is triggered and you run as fast as you can. Then later, when you feel safe, you have a ceremony to grieve for your friend.

That is what should happen, but we live in a fear-dominated society, with whole industries set up to keep us anxious and worried. The cost of doing this is illness — physically, mentally and emotionally.

With some people, it is preferable to experience physical pain rather than deal with the underlying emotional pain. Examples are people who cause harm to themselves by cutting, and those who use opioids, alcohol and other drugs to try and avoid emotional pain. However, it is also common for people to feel physical pain such as in the lower back as part of resisting overwhelming emotions. So, having tools that work on all levels is important in order to unwind the interplay between suppressed emotion and physical dysfunction.

We live in a society with incredibly high suicide rates, which is a sign we desperately need better tools and education for working on the emotional level. I have found the tools in this book to be the most efficient way to release emotional suffering as well as to work on physical dysfunction and pain.

On a physical level, our body is constantly under pressure from gravity, so let's have a look at how it deals with this.

Your Body Uses Your Bones to Support Itself Under the Constant Force of Gravity

Ligaments support your joints in a particular alignment. The postural muscles then support the ligaments. When there is a slight misalignment in the skeletal system, the weight of the body falls down through the ligaments at an angle, and the ligaments distort under the load. The body then recruits more muscle fibres to create support around the joint. You may have experienced this as having stiffness around a joint.

If there is more instability, the body recruits the global muscle fibres (your movement muscles). These muscles are not designed for constant load and you will often feel fatigue, aching, or pain.

If the joint is very unstable, the muscle supporting it will go into spasm, as it is constantly recruited beyond its capacity to function properly.

In order to try and reduce the load on the global muscle fibres and reduce pain in general, the body creates changes in posture. This can include shifting weight off the painful area, as well as bracing the area so it won't move. The postural adaptations use the fascia to draw load off the painful area. This shifts a localised, painful issue to a more global postural issue.

Changes in the posture also affect your resilience to impacts. Tight, rigid structures are more likely to break than bend. Also, your body's capacity to deal with gravity is reduced, so you will require more muscular holding rather than having more passive support of your skeletal system.

Although you have a rich supply of sensory receptors in the fascia that covers the bones (the periosteum), we do not seem to prioritise the information from these receptors.

You can check this for yourself. Move your arm, and you will be able to feel where it is in space, but you won't be able to feel where the bones are within your arm.

This is fine in most situations, but when you have a misalignment of the bones, your body doesn't know where the bone was, nor where it ended up.

One of the important pieces of information the body needs in order to reorganise itself is where your bones are and how they relate to each other across the joints. A slight rotation of a vertebrae can make a big difference to how stable the spine feels.

We can also add the hydrostatic pressure of the fluids within the body. Tension through the fascia also affects the movement of fluids, especially lymph. The fluids push out against the confinement of the fascia, your body then uses this pressure to rebound up against gravity. If you have an inefficient posture, this rebound mechanism won't be functioning properly and your muscles will have to work harder just to counteract the force of gravity. When the hydrostatic force is properly functioning, there is a springiness that rebounds out when compressed. Think about squeezing a water balloon and how there is resistance to the compressive force.

As the nerves originate deep within the body from the spinal cord and run to the muscles that are more superficial, they pass through layers of fascia. If there is a strong tension patterns in layers of fascia due to the body needing to adapt to inefficient postural patterns, there can be pressure on the myelin sheath around the nerves. This is one possible source of referred pain.

If your posture requires a lot of muscular support from your global muscles, it may take all your energy just to do day to day tasks, and the possibility of anything more challenging seems daunting. Fortunately, if you can find an Ortho-Bionomy practitioner, they will be able to help your system become more efficient.

We are not just physical beings. If you have ever had an emotion, you will have experiential clarity on how emotions can affect your physical body.

Of course, we are not just physical beings. Some of the most important forces that act on our physical system arise from our emotions and thoughts.

If you have ever had an emotion such as grief, anger, heartbreak, shame, humiliation, fear or terror, then you will have experiential clarity on how strongly these emotions can affect your muscular system as well as your digestive and immune systems.

When we allow ourselves to fully experience the emotion for a few seconds, the feeling flows through us and is gone. However, when we are in a state of overwhelm like when stressed or grieving, it is more likely that we will resist the emotion, and the tension from doing this will be held in the body. My personal experience leads me to feel that we use our fascia to hold these resisted emotional tension patterns.

There is a difference between holding the patterns of resistance to holding the emotions within the body. If you have a Facebook profile, you will probably have seen memes stating that a knee problem is associated with such and such an emotion. There is no scientific evidence to support this prescriptive model of the relationship between the body and a particular emotion. We are all different, and have different functional patterns so we create holding patterns that are unique to our system. In fact, emotions are not stored in the body. Rather, the resistance to an emotion is what is being held in the body.

In survival situations, it makes sense to repress emotions in order to continue to function.

Then when you are safe it is important to feel the repressed emotion to allow it to move through you.

Think of the traumatic situations our ancestors faced such as warfare, exposure to the elements, deaths of offspring — often many, early deaths of parents, famine etc. The human system is designed to recover from traumatic experiences, but our social conditioning and lack of efficient tools get in the way of the body/mind self-correcting.

The issue we have is, we often don't pause long enough to release the resisted emotions. As soon as we stop, the discomfort of our own resistance comes up and we find a distraction to make it go away.

This inability to stop will directly contribute to chronic health conditions, anxiety, issues with sleeping and relaxing, and therefore faster aging and reduced immune system function.

The truth is, you can either experience the emotional angst in all its discomfort for about 3 seconds, or you can resist it, and have it show up in different ways for the rest of your life.

To be clear, you only need to feel the underlying emotional pattern for about 3 seconds (in my experience). How long you feel the resistance is up to you. You can choose to dive into the discomfort or try and resist it. It is the resistance that increases the discomfort.
In chapters 6 and 7, we will give you some great tools to transform how you work with emotions and any malfunctions of the physical body that are of emotional origins.

Thoughts are another powerful influencer of the physical body. If you have a look at body language, you will see postural changes that are affected by thought processes. For example a low self-esteem will tend to have a person hunch forward with their head down, which is also the posture of someone who is depressed. In fact, this is a two-way street: your posture also affects how your mind works. In chapter 6 we will explore this in more detail.

The current theory of how the body/mind interacts is the Bio-Psychosocial model, which includes many different aspects when looking at causes of pain. The Bio-Psychosocial model includes things like tissue damage and misaligned vertebrae (Biological components), negative thought processes, trauma (Psychological processes) and things like poverty, financial stress, homelessness (social processes) as contributors to chronic pain. This is a much broader view of how humans' function than the narrower Bio-medical model that was the dominant theory prior to the findings from pain research and functional magnetic resonance imaging (FMRI) studies. The Bio-medical model viewed the human as a physical body that needed fixing. This is the basis for a lot of bodywork modalities where the focus is just on the muscles or bones.

Your ability to self-correct is affected by a broad range of contributing factors, so exploring what has the greatest impact on your system will help you find how to work with your dysfunction.

So, what do we mean by self-correction?

Our self-corrective response is what makes it possible for us to survive: our ability to balance our internal environment in response to changes in the external environment. All our systems rely on homeostasis, including biochemical balances, heart rate, carbon dioxide/oxygen ratio, balance, and body temperature. The body coordinates these systems in much the same way. You have a narrow band the body requires, and sensors pick up variations. Then the body has positive or negative feedback pathways to control the variable.
Imagine if you were standing up and started to slowly lean forward. As you near the edge where you were going to fall, your body will automatically either move a foot forward to take the load (we call this walking) or tighten up your back muscles to hold the weight moving further past your centre of gravity. If you have had lower back pain, you might find that your stress response might kick in, creating tension in your lower back with only a slight forward bend. This is an example of your protective mechanism at work.

Your musculoskeletal system (bones, muscles, fascia, fluids, ligaments) has this capacity to reorganise itself to create a more efficient way of working. In fact, the nervous system is constantly on the lookout for information that will enable the body/mind/emotions to adapt more effectively to the surroundings.

A number of things inhibit the self-corrective process from working. One of these is fear. This can be fear of being injured, fear of movement if you have acute pain, or fear of acute pain if there is chronic pain, or just fear in general.

The stress response is designed for survival situations, but unfortunately, we have a fear-based society, where there is a financial advantage for the media and politicians to keep us fearful. The scare tactics used around elections are a perfect example. One of the unintended results from having a fear-based reality is that the amygdala, the fear centre of the brain can increase in size, this was found to be common in children from abusive households. The more often you think fearful thoughts, the stronger the neurological pathways become. This makes it more likely you will feel fearful. It takes a deliberate effort to change this tendency.

One of the ways fear has this impact on the physical body is to tighten up the psoas major muscle, which runs on the inside of the spine from the base of your ribcage to the inside of the thigh bone.
 A tight psoas creates tension in your lower back, and if there is already pressure on a nerve in the lumbar spine, this increased pressure can increase/cause lower back pain.

Pain research has shown that financial stress and poverty increases the intensity of chronic pain. As chronic pain reduces productivity, disturbs sleep and increases the probability that you will be stressed, a tendency to be fearful is an important cause of dysfunction. Our current model of giving people in chronic pain insufficient money to live on, therefore creating poverty, increases the likelihood that they will never get out of the chronic pain trap due to the impact of fear on pain. Fortunately some of the tools in this book are useful for working with chronic pain and so may help break this pattern.

We will explore more of the findings from pain research in Chapter 4, but the takeaway message is that our whole system works as one unit with the physical body affected by the mental and emotional aspects, and vice-versa. In order to be more efficient at stimulating the body to self-correct, we need to have tools to work on all these levels and an understanding of when to use them.

How You Work on a Physical Level with the Self-Corrective Process Depends on what the Dysfunction Is

As our body is made up of different components, bones, muscles etc., there is the possibility that a dysfunction is related to a particular relationship in the physical structure. In order to be able to stimulate the self-corrective response, we need to be able to work with the different components in different ways to communicate with the nervous system what the dysfunction may be.

For instance, to stimulate a muscle to release, you bring the two ends of the muscle toward each other — that is, if a muscle is contracted concentrically (shortened), you will shorten the muscle further by positioning the joint, then add gentle compression to stimulate the proprioception (the receptors in the belly of the muscle and joint capsules that give you feedback about where your body is and any movements you make).

If you are working with connective tissue (fascia, ligaments or tendons), then often gentle traction will stimulate the connective tissue to recoil to the tension needed to support the joint.

If you are working with the alignment of bones, then touch is all that is necessary for the body to locate the bone and reorganise the joint.

The reason so little effort is needed is that the body is actively looking for this information. When the body feels safe, its protective mechanism is not engaged and the system becomes ready to use the information it receives, and changes the skeletal alignment very quickly.

While we do work with the components above, the main focus is to find what is driving the pattern of dysfunction. This can be a skeletal misalignment, an emotional holding pattern, or a dysfunctional movement pattern. Quite often, the painful condition such as a muscle spasm is part of a compensation pattern, so if you release it without changing the driver of the pattern, it will tend to wind up again over a couple of days.

On a structural level, with Ortho-bionomy, we work with the underlying joint misalignment, and the muscle spasm releases of its own accord. In this case, tight muscles become indicators of the underlying dysfunction and can be used to check if the skeletal structure is stable.

Exploring Your Nervous System

As you are a unique individual, what works for someone else may not work for you.

This is the key with stimulating the self-corrective process: you have to meet the body where it needs to be met.

So, the exercises in this book are designed to give you an opportunity to explore how your body/mind works. Some of them will work really well for you, some of them won't. This is not your failure, or the exercises, but rather the exercise wasn't suitable for your system at this time. It might however be exactly the right thing for someone else, or for you in the future.

Keeping a body healthy as you get older is really an ongoing experiment with the aim to collect as many useful tools as you can in order to keep your health for as long as you can. There really isn't much point in living to 100 if you spend the last 50 years with chronic pain.

The following exercises will give you an experience of your body and nervous system in a whole new way, and let you experience how finely tuned your body really is.

1. Stand in bare feet (or socks) with your feet close together.
    - Come up onto your toes then slowly back onto your heels, then come into a middle position.
    - Now with attention on where the weight is on your feet, move your lower jaw to one side.
    - Did your weight shift to the same side or opposite side or not at all?
    - Come back to the middle and move the jaw to the opposite side. What happened to your weight?
    - Now bring your weight back to the middle and just move your eyes to look in one direction. Did your weight move?
    - Try looking in the other direction.
    - Now glare at a point straight in front of you and track your weight shifting.
    - Then shift your attention to your peripheral vision and see if that changes where the weight is on your feet.
    - Sometimes, if your body is rigid, or senses the weight shift as threatening your balance, you may experience muscles contracting to prevent the weight shifting.
    - You can use this as an indication of change.

2. Now bring your attention to the muscles in your ears (did you know you had muscles in your ears?)
    - Keeping your head still, move your eyes from side to side and feel if the muscles in your ears move.
    - This is part of how you look for predators – like dogs move their ears to track sounds.
    - Next, feel the muscles in your ears and glare as if you were angry. What did the muscles feel like?
    - Next, smile with your eyes, so your eyes should be soft and the area around the eyes crinkle. How do the muscles in your ears feel now?
    - The amazing thing is that our social brain allows us to track these things in each other as it gives us information about whether a person is a threat or not. So, if you would like to help someone relax, and smile with your eyes at them. This is also part of the system we use to notice when a person is faking a smile or are pretending to be friendly.

3. Explore how it feels to turn your head from one side to the other.
    - Then turn your head slowly to one side but look in the opposite direction.
    - Repeat a couple of times on both sides.
    - Then recheck the range of movement of the neck: has it changed?
    - Sometimes the restrictions on our movement are due to limitations in automatic patterns we have built up over time. These functional patterns can be challenged with movements that upset the patterning and enable the body/mind to reset itself.

4. Feel your neck with your internal sense. Now, without actually moving, imagine you are raising your arm up to scratch your ear. Can you feel some muscles in your neck and shoulders engage?
    - The premotor neurons in your brain are goal focused. They turn on when you decide on an action, and a message is sent to the primary motor cortex that turns on the muscles needed to make the movement. As you are just imagining the movement, your recruitment of the muscles is minimal, but this is enough to create awareness in the body. In Ortho-

Bionomy, this is one way of releasing structural patterns when the client's body is very rigid, movement is painful or the person can't relax enough to allow movement with out control.
- In chapter 8, we will use this to stimulate your body to self-correct an elevated first rib.

The nervous system is far subtler and more fine-tuned than we often think, which is why it can respond to new information so rapidly.

Whenever we touch another person's body, we are really in direct contact with their brain. In Ortho-bionomy, we connect to the body with this in mind.

Things That Inhibit Your Self-Corrective Process

As chronic pain is a common problem in our society, there must be some things that inhibit the ability of the body to self-correct. As noted previously, fear is one of them, but also a number of other things interrupt the ability of our body to reorganise itself.

Stress, sleep deprivation or broken sleep, resisted emotions, chronic and acute pain, thoughts, beliefs and willingness to change them are among these. The story we tell ourselves about what is happening is also surprisingly important. But the key piece is often that we do not have the right information in order to self-correct. What this information is will depend on whether the dysfunction is on the physical, mental, emotional or energetic level, and often there is an interaction on all these levels. However, one aspect will be the driver and the other parts the compensation patterns.

In order for the body to self-correct, it needs to feel safe. If the protective mechanism of the body is recruited, the main concern of the body will be to protect itself against injury. As I've emphasised before, this is why there are no forced manipulation or painful techniques used in Ortho-Bionomy. It is more efficient to make the body feel safe and stimulate the self-corrective mechanism than to use force.

So, in the following chapters, we will look at ways of working with each of the areas that can inhibit the body's ability to self-correct, and give techniques to stimulate the body to become more efficient. Of course, you are an individual. Play with exercises, find the ones you like, and start building up a toolkit that enables you to take an active role in your own health care and personal development.

This is really an introduction to a way of working that has been around for decades but has been largely ignored as it requires more patience and listening from the practitioner and less fixing, force and doing.

If you like mindfulness, meditation, yoga or have chronic pain then you will love working in this way.

FACTORS AFFECTING YOUR ABILITY TO SELF CORRECT A DYSFUNCTION

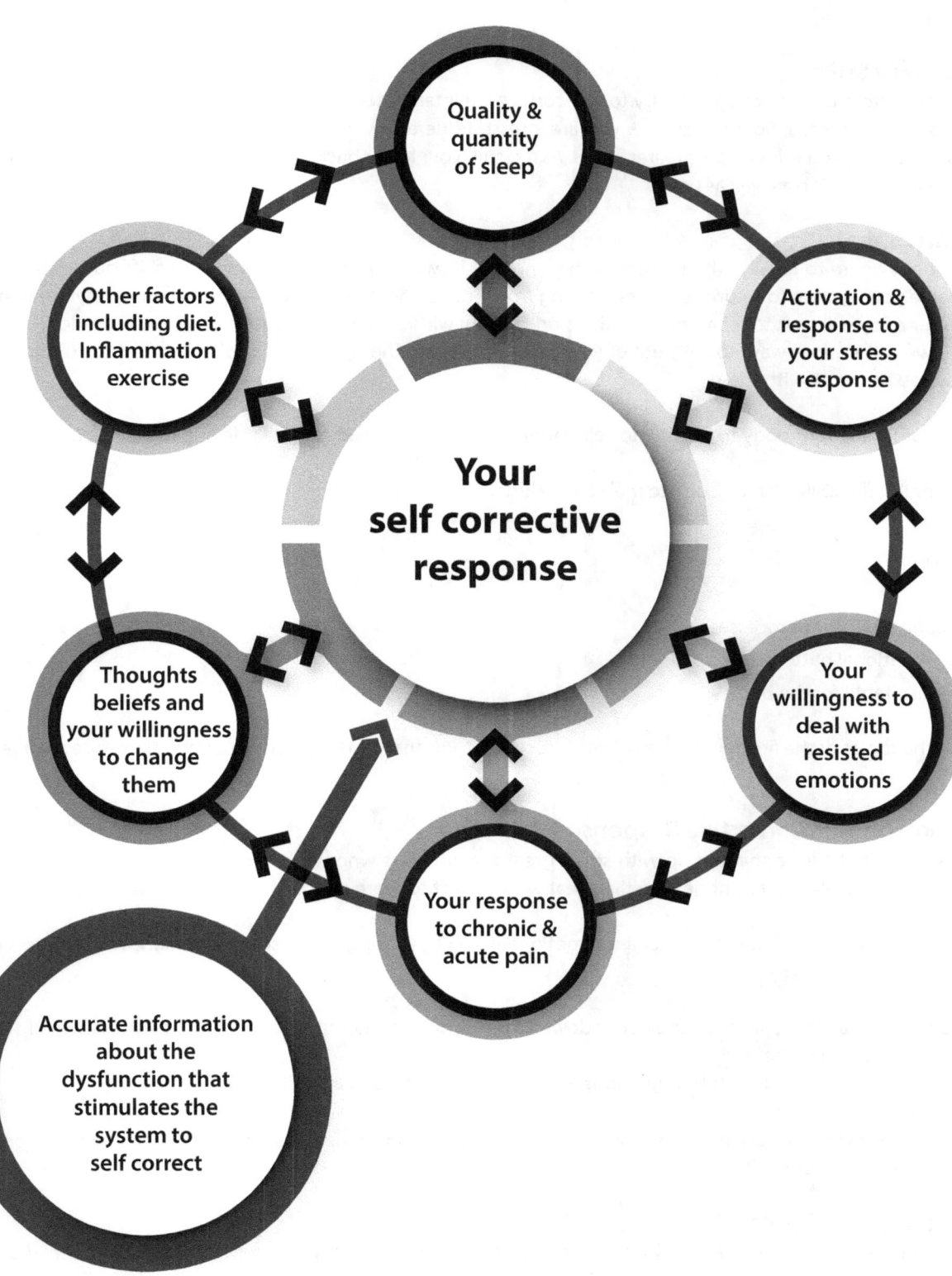

As this diagram suggests, all these factors interact with each other and affect your body's ability to self-correct. One challenge with breaking things down into different sections is that some of the interactions are missed. In essence, this is one system that interacts closely. So, throughout the book, I will mention these interactions, but in truth, the reality is much more integrated and complex than I have stated. The great thing is that using the tools, you will be able to change what you are experiencing, regardless of the complexity of the system.

The Downward Spiral

Because all the factors that affect your ability to self-correct are interrelated, when there is a dysfunction in one area, the whole system starts to be affected. So, for instance, you are stressed due to a work issue. This affects your sleep, so your emotional regulation is impaired, and this creates greater stress. As a result, your lower back, neck and shoulders are tight and your digestion doesn't seem to be working as well as usual.

The Upward Spiral

You can start anywhere to change the pattern of dysfunction. However, the quickest way is to shift out of the stress response. This will enable your system to return to normal cycling from your sympathetic (stress response) to parasympathetic (rest/digest response). Your body will start to relax and your decision-making will improve, as will your sleep and digestion.
In Chapter 2 we will explore ways to shift out of your stress response. The rest of this book will take each of the other areas and explore how you can work with them.

In essence, in order for your body to be able to self-correct, your system needs to feel safe and have the right information about the dysfunction.
Factors that inhibit the ability of the body to feel safe include:

- Stress
- Lack of sleep
- Pain
- Dysfunctional thought processes
- Resisted emotional patterns
- A diet not suitable for the body

So, these are the topics of the first few chapters, with a focus on tools that can help you notice and therefore change what is going on.

Stimulating The Self-Corrective Response

I am lucky enough to have connected up with some great practitioners who work in different ways to support people to heal themselves. In order to offer different perspectives that will connect to more people, I invited them to contribute to this book.

I have chosen to go from physical to mental and emotional aspects, looking at the science behind why the tools offered in this book work.

Lisa Tyree comes from a more spiritual perspective down to the emotional/mental level, which can also assist in unwinding chronic pain and physical tension in the body.
Hannah Moore, a naturopath, is contributing information from a nutritional perspective.

The idea is that wherever you start from, there will be somewhere you can connect to and improve your own awareness and ability to take an active role in your health.

An Overview Of The Process

Starting with the stress response is essential, because if you are in survival mode, your body and nervous system will have only one focus, to stay alive. Once you are more relaxed, we then want to ensure you are getting more sleep. This will improve your immune system and digestion, enables your system to return to a more balanced way of operating, and most importantly enables you to better regulate your emotions.

Next, we will look at pain, how it works, the difference between acute pain and chronic pain, and the effect of inflammation on how you perceive pain. Then we will offer you some tools for working with the system in pain.

We will then look at the way your thought patterns influence pain, health, and your ability to self-correct.

Following on from working with the mind, we will look at working with emotions. Because working with resisted emotions is something we all possibly need to improve on, there are two chapters in which we'll look at different ways to explore and release resisted emotional patterns.

We then look at ways of working with a painful musculoskeletal condition from an Ortho-Bionomy perspective, with self-care exercises for you to play with.

Then we look at the relationship between diet and the ability to self-correct, and finally look at how the tools can be used for self-development.

Throughout the book, there is a strong focus on easy-to-use tools that enable your system to change. Take the time to play with these as the real value is in your own experience rather than an intellectual understanding.

Enjoy the process 😊

CHAPTER 2.
WORKING WITH YOUR STRESS RESPONSE

WORKING WITH YOUR STRESS RESPONSE

Stress in modern society is a constant part of our lifestyle, with demanding jobs, time pressure, financial pressure, dealing with other humans on a regular basis. All of these can create stress that is a long-term constant state of being.

Stress is involved in many chronic illnesses such as heart disease, inflammatory issues and changes in immune function.[3,4]

A lack of tools to deal with stress is driving billion-dollar industries based around helping you escape from your life or feeling better for a short period of time. Ultimately, you go back to your life and the stress returns, so finding efficient ways of working with stress is a vital piece for creating a healthier, more fulfilling life.

There is positive stress, like having a deadline that makes you become more productive. Then there are also many examples of negative stress that make you less productive. This section is about negative stress and how we can shift out of our stress response in order to be more productive, healthier, and enjoy life more. If you can learn to shift your negative stress to a more positive approach to stress, then improve your resilience to stress in general, you will become healthier and more productive. Recognising when you are sliding into your stress response is the first step with this process.

There are two general strategies for working with stress.
1. The problem-solving strategy, which focuses on changing the external source of the stress.
2. The emotional/coping strategy, which focuses on increasing resilience, so you can remain functional under greater stress without going into your stress response.

The first strategy is useful and has been shown to reduce the impacts of stress on your physical health. The details of this strategy are as specific as the individual and need to be worked out by analysing your situation.

The second option is more about how you perceive the stress you are in. This is the area we will explore and offer tools for shifting your perspective about how threatening you find your stress level to be.

How you perceive the situation you are in depends on your view of the world. This in turn depends on what you have experienced, and your beliefs. Things often turn intellectual when we talk about beliefs, but the real place where we need to work is in the body.

What you experience is really the important part. We will revisit this later in the book.

Now let's look at the stress response in more detail.

When we become stressed, we slide into the more primitive part of our brain, which has four reflexive responses:
1. Fight
2. Flee
3. Freeze
4. Fawn

Our stress response is designed to help us survive challenging circumstances, and in the case of freeze mode, to disassociate from our body's sensory receptors, so we don't feel pain when we die.

All four of the modes of operating have physical tell-tale signs, which makes it easy to identify where you or someone else is operating from their stress response. Once you have that information, there are ways of shifting yourself or someone else out of the stress response back into a higher functioning part of the brain where rational thought is possible.

It is really useful to work out what your fall-back stress response is, and learn the indicator signs so you can more rapidly identify where you are operating from. Of course, you may visit each of these responses in different situations or fight first, then flee, then get overwhelmed and end up in freeze.

The way out is to as quickly as possible recognise which mode you are in and to shift out, so let's look at how to do that.

The Fight Response

The fight response is a highly activated mode that often includes muscle tension in the neck, shoulders and jaw; the eyes become very focused and often a bit squinted, which correlates with the narrowing field of vision. Your heart rate and blood pressure increase as your body becomes ready to fight. The increased blood pressure and muscular tension may lead to headaches, teeth grinding or clenching and tension in the neck, shoulders and jaw.

Being "stuck" in your head, thinking rather than feeling, being easily angered and exploding are also often signs of the fight response.

In the fight response, we suffer from tunnel vision in how we view the world, and how we think. We often consider it justifiable to punish people who do things differently or think in ways we don't understand.

We will also blame other people as the source of the conflict, and mistake our own activation level as being due to other people yelling at us. This is all normal, but being able to shift from this state will create more harmonious, productive relationships and enable more rational ways of dealing with the situation.

The Flee Response (also known as flight response)

The flee response is also a highly activated state. The desire to flee means that there is muscular tension in the legs and a tendency to be unable to sit still. Darting eyes, a nervous disposition, anxiety, jerky or shaky movements can all be tell-tale signs of being in the flee mode.

Your ability to focus on one task and finish it will be reduced, and this can create the tendency to multi-task without achieving much. If you start lots of things but finish nothing this may be where you are operating from.

Having a racing mind, having trouble focusing, not feeling your body, needing to move, being hypervigilant, expecting you will be attacked by others, may all be signs you are in fleeing mode.

The Freeze Response

The freeze response in a low-activated state. Low muscle tone, lowered immune system, low energy, low cognitive function, poor memory, being easily overwhelmed and depressed, feeling disassociated or out of your body are some of the signs of the freeze response. In short, freeze mode is perfect for when you are dying, but a really hard place from which to live for a long period of time.

If you find life a struggle, feel like a victim or have lowered energy levels or immune response, then you may be trying to live life in freeze mode.

The Fawn Response

The fawn response is a behavioural pattern where you become a people pleaser under stressful conditions. You often betray your own sense of right and wrong in order to appease someone who is more aggressive/dominant. This may explain a lot of duplicity that happens when people are under stress. The feeling of having no choice but to do something that is unethical when being bullied is the underlying scenario that pushes people into fawn mode.

My main focus in this book will be on the fight, flee and freeze responses. The tools will work equally well for the fawn response.

You may recognise some of these signs as your habitual response in stressful circumstances, or, as I said before, you may start in fight, wanting to challenge the whoever you perceive is responsible before shifting to flee and just wanting to get out of the situation before ending up in freeze and feeling overwhelmed— or go the other way.

The important thing is, if you can identify where you are, you can then start to make sense of why you do the things you do when you are stressed.

Lifting Yourself Out Of Your Stress Response

The exercises below all work differently. Find which works the best for your nervous system, and become familiar with those before you get into a stressful situation. This can be done by thinking about a stressful situation until you feel your body respond, then to use the exercise to help you shift out. Practice is the key to being able to shift when you need it. Particularly, Exercise 3 can be used for releasing many things, so we will revisit later in the book as well.

Exercise 1
Objective: To release the charge from the muscular system — great for fight or flee modes.

Do this exercise if you are currently in a highly activated state.
- Start shaking either your legs or arms, (you could also put some music on and dance).
- Keep shaking till the activation level in your body drops.
- Then do exercise 2.

Exercise 1 is really just a way to reduce the level of charge in the system, but it doesn't necessarily shift where you are operating from, so once you are more stable, use the other exercises to shift yourself.

Exercise 2
Objective: To overload the senses until you shift out of your stress response.

Think about a stressful situation until you notice you have shifted into one of the modes of your stress response — unless you are already there.
- Close your eyes
- Bring your attention to a sound in your environment.
- Now while listening to that include a second sound.
- Now a third sound.
- While you are listening to the sounds, become aware of the feeling of you clothes on your body.
- Now while maintaining your attention on the sounds and the contact with your clothes, feel the air passing in and out of your nostrils.
- Now wriggle your toes.
- Finally open your eyes and notice something shiny.

Do you feel like you have lifted out of your stress response?
If you are still feeling stressed, either repeat the above exercise, taking more time with each of the steps, or try one of the other exercises below.

Exercise 3
Objective: To stimulate the parasympathetic nervous system (rest/digest response) to reduce the sympathetic nervous system activation (fight/flee response).

Think about a stressful situation until you notice you have shifted into one of the modes of your stress response — unless you are already there.
- Notice any muscular tension or activation in your body.
- Become curious about what you are feeling in that area.
- Yawn and extend the exhalation— fake it till you make it.
- Repeat either yawning or faking a yawn till you feel a change in the tension or charge in the body.
- If you have trouble feeling your body, try to bring your attention to your feet by wriggling your toes, then yawn to release any tension there.
- Then move up to your ankles and first move them then release any tension with a yawn.
- Move to your calves, etc.

Do you feel like the level of activation has changed, and can you think more clearly? If not, spend more time feeling deeper into the body and keep yawning or trying one of the other exercises.

Some people have trouble yawning. If this is the case, then try one of the other techniques and revisit this one when you have shifted out of the stress response a few times.

Exercise 4 — Minding the edges
Objective: To focus on the peripheral part of your vision to shift out of your stress response.

This is a great quick way to shift out of your stress response while talking with someone in a potentially stressful situation.
- Bring your awareness to the edges of your peripheral vision on both sides.
- Hold your attention there until you feel a shift in your stress levels.

Minding the edges is a variation of a technique from the book Resurfacing by Harry Palmer[76].

This is a great technique, because our fight response creates tunnel vision and our brain prioritises visual data. Actually, shifting attention out to our peripheral vision activates the brain in a way that shifts us out of the stress response.

This is an easy way out of an emotion too, but it doesn't necessarily help that emotion integrate. Therefore, other techniques are needed to work with resisted emotions. We will explore this in chapters 6 and 7.

Exercise 5 – Using your reward system in your brain to shift you out of freeze mode

If you regularly feel being overwhelmed and unable to do much then this is a great technique for you.
- Choose a simple job that will take no more than a few minutes.
- Complete it then spend 20-30 seconds focusing on the sense of achievement from completing the job.
- Use the increase in dopamine to complete the next task.
- Do four or five small jobs and you will have shifted into a more activated state.

Helping others
It would be great if everyone was able to identify when they were stressed, and to do whichever exercise worked best for them (send them a link to this book and they might). However, helping someone else shift out of their stress response is a great skill to have. You could assist a person in circumstances such as after surviving a traumatic event, or going in for surgery, or giving birth for the first time, or working in a group on a project with a lot of stress and time pressure, etc.

First make sure you are not in your stress response. If you are, shift yourself first.

Then do this compassion exercise to help you have more understanding for the other person.

Compassion Exercise

Honesty with yourself leads to compassion for others.

Objective: To increase the amount of compassion in the world.

Expected results: A personal sense of peace.

Instructions: Run through each step with your attention on the person you are hoping to help shift out of their stress response.

Step 1: With attention on the person, repeat to yourself:
"Just like me, this person is seeking some happiness for his/her life."

Step 2: With attention on the person, repeat to yourself:
"Just like me, this person is trying to avoid suffering in his/her life."

Step 3: With attention on the person, repeat to yourself:
"Just like me, this person has known sadness, loneliness and despair."

Step 4: With attention on the person, repeat to yourself:
"Just like me, this person is seeking to fulfil his/her needs."

Step 5: With attention on the person, repeat to yourself:
"Just like me, this person is learning about life."

Adapted from Resurfacing: Techniques for exploring Consciousness
Harry Palmer, 1994[76]

Then identify which mode the other person is in by asking questions and observing how they respond.
- Do you feel tight in the neck, shoulders and jaws? (fight)
- Do you feel like having an argument or yelling at someone? (fight)
- Do you feel frustrated? (fight)
- Do you want to go for a walk? (flee)
- Do you feel agitated (flee)
- Are you anxious? (flee)
- Do you feel overwhelmed? (freeze)
- Is it hard to make decisions? (freeze)
- Are you struggling with life? (freeze)

Each mode is then treated differently.

Fight mode
Make sure you remain neutral.

Use open questions — what can I do to help?

If the energy can be used in a productive way, work on removing distractions from that person, allowing them to focus on one thing. For instance, offer to take their phone and deal with anything that isn't an emergency in order for them to focus on the main project.

Ignore challenging things they say while they are in fight mode. If the issue is important, choose another time to discuss it, once the person is out of fight mode. Often people who visit fight mode regularly will see any discussion as an attack, so creating a discussion about issues can trigger them. Being able to stay in neutral and bring their attention to what you have said can make them observe their own state of activation and that they are projecting their own aggression onto you. This is challenging as most people don't like noticing that they are doing this.

Bring their awareness to the fact that they may be in fight mode, (without judgment) and therefore may be a bit hard on people around them may help.

Ask if they would like a hand to reduce their stress levels, and if yes, show them the techniques above.

Most people in fight mode don't want to hurt the people around them, and regret saying things that create suffering after they shift out of their stress mode. However, they often struggle to regulate their own activation level. Offering tools to help them shift out of this state will often be gratefully received if done in a compassionate way. If they perceive your attempts to connect as conflict, wait till they calm down. There is no point in creating conflict with someone in fight mode unless there is the risk of them hurting someone else.

Flee mode
Before anything else, get the person moving.

If they are able to walk, go for a walk with them.

If they are bedridden, get them to shake their hands.

Get them yawning.

Once they have become more stable, then they will be able to function better. Help them become aware of the feelings* associated with flee mode, so they can become better able to self-regulate.
*feelings associated with flee mode might include anxiety, agitation, irritability. These can be used as an indication of when a person is in flee mode.

Freeze mode
Help them feel safe. This maybe by touch, e.g., a hug (if appropriate), or holding a hand.

Keep warm

Use closed questions — would you like a cup of tea now?

Avoid open questions, for example — would you like a cup of coffee or tea? How do you have your coffee, flat white, cappuccino? How many sugars? What milk?

Get them yawning or teach them Minding the edges (exercise 4).

The idea is to get the person to shift to a higher level of operation so they can return to being productive. It's best to teach them the skills to do it themselves.

In a work environment, productivity will depend on a certain level of stress to create motivation, without pushing people into their stress response. A person in fight mode will be great at getting one task done but will mistreat people around them, reducing their productivity.

A person in flee mode will be busy looking for another job, trying to multi-task and getting little finished.

A person in freeze mode will forget things, be very unproductive and feel unsafe because of being unproductive.

To maximise productivity, everyone needs to be able to shift out of their stress response and assist others around them to do the same. The first step with this is the recognition that this is the level they are operating from.

What Happens When We Yawn?

OK, here's a bit of science you can skip if you like, but check out the exercise at the end of this box.

Three different neurotransmitter-activated pathways can be triggered by yawning.
When the Adrenocorticotropic Hormone (ACTH) pathway is triggered, there is a noticeable increase of cortisol in the saliva, which correlates with increased stress and maybe associated with conditions like Cushing's syndrome (excess cortisol production)[5]. This is the sort of yawn that would occur if you were bored or tired, since it increases arousal.

The two other pathways stimulate the neurotransmitters dopamine and oxytocin.

You may have experienced a yawn that stimulates a dopamine release when you have been working toward a particular outcome and get a good result. There is a sense of achievement as well as being tired and happy with the outcome[6].

The oxytocin pathway is the one I'm most interested in. Oxytocin creates a sense of safety, which is useful for relaxing the body and helping emotional states like fear release. Oxytocin is produced in the hypothalamus, and released in the pituitary and the amygdala.[7]

The pituitary gland regulates the stress response and the amygdala creates the fear response. The ability to stimulate the release of oxytocin in the pituitary and amygdala gives us a way to interact with the body's response to fear and stress.

This is probably what Dr Stephen Porges means when he states, "one of the roles of oxytocin is to allow you to be immobilised without fear".[8,9]

The amygdala, hypothalamus and pituitary are all parts of the limbic system — the emotional part of the brain. These areas are rich with receptors designed for specific neurotransmitters. These neurotransmitters are produced in the nerves and send information through the nervous system.

One of the roles of the hypothalamus and pituitary is to regulate the balance between the sympathetic (fight/flight response) and the parasympathetic (rest/digest response), so it is interesting that this is the site of oxytocin production and release. This is likely to be part of the reason that stress levels change when we fall in love. So, being able to stimulate oxytocin release is excellent for changing how we feel. Oxytocin can also be considered a stress hormone that encourages you to seek support of family and friends when you are in a stressful situation.

On a physical level, the action of yawning stimulates the vagus nerve at the back of the mouth, around the larynx, though the ribcage and diaphragm. By extending the exhalation, you can also maximise the stimulus of the parasympathetic nervous system.

This, coupled with the possible activation of oxytocin in the brain, means yawning is a useful tool for releasing emotional charge as well as releasing tight muscles.

Feeling the difference between the three different pathways stimulated by yawning
The key to which of the three neurotransmitter pathways is activated seems to be the length of the exhalation. Experiment with the three options below and see what you experience:
1. Yawn with a short sharp exhalation and feel if it feels more stimulating or relaxing
2. Yawn with a similar length exhalation to inhalation how does that make you feel?
3. Yawn and extend the exhalation as long as possible, how does that make you feel?

From now on, whenever yawning is mentioned as a method of release, the idea is to extend the exhalation longer than the inhalation.

> **A yawning exercise to play with**
> - Find a tight or sore muscle in your neck or shoulders.
> - Gently put a finger on the area — there doesn't need to be any pressure.
> - Feel the area and yawn a couple of times.
> - Check to see if the tension in the area has changed.
>
> Later, I'll describe other ways of using yawning as a tool to release the body/mind and emotions.

Creating Structure Reduces Stress Due to Unknowns

One of the principles of Ortho-Bionomy is, structure governs function, and this works beautifully for shifting negative stress to enable a more productive response to the situation.

Often, unknown aspects of a situation add to stress. These tend to be things we can't control, so we don't have the ability to create change.

Therefore, a useful assessment tool is to write down what is known about the issue:

What areas are unknown? Is this due to missing information that can be obtained but hasn't yet been? Can you find an adviser who can fill in the missing information?

Is the missing information not available at all, for instance will the housing market rise or fall in two years' time? If this is the case, then it is a question of being comfortable with the level of risk. If you are not, then get out to avoid ongoing stress.

Is this unknown important? If this area doesn't work, what can be done to create alternatives, and can any of these be put in place?

If there really isn't anything you can do at present, can you focus your attention on something else, which might create a more productive outcome than being stressed?

> *A problem either has a solution or it doesn't.*
> *If it does, then working on the solution is better than worrying.*
> *If it doesn't, then there is no point in worrying.*
> The Dalai Lama

If you can use the tools above to step out of your stress response and start being productive, you may find you don't fall back into your stress response till you stop.

If the stress is due to domestic arrangements, take a structural approach to working out where the stress is coming from, and who can assist in changing this. Are they willing to help? If not, what can you do to change the situation? So, for instance if cleaning is the source of constant stress, can you hire a cleaner for two hours a week to take the load and stop the stressful interactions?

If this is a lifestyle issue — you are stressed all the time and fall apart whenever you stop — then you probably need to process the underlying resisted emotions. Chapter 6 will be very useful for this. If you have been traumatised, you will need to work with someone for support to help you maintain stability while you are working your way through your trauma. The tools in this book can assist with this, but getting support will be very helpful.

Social Standing and Your Stress Response

One of the interesting things about the stress response is that it is often governed by social hierarchy. So, a stressed person in a position of authority will often go into fight mode. If workers do not respect the position of authority or the person involved, conflict will occur as they shift into fight mode. Alternatively, they may shift into flee mode and start looking for another job, planning a holiday or going out for lunch or taking a sickie. If the boss is dominating or the worker is inclined to become overwhelmed, then they will end up in freeze mode. Then, memory is impaired, productivity suffers and the worker will be stressed about being unproductive and losing their job.

Of, course when people go home, the social hierarchy is different, and the stress response may completely change. So, it is more likely that you may "take it out" on your partner or kids by going into fight mode and they will slide into one of the three modes of operating and this will either create conflict, separation/isolation or depression in those around you. None of these are preferred outcomes.

One of the interesting connections is that resisted emotions within your system will have an impact on how easy it is for you to go into your stress response and what your habitual response is.

If you have been physically abused and you have not managed to escape, you will probably end up in freeze very quickly when you get stressed.

In order to protect itself during an assault, the body/brain goes into freeze mode and a disassociated state occurs. It's like watching what is happening but being numb to it.

Many sexual assault survivors report not being able to yell, say no or fight back during the attack. This sets the stage for a disassociated state to reappear when they are stressed.

If you have ever gone away from a situation where there was verbal conflict, and ten minutes later you start thinking of all the things you could have said to better represent your position, then you have experienced slipping into your stress response and losing your ability to think clearly.

When we are children, our brains develop slowly over many years with various milestones being identified. One of the most noticeable is the emotional regulation area in the pre-frontal cortex. In the absence of this development, temper tantrums are frequent. If a child experiences abuse, the age when this happened is a critical factor in how the developmental process proceeds. MRI studies of children who have experienced abuse have been found to have an enlarged amygdala (and therefore increased fear response) and reduced hippocampus volume (therefore impaired memory). The story assigned to the abuse is also important as that is what the person identifies with.

If someone disassociates whenever they have a potential conflict situation, then they are in freeze mode. This can be observed by their body language: not making eye contact, collapsed in, heavy feeling, tired/fatigued, needing to sit down, shaking, not being able to stand up for themselves.

Helping them become grounded by having them walk with bare feet on a textured surface (grass is good) and touching different textured surfaces will assist them returning to their body.

None of us are at our best when we are stuck in our stress response. It's a great set of skills to be able to recognise when we are reacting from our stress response, and being able to shift out of it.

Stress and Children
There is a large size difference between children and adults, and there is a natural inclination to become stressed when yelled at. This occurs until they become habituated to it, so children are often stressed where they live. This has an impact on self-esteem, digestion, sleep and the ability to learn.

Stress in children is also quite often directly related to the stress in the parents, not just by being yelled at but also the subconscious tracking of the care giver's stress response enables the child to avoid threatening situations, and this can create the feeling of being on edge when around a stressed parent.

One of the best things you can do for your children is to work on dealing better with your stress, processing your own resisted emotions. Upskilling in how you deal with stress, doing internal work to deal with your resisted emotional states and some form of meditation can be a great way to do this.

The Cost to Your Health of Cortisol

Cortisol is a stress hormone that is produced in your adrenal glands, which sit on your kidneys. It is an important hormone for glucose metabolism, has an anti-inflammatory effect, and influences blood pressure, so the correct balance is important for your health.

In an ideal situation, when you are faced with a short-term stressful situation, for example needing to escape from danger, your stress response will turn on. When the danger is past, your stress response will relax, and your body will return to a more balanced flow between activation and relaxation.

How this should work:
You perceive a threat.
Your hypothalamus stimulates the pituitary to activate your flight response.
Your pituitary stimulates the release of cortisol and epinephrine from your adrenals.
The cortisol creates a glucose spike and inhibits insulin production, so that the body doesn't store the glucose but rather has it available for immediate use.
The cortisol narrows the arteries while the epinephrine increases the heart rate, which makes the heart pump harder and faster.

In fight/flight mode, the activation is designed for fighting or running away, so your blood flow increases to your muscles and reduces to your digestive and immune systems, because both of those use a great deal of energy that's now needed to cope with the danger.

Once the threat has been avoided, the cortisol levels drop to a lower rate, allowing the body to recover.

As you can see from the effects of the hormones, when there is long term stress, high cortisol levels can cause issues such as:
- Anxiety
- Depression
- Digestive problems
- Diabetes
- Headaches
- Heart disease
- Sleep problems
- Weight gain, especially around abdomen and face
- Memory and concentration impairment
- Reduced immune system activity

Stress is a core piece to so many chronic health conditions that it is too important to ignore.

Background Stress Levels

One interesting thing is that we need a certain level of stress to make us productive.

However, sometimes people become addicted to stress and will create drama or take on someone else's drama in order to maintain their customary levels of stress.

You may know someone who creates stress and drama as soon as there is no external pressure on them.

Another example is when people are always involved in fixing/rescuing others. This doesn't mean you shouldn't be helpful, but you should be able to stop, relax, be completely still within yourself, which helps recharge your own system, enabling you to be grounded and healthier.

Your need to have an ongoing level of stress is really a way to avoid stopping, so you don't need to feel your own resisted emotions. Once you have the tools for dealing with the resisted emotions (chapter 6 & 7) and the intention to explore and unwind, you will experience much less drama and stress in your life. From this space, you can assist people by helping them find their own answers rather than trying to "fix" them.

Stress, Resilience and Safety

Resilience can be defined as the ability to remain functional while experiencing stressful conditions. This can be seen as the ability to avoid going into your stress response and therefore maintaining the ability to think instead of just reacting.

The ability to remain functional while under stressful conditions will be affected by a number of things, previous experience being one of them. If you feel safe within yourself, you are more likely to see a stressful period as a challenge to be met, and therefore remain functional. If you feel unsafe, you will be more likely to interpret the situation as a threat to your survival, and therefore drop into your stress response.

The sense of feeling safe will appear in a number of different places in this book, as it seems to be important to things such as perception of pain, sleep, digestion as well as working with resisted emotions.

Your internal sense of safety is the key to whether you are resilient or react to a stressful situation by slipping into fight, flee or freeze.

You will already know some activities you enjoy that increase your sense of safety. Making a list of these is a great idea so that when you are going into a stressful time of the year you can deliberately make time to include some of these. Programming time for a bath or catching up with a friend and creating down time can make a huge difference and allow you to recharge.
 A walk in nature, breathing exercises, listening to music, being with friends or by yourself can also be useful for a short-term shift from your stress response. Prioritising "me" time will actually improve your productivity and health which will enable you to be more present and stay out of your stress response.

However, to really change how you function, you need to work deeper and help your system reorganise your response to stress.

Being deeply connected to who you are as a being creates a space that is stable despite external stressors. The internal sense of your own value creates a base on which your sense of safety can rest. Being internally coherent is really the only way to create safety in a dynamic world.

So, how can you connect to the you that is safe and stable within yourself?

This initially requires a decision to change.

Then it requires the determination to be willing to be uncomfortable and stay present until you can relax in the situation.

And then you need to do the internal work, releasing the resisted emotional content that is holding you from that sense of inner cohesion: the oneness that is stable.

Once you have created some space, then small incremental exposure to stress increases your ability to deal with more stress and stay present and productive.

So, the process is twofold:
Explore and release the patterns that lead to stress being overwhelming, which we shall discuss in chapter 6.
And
Once you feel able, start to take on challenges that stretch your ability to deal with stress.

If you have a pattern of slipping into freeze mode, attempt small things at first, and do them with someone who can support you.

In freeze mode, you are likely to disassociate easily. Noticing the feeling of disassociation and just relaxing will help you come back into your body.

What you Believe About Stress is Important for How Stress Affects Your Health
Recent studies have shown that what you believe about the physical changes in response to stress play a big role in how much of an impact the stress has on your health.[10]

Believing that the physical effects, such as increased heart rate and level of activation in the body are positive in order for you to meet the challenge will improve your performance, make you more functional and keep your blood pressure lower.

People who viewed stress as negative had greater vascular constriction, which made blood pressure increase, and increased the likelihood of having a heart attack.[10]

Creating the attitude that stress is your friend and helps you perform at a higher level makes stress healthy. So, if you feel you are getting stressed, love the activation of your physical body, because it is there to help you become more productive.

Exploring Your Physical Response to Stress
- Place one hand over your heart and tune into your heartbeat.
- Spread your awareness a bit broader to get a sense of the area around the heart.
- When you have a sense of that think about something stressful.
- Did you experience a contraction in the area around the heart?
- That is the vascular constriction mentioned above.
- Now think about how great it is that your body is getting ready for action to help you be more productive and meet the challenges of your life.
- Did you notice the area around your heart relax when you shifted to a positive mindset about what the physical changes meant?

Whenever you notice you are stressed you can deliberately choose a positive mindset that will reduce the physical impact on your body

Stress and Inflammation
The inflammatory process is a response of the body to cell damage, but is also a chronic response stimulated by other things such as broken sleep, increased long term stress, a diet not suited to your body, and digestive issues. So, we will discuss inflammation at various places in the book.

Inflammation is an important part of the healing process when it occurs in the short term. However, like stress itself, long term inflammation can lead to a range of negative consequences that include increased sensitivity to pain, damage to the joints, as well as changes to how well the digestive system works, which in turn affects the absorption of nutrients from food.

Cortisol initially has an anti-inflammatory effect on the system, but as the stress continues, this changes to a pro-inflammatory effect.

Chronic inflammation has been found to be associated with health conditions like depression,[11] obesity, and heart disease.[12]

The common way of dealing with this is taking an anti-inflammatory drug, but this is putting a band-aid on the underlying problem without looking at what is actually going on, and taking a drug every day is not a solution, as the side effects can lead to further symptoms.

Interestingly, what you believe about life actually has an impact on the level of inflammation in your system. People who are conscientious about life were found to have lower levels of a reactive protein called interleukin (IL6), which is associated with inflammation[77]. So, playing with your mindset about life can be a useful way to influence your biochemistry.

Stress and the Digestive System
The stress response is an activation of the sympathetic nervous system, which is part of the autonomic nervous system. The other part of the autonomic nervous system is the parasympathetic nervous system. When stimulated, the parasympathetic nervous system creates relaxation, and stimulates the digestive system.

The sympathetic and parasympathetic are in a constant dance: each inhalation activates your sympathetic nervous system and each exhalation activates your parasympathetic.

There are also larger swings with activities like after meals, when the parasympathetic should be dominant, and times of exercise when the sympathetic dominates. When you are stressed, your sympathetic nervous system is dominant, which reduces the activation of your digestive system.

This can have an impact on the movement of food through the gut (peristalsis), which can lead to constipation. The food sitting in the gut for longer periods can cause inflammation and sensitivities to some things, which if eaten under relaxed situations would not be an issue. Stress hormones also affect the blood flow in the body: as we become stressed, our blood flows to our muscles, readying our system for action and this reduces the efficiency of our digestive system. Supplements are much less effective if the nervous system is stuck in sympathetic dominance.

Part of the parasympathetic nervous system that has been getting a lot of attention recently is the vagus nerve. The vagus nerve, also known as the 10th cranial nerve, runs from the brain down the back of the throat and innervates the heart, lungs and digestive system. The vagus nerve is unique, as a majority of the information it carries is sensory information from the organs to the brain (80-90%). Our visceral nervous system is a major source of information, not only from what we have eaten but also for perceiving the world around us. Our sense of safety can be strongly affected by the feedback through the vagus nerve. Stephen Porges refers to this a neuroception.[9]

There are a number of ways to stimulate the vagus nerve and therefore activate the parasympathetic nervous system. Singing, humming, gargling will all stimulate the vagus nerve, but as I mentioned before my favourite is yawning with a focus on extending the exhalation.

Stress and Fear
There is an obvious relationship between what we fear and the stress response. However, what we fear can be due to both an external situation and to the internal environment of beliefs. When you feel fearful about something like public speaking or heights, it is not primarily about the external world. If you deal with the resisted emotions and then "pressure test" yourself — choose to expose yourself to the same stress in smaller amounts to build resilience so you can remain functional under pressure, then your fears become more manageable or turn into excitement.

Breathing as a Gateway To Work with Stress
As mentioned before, on each inhalation we activate our sympathetic nervous system, on each exhalation we activate our parasympathetic nervous system. This gives us a direct way to influence the balance between our stress response and our rest/digest response.

Increasing the length of the exhalation can help your system drop into a more relaxed state.
Play with various lengths of inhalation vs. exhalation, for instance:

Square breathing to stabilise yourself when in emotional crisis

Breathe in for a count or 4.

Hold for a count of 4.

Breathe out for a count of 4.

Hold for a count of 4.

Once stable, you can increase the exhalation to stimulate the relaxation of the body.

Inhale for a count of 4

Hold for a count of 4

Exhale for a count of 6
Add to the exhalation length till you feel you are able to do it without feeling out of breath.
Alternatively, you can just yawn and extend the exhalation.

There are a lot more ways of working with the breath, if breath work interests you seeking out a breathwork practitioner maybe useful.

Stress and Your Body's Ability to Self-Correct

The process of healing is set up to happen when you are not in a survival situation. It is therefore important to be able to give your body extended periods when your stress response is off. This enables your body to become more efficient at digestion, absorption, and for self-correction to work more efficiently. This is why we sleep more when we are sick or have a broken bone.

Our system requires downtime to handle the integration and reorganisation involved in self-correcting a dysfunction.

Being able to deal with stress effectively enables you to spend more time with a balance between activation and relaxation modes of the autonomic nervous system. This improves your health dramatically.

Ultimately creating a life where you have longer periods of reduced stress will be the best investment in your health and longevity that you can make.

In the next section, we will look at the importance of sleep and its impact on your health.

Coffee and Stress, by Hannah Moore, Naturopath

There are a few things you can do to reduce stress, such as doing yoga, meditation, employing time managements strategies, deleting toxic relationships, and working in a job you love. However, there is one very simple food-based measure that always makes a significant difference to my clients' health, and this is quitting all coffee for good!
They all hate it and put up a fight initially, but as soon as they do, it they feel an immediate reduction in their stress, anxiety and an improvement in their moods and energy levels. It really is a no brainer when you look at it like this.

The coffee industry is booming, and this is purely due to the addictive nature of caffeine. Like any addictive substance, the more you have the more you need to get the same hit, and this is where the problem starts.

Coffee has been scientifically proven to increase cortisol levels for 12 hours after drinking. Therefore, the simplest way to think of coffee is that you're drinking a cup of stress.

If you are already stressed, then having more stress in the form of caffeine from coffee is not a good idea. Even if you aren't stressed, multiple cups of coffee daily can put your body into a chronically stressed state, which can lead to hypothalamus-pituitary-adrenal (HPA) dysfunction (we naturopaths used to call this adrenal fatigue but it's now more accurate to call it HPA dysfunction).

For those of you who've read the positive studies on caffeine, that's great. However, stress is the number one contributor to all health conditions, so the increased stress induced by caffeine intake ends up negating the positive effects. This is especially true in this day and age where stress levels are already through the roof without the addition of coffee.

HPA Dysfunction occurs with extended periods of stress either induced by overuse of energy drinks, hidden chronic infections, caffeinated beverages and/or stress caused by traumas, or just life's normal events and challenges, which of course can be numerous.

To understand HPA Dysfunction, we need to understand the stress response. Stress is primarily governed by the hypothalamic–pituitary–adrenal (HPA) axis. When stressed, the HPA axis is stimulated to release stress hormones and neurotransmitters such as cortisol, norepinephrine (noradrenaline), and epinephrine (adrenaline). These hormones have far-reaching effects that range from maintaining blood pressure, stimulating sex hormone production, regulating immune function, thyroid, gut health, brain function, fertility, weight and regulating energy, plus a lot more.

The effect of stress on the immune system: When stressed, immune function is reduced and infections that would normally get dealt with are able to take hold in the weakened body. This can lead to what we naturopaths call chronic hidden infections and/or stealth infections. Infections cause inflammation and when the body detects inflammation, cortisol is secreted to dampen it down, as cortisol is one of our body's main anti-inflammatories. So, it's in this way that immune dysfunction caused by chronic stress can also cause an imbalance in HPA axis.

In so called "normal daily life" (or more accurately a non-chronically stressed environment), small amounts of stress hormones are secreted throughout the day to wake us up, maintain consistent energy levels, and keep us alert. However, with long-term stress, HPA Dysfunction can occur, eroding the body's resilience to stress, depleting metabolic reserves and scrambling hormonal signals. This dysregulation can result in what I commonly see in clinic as people being tired in the morning, really tired between 2-4 pm and wired and tired (not able to sleep even though they are exhausted) at night. People may have one of these or all three, depending on the severity.

So, hopefully you can see that prolonged stress, chronic hidden infections or too much caffeine can create a very negative syndrome that can affect nearly every organ, gland and system of the body. This explains why the symptoms of prolonged stress are diverse and can be so devastating.

Additional TIP:
Tea contains caffeine, but it also contains l-theanine: a relaxing plant chemical. This is why it gives a gentle waking and relaxing effect. So, tea in moderation, especially green tea, is very beneficial due to antioxidant levels.

Chocolate, everyone's favourite, made from the cocoa plant, also wakes us up due the caffeine-like substance theobromine it contains. Theobromine does gives us energy + mental clarity but doesn't overstimulate the body like the caffeine from coffee does, so yes, hot cocoa sweetened with a mix of maple syrup and stevia is the best option in my opinion. Enjoy.

CHAPTER 3.
SLEEP

SLEEP

Our society seems to treat sleep as an unimportant aspect of life, yet the research shows very clearly that sleep is essential to many aspects of health and self-regulation.[13]

I'm sure you have experienced the day after a crappy night's sleep: feeling fatigued, inability to learn and remember things, compared to after a full night sleep where you feel refreshed and ready to take on the world.

Our body/mind/emotional health relies on sleep. Your ability to self-correct will be impacted by your ability to be present, and to feel.
Sleep is so important that if you are sleep-deprived, you will sleep as soon as you stop.

As sleep makes the individual vulnerable to predation,[14] there must be something very important that occurs, otherwise evolution would have found a way to eliminate it.

Animal studies have demonstrated that if deprived of sleep, animals will have issues with temperature regulation, gain weight and ultimately die of infections and tissue lesions as the immune system fails.15 This should sound warning bells for people with cancer in their family history.

Sleep is the best and cheapest health supplement you can ever get. It is also a great way to measure your stress levels. If you have trouble sleeping, it may be time to do emotional release work, increase the level of exercise you do, and eliminate stimulants like caffeine and screens at night.

All sorts of interesting things can happen when we get broken sleep, including impairment of our ability to regulate our emotions. In this section, we will look at what happens in the brain when we don't get enough sleep.

The brain is 2% of your body weight, yet gets 20% of your blood flow, so there is a serious amount of energy used and metabolic waste produced in the brain. The volume of blood flow that is pumped through the brain and the hard-external casing your brain sits in means that the venous return — where the blood flows out of the skull — is vital for the brain to function properly.

One of the possible causes of migraines is a restriction in fluid movement exiting the skull. This could be from fascia tension patterns running up the neck and around the base of the skull. There are other causes for migraines such as genetic disposition and sensitivity to chemicals in foods, however getting the spine stable makes a big difference to many migraine sufferers that I see in my clinic.

The brain is made up of approximately 100 billion neurons (give or take a few billion) and 10 times that number of glial cells. This is probably where the misconception occurred that we only use 10% of our brain. However, the glial cells have many uses and therefore we use 100% of our brain. Mother nature doesn't waste capacity.

Glial cells have a number of different functions. These range from acting as the immune system of the brain, supporting the highly branched neurons and maybe even guiding the neurons where to make new connections.18 Chemical signalling also occurs between glial cells. So, there is a lot going on that was not appreciated until technology allowed us to track deeper in the living brain.

When we drop into deep sleep, these glial cells shrink in size, to allow the cerebrospinal fluid (CSF) to flush out the metabolic waste of the day.

Metabolic waste builds up relatively fast. This creates the need for us to sleep every 14-16 hours or so.

One of the neurotransmitters found in the metabolic waste is called adenosine. Adenosine builds up in the brain and inhibits the areas of the brain that lead to arousal, which creates the experience of sleepiness.

The CSF flushing the brain acts like a garbage disposal service. Waste builds up if this doesn't happen. One area that is affected relatively quickly is in the pre-frontal cortex where emotions are regulated. This leads to wide swings of emotion and increases reactivity even after relatively short period of sleep deprivation or broken sleep.[13] I think every new parent can relate to this.

This has implications for conditions of the brain such as Alzheimer's, a disease where amyloid plaques build up in the brain, affecting brain function. These are fragments of the proteins that are usually broken down and eliminated. In a recent study, reduced rates of rapid eye movement (REM) sleep instead of deep sleep were correlated with an increased likelihood of Alzheimer's[78].

It is fairly safe to say that if the metabolic waste of the day is not removed by getting sufficient sleep, then dysfunction is more likely to occur.

Sleep and Memory

During our waking hours, our brain is optimised to encode memories. During sleep, these memories are consolidated into long-term memory.

Sleep can be divided into slow-wave sleep (SWS) and REM sleep. These two different states occur sequentially over a 90-110 minute cycle. The early part of the night has more SWS and less REM sleep. Later, this changes to be more REM dominant.16

SWS has a number of different frequencies associated with it, which include sharp bursts of activity called sleep spindles. These are thought to be what shifts memories from short term to long-term memory.
REM sleep is characterised by rapid eye movement and the short-term paralysis of the body, allowing the brain to rapidly replay experiences. This is thought to be part of the consolidation process of the memories.

This means that what happens in your brain during an hour's sleep varies, depending on what time of the night the sleep occurs.

This then impacts your memory and ability to learn.[81]

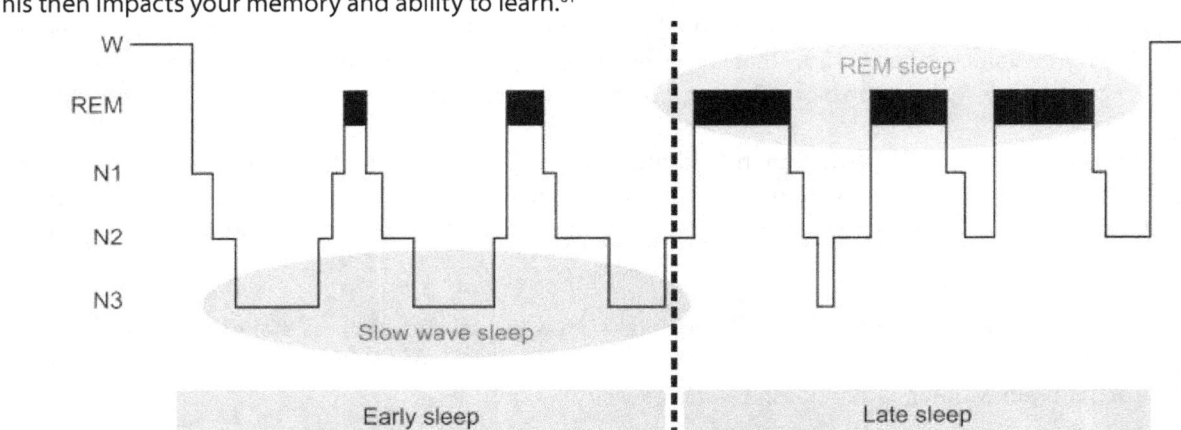

Memories are interesting as they are potentially made up of input from our different senses. However, a majority of people will have memories in visual format.

Approximately 3% of the population have a condition called aphantasia.[17] These people report that they don't remember in pictures, rather in things like lists or with words.

So, it appears that there can be many triggers for memories, for example a song or sound or smell, etc. But the actual memory in a majority of people seems to be visual in nature.

What is the format of your memories?
Recall a memory. What information from your different senses is involved?
Do you get visual, emotional, auditory, olfactory, tactile or taste aspects to the memory?

Sleep and the Immune System
Poor sleep also impacts on the immune system.
Sleep researchers have found that 711 genes were affected when they restricted participants to 6 hours of sleep each night for a week.
Half of these are down-regulated and are from the immune system, including the genes responsible for the killer T cells, which are our primary defence against tumours.[18]

The other half of the genes are upregulated and have to do with inflammation, and encourage the growth of tumours.

In one study where participants were limited to 4 hours sleep for one night, there was a 70% decrease in killer T cell activity the next day.[19,20]

In animal studies, rats with tumours were divided into two groups: one that got normal sleep, the other with interrupted sleep. The group with interrupted sleep had much larger tumours that metastasised. The control group that had normal sleep showed smaller tumours and no signs of spreading.

This research needs to be integrated into how we treat people in hospital.

As mentioned above, reduced sleep increases the inflammatory response in the body. This has a number of impacts. We will explore inflammation more in the next section.

Sleep and Hormonal Health
Men who get less than 4 hours sleep a night have lower testosterone levels than men who sleep longer. Testosterone naturally declines with age, so on average the testosterone levels seen in men with less sleep was equivalent to men 10 years their senior.[21] Lower testosterone levels have been connected to increased insulin resistance and therefore increased risk of developing type 2 diabetes.

Sleep and Larger Body Mass
Broken sleep is also correlated with a larger body mass.

You may have noticed that when you have poor sleep, you feel hungry more often.

The hormone ghrelin, which is released mainly in the stomach but also in the brain and small intestine, stimulates your appetite and is released more when the emotional regulation area in the pre-frontal cortex is dysfunctional due to broken sleep.

The sensation of hunger can also be a response to resisted emotions coming up, which is why comfort eating is a thing.

The solution is to release the resisted emotions, and this unwinds the stress within the system. The tools in chapters 6 and 7 will help with this.

So, if you have more weight than is ideal, make sure you get 8 hours of sleep a night, and work on releasing resisted emotions as well as work with what you put in your mouth and increase your exercise.

Sleep and Learning
Sleep has a major impact on the ability to learn and remember. Good sleep both before a period of learning and after massively increases the retention of information.

Sleep also has an impact on your cognitive ability. In school-based trials where they delayed the start of school by an hour, they saw a massive jump in test scores and reduction in behavioural problems.

In an experiment looking at testing if pulling an all-nighter affected memory, there was a 40% decline in memory due to lack of sleep. As such a large margin is the difference between a HD and a pass, so, are exams really testing knowledge, or just how well as person deals with stress and how well they sleep?[22]

Sleep and Heart Attacks

Less sleep has also been found to increase the risk of heart attack. Every year, the morning after daylight savings starts, in areas where people get 1 hour less sleep, there is a 24% increase in cardiac arrests.

When daylight savings reverts and people get an extra hour sleep, there is a 21% drop in heart attacks[79]. More research is being done on this, but if validated, could be the best reason for not having daylight savings time changes.

Sleep and Mental Illness

Disturbed sleep patterns have also been found in all of the mental illnesses that have been studied. These include depression, PTSD, schizophrenia, anxiety and suicide.[23]

The ability to regulate our emotions is essential to our health and how well we interact with each other.

Humans are the only species that will sacrifice sleep for entertainment. Therefore, our natural systems do not have a coping mechanism to deal with it.

So, sleep seems rather important to the body's ability to self-regulate on all levels.

One of the common ways we distort our system that affects sleep is caffeine. The caffeine molecule fits into the adenosine receptors in the brain, blocking the feeling of sleepiness.

The sheer size of the coffee industry worldwide suggests we have a massive problem with sleep deprivation, and possibly in future a large proportion of people that will experience neurological dysfunctions such as dementia and Alzheimer's.

> **The real question is, why do we choose to not do something that feels good and is incredibly good for our health?**

For some people, one answer might be that when we stop and relax, our resisted emotions show up, which feels uncomfortable — there is a good reason we resisted the emotions in the first place, we shall explore this in the section on emotions.

Sleep and Aging

One of the commonly observed patterns is that as we get older, the quality of sleep declines. This then becomes a chicken and egg scenario. Do the changes in the brain and cognitive function reduce sleep quality, or does a lack of good quality deep sleep affect the brain and create cognitive dysfunction such as memory loss, etc.?[24]

If you think it is all due to aging, there is nothing much you can do about it, but if you look at it the other way, then focusing on improving your sleep patterns may improve or at least maintain your cognitive function for longer.

While we are talking about cognitive function, a couple of supplements might help improve your memory. Lionsmane mushroom has been found to increase the neural growth factor in the brain and has been shown in randomised controlled trials to improve cognitive function in people with mild dementia. 3 grams/day in a cup of hot water (or herb tea) is the recommended dose.

One warning with medicinal mushrooms is that you need to find a good source as they need to test each batch for heavy metals. I would recommend either Teelixir (www.teelixir.com) or Fungi Perfecti in the US (or online).

The second supplement is docosahexaenoic acid (DHA), which is a fat found in the brain, myelin sheath around the nerves, the skin and in the retina of the eye. Avoid fish oils, as these are often rancid and therefore damage the health. If you can find an algae based DHA-EPA supplement like green omega 3 by Green Nutritionals, then you are not funding the industrial vacuuming up of huge quantities of krill from the ocean, which is the basis of the whole food chain.

Improving Your Sleep

A number of easy things can increase the likelihood of getting a good night's sleep.

Exercise at some point throughout the day increases overall health and has been shown to improve sleep patterns.

Reducing screen time after 5 pm can be a great help, as blue light acts to stimulate the nervous system. Putting screens on night mode will help, but being screen-free is better.

Have red coloured lights on — (e.g., a salt lamp), which imitates the red light of a sunset. This starts the brain to wind down.

Eat pistachios before bed — pistachios contain a small amount of melatonin, which can help the brain relax.

On a physical level, having a hot shower or bath in the dark or by candlelight can really help the whole body to relax. Then sleep in a slightly cool room. 18 degrees is meant to be ideal, but I think this will vary from person to person. The idea is to drop the body's core temperature down by 1 degree.

The brain wave frequency of deep sleep is between 1-4 hz. You can try and stimulate this frequency by playing a tone generator just prior to going to sleep. So, close your eyes and adjust the tone from 1-4 hz, finding where it is comfortable for you. Play for a couple of minutes and then turn it off.

Free online tone generator https://www.szynalski.com/tone-generator/
One of the key aspects of the ability to fall asleep is whether you feel safe or not.
As sleep makes you so vulnerable, the ability to relax is directly affected by how safe you feel.

Feeling Safe

Our brain has evolved to maximise the chances of survival in times of danger. This means we prioritise information about threat in our environment. However, most of us live in places where the threat of predation is very low. So, feeling unsafe is often created by a mistaken perception of reality. This sense of not being safe can create hypervigilance, anxiety, stress, and being more reactive to people around you.

These behaviours maybe great survival strategies in a dangerous situation, but as a lifestyle will cause exhaustion and ill health over time.

Two separate aspects can affect your ability to feel safe.
1. Being in a situation where you are physically at risk — such as living with an abusive partner or parent. In this case, changing that situation is the first step. This will probably require external help and support. If you are in freeze mode, you will be unlikely to cope with big changes easily. Having the courage to ask for help is the first step.
2. Feeling unsafe because of internal causes such as beliefs that the world is a dangerous place, or that you are a victim, etc.

It is this second aspect we are talking about in the next section.

The feeling of being safe is directly tied to the neurotransmitters in the brain. These are of course affected by what we have experienced before, so for instance if you have been assaulted or had a break-in at night, your system is going to feel unsafe when going to sleep. If this is the case, this trauma needs to be released before you will feel safe to sleep deeply again.

One of the neurotransmitters involved with the sense of safety is oxytocin. It is thought to allow the body to be immobilised without fear. This plays a part in reproduction, as having a person lie on top of you without feeling safe will create fear.

Oxytocin's sister neurotransmitter, vasopressin, creates mobilisation when faced with fear or anxiety. Vasopressin fits into the same receptor sites on cells as oxytocin and is probably involved in creating the fight/flight response.[25]
So, what factors influence whether oxytocin or vasopressin is released?

Dr Stephan Porges, a professor of Psychiatry at the university of North Carolina, coined the term neuroception,[9] which he defined as the nervous system's perception of threat in the environment. This perception may not be based on actual threat, but your system perceives threat and responds accordingly.

So, safety is in part an internally generated state. It is based on the stories we have created about how life is. In chapter 5, we will explore the importance of your stories about reality.

In any case, this means we can create the sense of safety within our own systems if we know how to stimulate the system to release oxytocin.

You can work with your nervous system in a number of different ways, and different things work for different people.

Techniques For Stimulating Oxytocin

1. Body-oriented oxytocin release
   - Lie on one side with a pillow between your bent knees — think of foetal position but your legs don't have to be so close to your chest; whatever is comfortable.
   - Place one hand so the palm touches your sacrum.
   - Place the other hand so the palm is on your sternum.
   - Ensure you are warm enough so you can fully relax.
   - You can either yawn, hum or listen to calming music.
   - If you get an intense pins and needles feeling in your hands, just lift a finger off your body.

2. Mind-oriented oxytocin release:
   - Think of getting a hug from someone you love.
   - Feel the pressure of their arms on your body.
   - Breathe out with a longer exhalation than inhalation.

3. Emotion-oriented oxytocin release:
   - Create the feeling of love till the muscles around your eyes wrinkle.
   - Bathe all your body in the feeling of love or kindness.

Play with these, do one at a time or try all of them together, see what makes you feel safe in your body.
The next step is to become relaxed enough so that you can feel safe with others.

When you are trusting your mind/body to a therapist, examine if you can feel safe with them. If you can't create that sense of safety, then your protective mechanism will be activated and whatever you are working on will take longer to change. This may not necessarily be about the therapist but about some of your resisted experiences. So, you may decide to work with a person that triggers you in order to integrate this area, but do it deliberately.

As we will see in the next chapter, when the body feels safe, there is a reduction in the intensity of pain. The sense of safety also allows a change in the protective mechanism of the body, from resisting change that feels threatening to allowing change to occur. This is fundamental to the body reorganising itself. In some cases, the dysfunction is primarily the body being unable to feel safe with movement, or just feeling unsafe in general.

Your ability to self-correct will depend on your internal sense of safety. This is why the use of forced manipulations or painful techniques in bodywork may interfere with the body's ability to self-correct. If the body is able to relax, trusting that no harm will come to it, then the brain can prioritise the information about the dysfunction. If there is the perception that an injury or tissue damage is likely, then guarding against that possibility is the priority.

So, what aspects are important in order to create the sense of safety as a background default setting?

The sense of being unsafe even when there is no external threat is due to sensations from our body that we are not safe. This creates hypervigilance — the sense we can never relax. The stress within the system also impacts on the digestive system, sleep and emotional regulation.

Unless you are currently in an unsafe place, any sense that you are unsafe is due to resisted emotions associated with an unresolved experience or thought process.

> During an Ortho-Bionomy session the way the body is contacted and the way the releases work continually stimulates the parasympathetic nervous system. This creates a deep sense of relaxation and often people feel in an altered state as their body goes through the process of releasing long held patterns on the physical and emotional levels.

Feeling Safe Exercise

Do the following when you are in a safe, comfortable environment.

- Imagine you are face to face with something you consider scary (a dog, heights, blood, or whatever freaks you out). How does your body feel? We will call that 0.
- Take a few deep breaths and look around you, wait until your nervous system feels "normal," whatever that is for you.
- Now imagine you feel incredibly safe, with someone you love holding you — we will call that a 10.
- Take a few deep breaths and look around you.
- Now assess how safe you feel in your everyday life, in the absence of any new external threats?
- If you do feel unsafe, can you recognise what makes you feel that way?
- Is it due to an external factor? If so, is there a way to change that situation?
- Is it due to an internal factor that you can work with?
- If you don't recognise the threat, you may need to do work on your emotional state to get more clarity.

One aspect of feeling unsafe when there is no external threat is a belief that you cannot cope with life. This is possibly part of the pattern of going into freeze mode.
If this feels like it is part of your pattern, tune into it and yawn until the feeling clears.

If you do feel unsafe, you can create a sense of safety by hugging yourself:
- Place your right hand under your left armpit.
- Place your left arm on your right upper arm.
- Apply gentle but firm pressure with both arms.
- Yawn.

The internal sense of safety on the emotional level is one of the rewards for processing resisted emotions, so we will revisit this in chapter 6.

The sense of safety in the body on the physical level affects the range of movement of joints.
When the body feels unsafe in a movement, the muscles surrounding the joint will contract to prevent injury. This is the protective response at work, some conditions such as whiplash, chronic lower back pain and frozen shoulder are created or made worse by this process.

One of the ways we work with the body from an Ortho-Bionomy perspective is to make the body feel safe, both from being injured due to techniques, and by feeling held without pressure to change. When the body feels safe, the protective mechanism turns off and the self-corrective mechanism engages. This is the ideal situation for the body to work out how to function more efficiently.

Safety and Uncertainty

Our brains are set up to put things on automatic as fast as possible. This is how we create the illusion of certainty. The idea that today is the same as yesterday is quite bizarre, since there is ample evidence that change occurs, for instance the weather, yet we have routines, we eat at the same time, work the same hours (well, some people do), and create this pretence that things are certain.

However, reality has a habit of crashing that occasionally: natural disasters, terrorism, climate change, financial meltdowns, being sacked have a greater impact if you are pretending that life is certain and then it isn't.

You will be better able to deal with change if you base your internal sense of safety on your ability to adapt to a changing reality. This is what being flexible in your approach to life means, and this is really the only certainty. By this is I don't mean you should compromise your values, but become flexible about how you think about reality and consider that the things you hold onto now

A bird sitting on a branch is never afraid of the branch breaking, because he trusts his wings not the branch.

Creating safety in your body creates greater adaptability to the dynamic nature of life

to create safety actually make you more vulnerable to a changing world. For instance, during the GFC there were billionaires who committed suicide because they had lost a significant amount of money. The fact that they still had more money than most people will ever have in their life was irrelevant to them.

So, what helps you create certainty in your life?
Is it your family, friends, your pets, owning property, your job, how much money you have, your house, what car you drive? Research suggest that the more social engagement a person has, the more stability and safety they have in their life[80]. Therefore, if your relationships with other people help you create certainty and safety in your life, then investing in making them strong is a good external strategy.

However ultimately your internal sense of safety is created internally so that is where you need to work.

Safety and Rejection
When we do not feel safe within ourselves we can often look for others to supply that for us. This can make us put up with all sorts of negative behaviour by the people around us as the fear of rejection is worse than the suffering due to their behaviour.

The key is when you create your own safety within yourself being treated poorly becomes unacceptable and you can move on. If you recognise that you may be doing putting up being treated badly by people who are meant to care for you then make sure you explore what is making you feel unsafe within yourself. The tools in chapter 6 & 7 will be handy for this.

Safety and Resilience
When we feel that we can cope with change in the external world, this will naturally make us feel safer. So, is it possible to create more resilience in your life?

One of the interesting things about the human brain is that a majority of humans are wired to offer assistance to people they don't know. You can see this when there is a natural disaster, even if it is in a different country. People donate money and other things in order to help out.

This behaviour is wired into our brains and has helped humans become the successful species we are. Our brain chemistry rewards us for doing this. When we do things for ourselves, the dopamine reward we feel is much shorter-lived than when we help someone else.
From a personal development perspective, the way to avoid the ego is to step beyond endlessly being in service to self and become active in service to others, or being in service to something bigger than ourselves.

So, even if you currently do not feel you have a good support network, asking for help will improve your resilience, and you will quite likely get the support you need. It just may not be from the people you know.

Another option to create a better support network is to find people who need assistance. The stronger the community you create around you, the more resilient you will feel, and if/when you need help there will be people keen to help you out.

Integrity

As having a strong connection to your community creates resilience, your level of integrity is vital for maintaining that connection. Establishing a good reputation by doing what you promise builds trust. Anything that erodes trust will impact on your sense of safety within the community. One of the costs of being out of integrity is the loss of trust from the community, but also the fear that if the other members of the community found out what you have done, you would be excluded. We are social animals and being ostracised has a psychological effect of making the world a more dangerous place.

Let's return to the theme of this chapter. From the perspective of the ability to self-correct, sleep is vital, and the quality of your sleep depends on your levels of stress, which in part depends on your internal sense of safety. Your sense of safety depends on your internal emotional state as well as the quality of your connection to your community.

Your connection to others influences how you respond to the people around you, which is directly related to whether you are in your stress response. This in turn is related to the presence of any unresolved emotional baggage. It really is a highly inter-related web. The good news is, you can pull it apart and optimise each piece as you go.

A good place to start is to set aside some time and feel your sense of internal safety — as you did above. If you are not feeling safe, then do the exercise below. Track to see if your internal sense of safety changes the more you do this. Give yourself 10 - 20 minutes. Either when you wake up or when you are about to go to bed are ideal times to do this.

Body-oriented oxytocin release
- Lie on one side with a pillow between your bent knees.
- Place one hand palm touching your sacrum.
- Place the other hand palm on your sternum.
- Ensure you are warm enough so you can fully relax.
- You can either yawn, hum or listen to calming music.
- If you get an intense pins and needles feeling in your hands just lift a finger off your body.

Pineal Gland Meditation to Help You Drop into Deep Sleep Faster

The pineal gland is a small pinecone-shaped lump that sits between the two hemispheres of the brain. A line from between your eyebrows straight back to deep in your brain is close to your pineal gland.

Your pineal gland takes serotonin (your happy hormone) and when it is dark, converts it to melatonin.

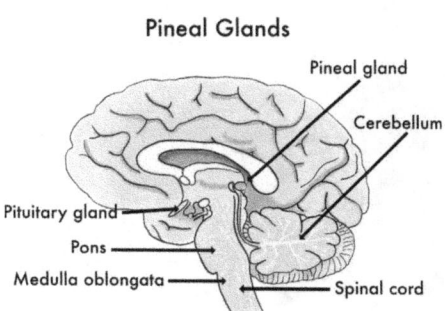

Pineal Glands

To help stimulate this production, you can do a neat little process.

1. Do all of the things mentioned above – hot shower, pistachios, no screens after 5pm, red lights etc.
2. Lie on your side and do 10 minutes with your hand on sternum/sacrum.
3. Bring you attention from between your eyebrows in a straight line to where your brainstem is and have your intention that your focus will shift to your pineal gland. Hold your attention there in a relaxed, calm way as long as you can. Notice how you feel.

When I do this, I initially start to feel the pulsing of the blood flowing in my head, then fine-tune my awareness to deep in my brain, and within a couple of minutes this beautiful softness spreads through my brain, and deep sleep swallows me.

If you are depressed, you may want to add a few minutes of focussing on things that make you happy before you do the above process. This could be recalling memories that make you smile, listening to comedy or just deciding to create the feeling of being happy.

CHAPTER 4.
HOW PAIN WORKS

HOW PAIN WORKS

No discussion of the body's ability to self-correct can be complete without looking at how pain works. The last 15 years of research has completely changed how pain is viewed.

Let's take a simple painful incident and follow what happens.

You stub your toe.
The receptors in your toe, which were known as pain receptors but are better described as threat receptors, fire, sending a stimulus (this is not what you experience as pain) up to the dorsal ganglion near your spine. If the stimulus is over a certain threshold, the message moves to the dorsal horn of the spinal cord and then travels up to the brain.

Initially, the stimulation goes to the thalamus, then one branch goes to the primary sensory cortex, which gives you the location of the sensation and tracks the intensity of the signal.

The other branch from the thalamus goes to the amygdala, which is part of the emotional region of the brain. The amygdala looks for information from the hippocampus about what the brain knows about this stimulus. This is where your past experience, beliefs and thoughts create your response to the stimulus. The amygdala then creates a response that is connected to the location from which the stimulus came. This response is what you will experience as pain.

This means that your thoughts, beliefs and past experiences have a major impact on how you experience pain in your body.

There is a difference between acute pain and chronic pain from the perspective of what happens in the nervous system.

> **Acute pain is usually less than 3 months, usually associated with tissue damage.**
>
> **Chronic pain persists beyond 3 months and is associated with output from the limbic system of the brain**

From FMRI work, we know that acute pain stimulates areas of the brain that are associated with input from the body.

With chronic pain, the emotional areas of the brain are giving off a stronger signal. This means that to effectively treat pain, you need to do different things to work with chronic pain vs. acute pain.

With acute pain, the main focus is on alignment of the skeletal structure, releasing the soft tissue and allowing the body to heal itself.

With chronic pain, there can be physical misalignments of the skeletal structure and soft tissue holding patterns, but also the emotional aspect, such as fear of more pain or fear of movement. This fear is not usually on a conscious level, like a fear of spiders, but more like a resistance to movement held within the soft tissues that is holding the body out of alignment.

Any fear of movement will arise when the body moves to self-correct.

We can release this fear by making the body feel safe. Then the body is more likely to allow the skeletal structure to change.

Another thing that can change is the sensitivity to feedback from the area where you have chronic pain. The nociceptive receptors that give your body information about the threat of damage in an area are replaced every 3-4 days. One theory about chronic pain is that when the pain becomes constant, the body increases the number of nociceptive receptors in the area. This leads to an increase in the sensitivity to the stimulus from the body. Part of the way to reverse this is to make the body feel safe and if possible break the constant pain cycle. This may require painkillers along with Ortho-bionomy.

The Difference Between Pain and Suffering

The distinction between pain and suffering can be subtle. As we all experience things differently, how we define pain and suffering is individual, but there does seem to be a relationship between how much we resist our experience and how much we suffer.

I recently had a hip replaced due to a congenital hip issue. After surgery I had 1/10 pain despite having had my femur cut off, my acetabulum ground out and a titanium shaft hammered down my femur. Evidentially, most people experience quite a lot of pain as I was given opioid based pain killers and put on a fentanyl drip.

After an adverse drug response on day 2, they removed all the painkillers except Panadol and I continued to feel 1/10 pain. So, I'm not sure why I didn't suffer to the point of needing opioids and fentanyl. Maybe I'm a bit thicker than the average person, or maybe I accepted the stimulus from my body willingly and so the emotional component from my brain, which creates suffering, wasn't engaged.

It does seem that our approach to life has a bearing on whether we suffer or not.

Next time you are in pain, experiment with resisting it and seeing if the pain increases or decreases, then fully embrace the pain, feel into it and yawn.

*This works a treat, except when you have major jagged nerve pain associated with nerve impingement for instance severe sciatic nerve pain. The high-level pain is therefore more from the nociceptors in the body screaming, not the emotional centres in the brain.

Meditation To Help Reduce Chronic Pain, Anxiety and Fear

The periaqueductal grey (PAG) is a small area of the brain that is rich in opioid receptors. These are part of the inhibitory pathway that reduces the sensitivity to pain within your nervous system.[26,27] As the stimulus from nociceptors (threat receptors in your body) enter the brain, it goes through the PAG and from there to other parts of the brain. The PAG has been a target for deep brain stimulation, that is, neurosurgeons have tried to insert electrodes to stimulate this area to suppress chronic pain. Unfortunately, the side effects of stimulation were highly unpredictable. The good thing is you don't need an electrode to stimulate this area of the brain. Your attention will do just fine.

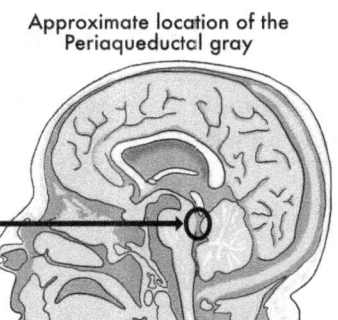

Approximate location of the Periaqueductal gray

The best part is, we don't need to get it right, it is the intention that is actually the most important part. Having a location to focus on does help.

As depicted in the picture, if you bring your awareness from the bridge of your nose backwards to behind your brainstem you will be in the area of the PAG.

Then in a gentle way focus on the PAG and see what you feel.

Keep refining your attention until you feel a wave of relaxation spread through your system.

I find that when I use this, for instance at the dentist, it helps relax the body right up until the dentist jabs a nerve with his probe, or just exploring what it feels like I get a deep numb sensation that is quite calming and reduces pain.

If your typical stress response is freeze and disassociate, then you might actually find this easier to use as the PAG is thought to activate strongly during that process.

So, if you are experiencing chronic pain, fear or anxiety, then spend some time accessing the PAG and see what that feels like. Practicing this technique makes it easier to access the right area of the brain.

The presence of inflammation also increases sensitivity to pain and causes pain in tissues. There are also changes in the brain that can occur when pain persists. All of these things can influence your ability to change painful conditions. The great thing is that your body is trying to find a way to change and become more efficient. It just needs some help.

Inflammation, Pain and Emotions

As we saw in the chapter on stress, inflammation is an important part of how your body heals damaged tissue. There is however an interaction between inflammation and the intensity of pain. When you have an injury, it makes sense that the area needs to be protected from further injury. The chemicals released that create inflammation also increase the feedback from the nociceptors. This increases the pain from the area and makes the body reduce the movement, thus allowing the damaged area to heal.

In chronic inflammation, the irritation of the nociceptors can lead to greater sensitisation of the area. This then increases the amount of feedback from the area and is part of the chronic pain pattern.

As well as the relationship with stress, there is some evidence that how we think influences our levels of inflammation. Hostile attitudes were found to increase inflammation and be associated with increased pain, coronary heart disease and depression.[28,29] As mentioned before in the stress and inflammation section, being conscientious was associated with a reduction in inflammatory markers in the body.

The digestive system is one of the common areas of inflammation. This can be due to eating foods you are intolerant to on a regular basis. With the huge increase of gluten intolerance, IBS, Crohn's disease and other bowel issues, it is interesting to ask what has changed in our diets in the last 10-20 years that could be creating this ill health.

Of course many things have changed, but one of the stand-out chemicals that has increased massively in the food chain is glyphosate, the active ingredient of Roundup. As you may have heard, Monsanto (now Bayer) has lost two large court cases for Roundup causing lymphoma, and there is a large class action in process at the moment.

In pigs, GMO soy in the feed increased the inflammation of the gut compared to non-GMO soy.

Glyphosate has also been found to increase the proliferation of estrogen-sensitive breast cancer cells in humans[30] and create celiac and gluten intolerance symptoms in animal studies.[31]

The key here is that GMO foods are designed to withstand roundup, so they are sprayed more often, since weeds are becoming resistant to glyphosate.

Unfortunately, most grains/legumes including wheat, lentils, chickpeas, rye, buckwheat are sprayed with roundup just before harvest in order to desiccate the crop (dry it out so there is less likelihood of mould or sprouting when the crop is stored). In some countries, sugar cane is also sprayed just prior to harvesting.

So, in a diet with processed foods, you will be exposed to some glyphosate. The glyphosate kills off the microbes in your gut, changing how your digestive system works. Since our gut microbes make our Vitamin Bs, serotonin and dopamine, it is realistic to expect this will impact not only our health but how we feel as well.

Once the gut is inflamed, the gut lining is less able to absorb nutrients and is more likely to become sensitised to other chemicals. Bloating, gut pain, diarrhoea, constipation, a constant need to eat can all be signs of inflammation of the gut. If you have any of these, you may benefit from working with a naturopath to heal the gut.

If you would like more information on this, check out *What's Making Our Children Sick?* by Perro and Evans[81], or Dr Zach Bush does a great talk exploring the effects of glyphosate on the digestive system. The link is in the reference section.

Your Protective Mechanism

The body has a built-in protective mechanism when experiencing musculoskeletal pain. Common responses are to reduce movement to prevent further damage to the area, and creating adaptive changes to get the bodyweight off the area, for instance limping if you have a sore ankle.

Contracting the global muscles (muscles we use to move) is one way to brace an area to stop movement. If you have ever had a muscle go into spasm, you will recognise this process.

Adaptive patterns can include changes to the posture to prevent movement of the area. For instance, if you have an apparent leg length difference (some difference in leg length is normal, but if the pelvis is jammed in either posterior rotation (like when you are in sitting position) or anterior rotation (the position of the back leg when you are striding forward), you will get an apparent leg length difference. This is really a compensation pattern which will often self-correct once the 4th and 5th lumbar vertebrae are in a more stable position.

Many Chiropractors will treat an apparent leg length difference by using wedges under the pelvis. However, as the leg length is a compensation pattern it will return within a few minutes once you start moving around. If you fine tune the relationship between the lower two vertebrae you can often see the leg length difference change when the body recognises the increased stability in the lower back.

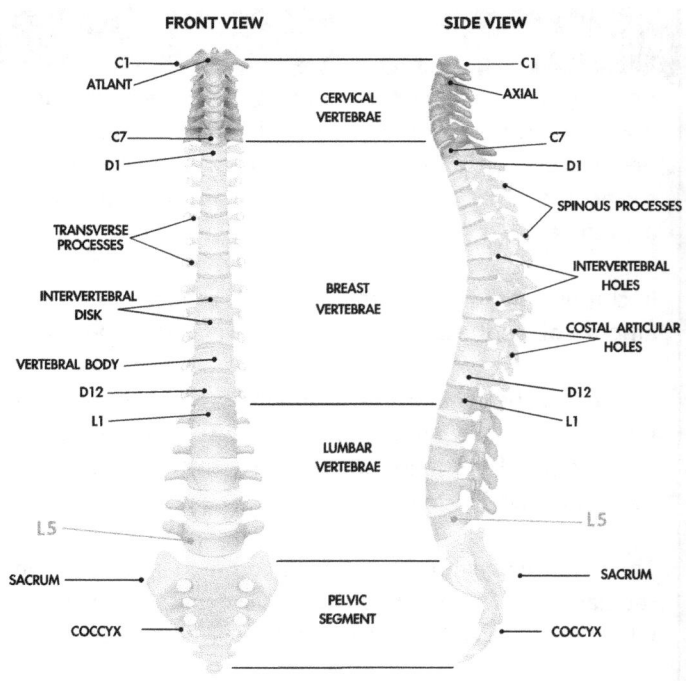

One of the findings from pain science is that the perception of fear within the body can influence the intensity of pain. Lorimer Mosley and his co-workers invented the acronym DIM SIM as an easy way to present this. Danger in Me increases the intensity of pain, Safety in Me reduces the intensity of pain.[32] This ties in beautifully with how we approach the body in Ortho-Bionomy in order to stimulate the self-corrective process. When you are in a position of comfort, your body is ready to pay attention to novel information that can help it understand the dysfunction. When the body understands what is going on, it has the capacity to change it.

In contrast, when there is a lot of pain, there is resistance to feeling into that area of the body, which reduces the likelihood of the information from the area being used to understand the dysfunction. Pain is much louder than the feedback from proprioceptive reflexes in the painful area. This is part of why there is often a sense of confusion about the area of the body that is painful. This creates the situation where the dysfunction creates the fear and pain that prevents the nervous system making sense of the underlying dysfunction. In this situation, change becomes scary as it often leads to more pain.

Anything that is perceived as a threat to the body such as a painful technique or forced manipulation of the skeletal structure can engage the protective mechanism, which in turn will inhibit the body's ability to change. Some areas of the body are far more guarded than others. For instance, the neck often has a strong protective mechanism, as it is fairly susceptible to injury.

Shoulder pain will also often be accompanied by the body protecting the area. This often includes the Pectoralis Minor (one of the chest muscles) pulling the shoulder forward and the rotator cuff holding to create more support for the humerus (upper arm). This reduces the range of movement and is often an underlying condition to painful dysfunctions such as bursitis and rotator cuff tears.

If we want to work effectively with the body's intelligence, we need to make the body feel safe. This starts with how we welcome a client into our clinic, how we talk to them, how we touch their body. The nervous system is finely tuned to assess threat, especially when there is existing intense pain threatening the system. If we can create a safe space, our ability to help the body recognise what is happening with a dysfunction improves dramatically.

This is Basis Of What we do With Ortho-Bionomy

The core of Ortho-Bionomy is connecting to a person in a way that stimulates the body to self-correct. A painful musculoskeletal dysfunction can be the result of a number of different causative factors, including physical tissue damage, increased sensitivity to movement which the body reads as a threat and therefore triggers pain, and emotional holding patterns such as fear. Negative thought processes such as "things always get worse," structural misalignments and asymmetric functional patterns are also possible causes. We need to be able to work on all these levels in order to meet the mind/body and assist it to self-correct.

Let's explore how these factors may interact.

Suppose you have just got off a plane from a long flight, you grab your bag, but instead of keeping your bicep contracted (your elbow slightly bent) your arm is straight. The weight of the bag pulls down on the postural muscles fibres and ligaments supporting the joints at the elbow and shoulder. The next day, you get a deep ache in your shoulder and it hurts to bend your elbow. Your shoulder looks like it is forward of your body and there is pain in a few different places. The pain increases, and disturbs your sleep, and any shoulder movement creates more pain. After a while it is only comfortable to hold your arm close to the body.

A few things may be happening. One is that the initial pull of the bag distorted the ligaments at the elbow and the ligaments and joint capsule in the shoulder.

The body has then engaged the pectoralis minor to bring the shoulder forward. With the shoulder in the forward position, the rotator cuff muscles are recruited to support the humerus in the glenohumoral joint (the cup of the shoulder). When the shoulder is in the forward position, the space around the subacromial bursa is reduced and the constant pressure from the supraspinatus muscle aggravates the bursa, which gets inflamed and painful. The bursa is normally about 0.74 mm thick, but once inflamed, this can almost double (sometimes up to 1.25 mm). This then leads to constant pain and aggravation.

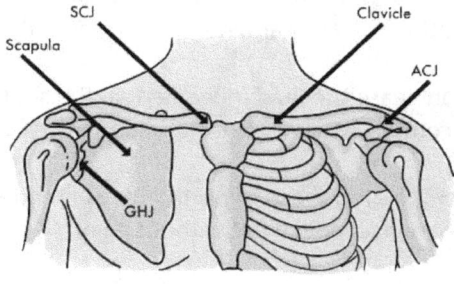

Acromioclavicular joint (ACJ)
Sternoclavicular joint (SCJ)
Glenohumeral joint (GHJ)

When the shoulder joint isn't moved for a period of time, the synovial fluid (the lubricant in the joint) isn't distributed and the joint becomes more painful.

Once you have a pattern of "movement = pain," the protective mechanism becomes more sensitive to movement and the muscles around the shoulder contract to control and reduce movement. This the precursor to your bursitis and/or frozen shoulder.

The way we might work with this in an Ortho-Bionomy session is to start with the psoas major muscle. The psoas muscle is on the inside of your lower back and stabilises the lumbar spine, as well as acting to flex your hip, but more importantly in this case, it has a connection to the parasympathetic nervous system (your rest/digest response). When you release the psoas without causing pain, the whole body starts to relax and feel safe. We might then work up though the ribcage with a particular attention to the upper three ribs.

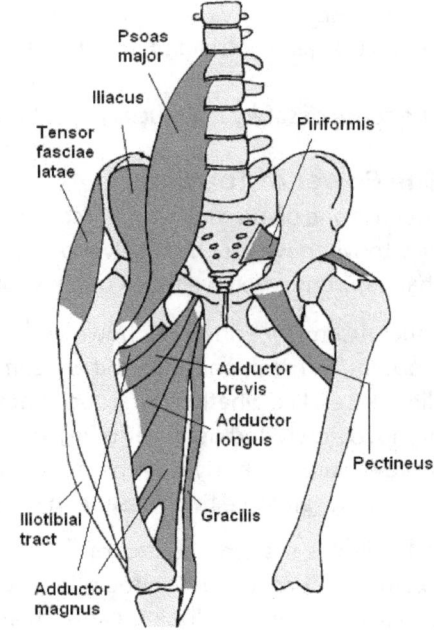

As there is no force or pain created by Ortho-Bionomy, your body learns that you won't be hurt by anything that is happening.

So, when we start to touch the shoulder, we cradle it, allowing it to feel supported and safe. The protective mechanism can start to relax, which starts to open the body to new information about what is happening in the shoulder and new possibilities of how it can move without pain, rather than just focusing on stopping the pain by stopping any movement.

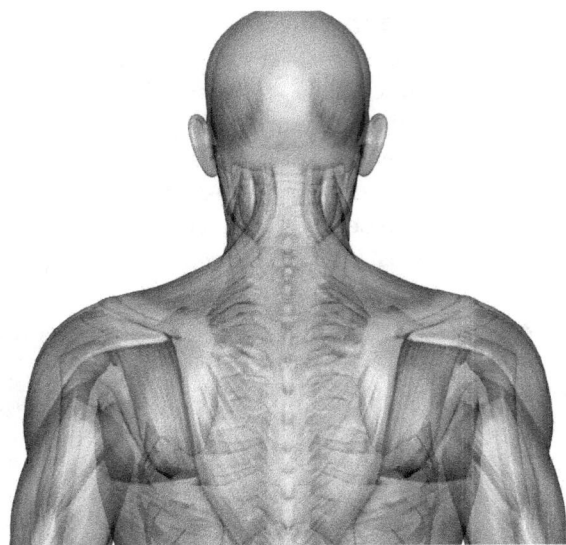

Then, slowly and carefully, we work out what is happening with the alignment of the bones at the joints, starting at the sternoclavicular joint (SCJ), where the collarbone meets the breast bone, then the acromioclavicular joint (ACJ), at the far end of the collarbone, and finally the glenohumoral joint (GHJ) (see picture for locations). We check and release what is happening with the three small ligaments at the front of the shoulder and the muscles of the rotator cuff.

To increase the fluid movement in the shoulder joint, we use a slight pumping movement, but always with the arm in a position of comfort.

All of this is done in a way that doesn't threaten the body, which increases the ability of the body relax, and this helps the body to experience movement without pain.

This challenges the protective mechanisms pattern that "movement = pain" in that shoulder.

With the ligaments at the elbow, we use very gentle traction.

The approach of making the body feel safe is a great first step with any chronic painful condition and greatly improves the effectiveness of any gentle techniques used. Making the body feel safe assists it in changing alignment on a structural level and allows the fascia to release, which alters the functional patterns in the body.

The sense of safety is a crucial part of enabling the body to self-correct.

The Power of Touch

Touch is one of our fundamental senses for conveying love. Our brain pays attention to touch from someone else in a very different way to when we touch ourselves. An example of this is that we cannot tickle ourselves. There is actually a neurological inhibition that happens when we touch ourselves that turns down the stimulus from the area touched.

Touch from someone else, however, is monitored very closely by the nervous system. Initially the touched maybe assessed as a potential threat, and then if it is deemed safe, the body will relax and shift into looking for information from that touch. Small differences, like whether you touch another person with a hard hand or a soft hand, whether you move in an abrupt forceful way or move slowly and gently all give the body information about your intention and whether the protective mechanism needs to be on to ensure the body is prepared to withstand force. In order to create the best chance for the body to self-correct, we want to constantly reinforce the message that it is safe.

In the limbic system, the part of the brain that creates emotions, there is an area called the hypothalamus this is one area where oxytocin is produced. Oxytocin is a hormone/neurotransmitter that is involved in creating the feeling of being loved. It also enslaves parents into looking after their children for decades. Oxytocin is also involved in behaviours such as being generous to strangers, and trust,[33] as well being associated with envy and gloating.[34] The variation in these behaviours is probably due to the combination of other neurotransmitters that are being released at the same time. This would be associated with how we interpret the social situations.

Oxytocin is probably also involved in many other processes that we don't know about yet.

As I mentioned earlier in the section on yawning, the area of the brain that regulates the fight/flight response with the rest-digest response is called the pituitary. Oxytocin is released in both the pituitary gland and the amygdala (which creates the fear response), which means oxytocin has the potential to interrupt stress and fear.[35] This is why a hug from someone you love can make you feel better when you are upset.

So, if we can get the brain to release oxytocin, then the fear and stress in the body can be reduced for long enough for more information to be put into the nervous system. This enables the body to unwind the dysfunction. This may be what creating the feeling of being safe and using positions of comfort does on a neurological level and why the results of working this way exceed the use of force.

Every time you come in physical contact with another person's body, you will create a change in the neurotransmitters being released. This can be an increase in stress hormones such as cortisol, or creating the sense of safety, which allows the stress response to reset in the body.

Our nervous system is set up to take notice of external touch, as this could be associated with a threat, for instance a spider walking on your skin. This focused awareness can therefore be used to increase the awareness of where the bones are, and their alignment. This can be done by gently touching the bones on either side of a joint. The body recognises the touch but is not threatened, so it starts to use the information about bone location, and fine tunes the alignment. If force is used, the body focuses on protecting itself from possible injury and therefore does not utilise the information in the same way.

Pain In Detail, and How We Work With It in Ortho-Bionomy

There is a lot we don't know about how the body works, and there is more being discovered every year. So, this is definitely a section that will change and evolve as we learn more.

When the body is treated in a way that makes it feel safe, there is a shift from sympathetic dominance (fight/flee response) to parasympathetic (rest/digest response). In order to maximise this, Ortho-Bionomy sessions are usually an hour long, and as mentioned before, there are no forced manipulations or painful techniques used.

The way we contact the body is with soft hands that mould to the client's body, allowing the body to show the practitioner where they are in space, which give us an indication of what the dysfunction might be. We can then find what is comfortable for the client, which is usually a slight exaggeration of the dysfunction. When we slightly exaggerate the dysfunction, we stimulate the nervous system both with the touch and with any movement used. This enables the nervous system to gain new information about what is happening on a structural level.

Because the body feels safe, the protective mechanism is not engaged and the body starts to look for more information about the dysfunction.

A deep ache in a joint often comes from the type 4 receptors in the joint capsule. Finding a position of comfort for the joint and applying gentle compression stimulates type 1 receptors in the joint capsule, which in turn inhibit the type 4 receptors. In effect, the gentle compression turns off the sensation that is being interpreted as pain.

Where muscles are in spasm, we look for the unstable joint that the muscle is crossing. By working with the joint alignment we enable the body to find a more stable way to use the bones. Once the joint self-corrects, the body no longer needs to recruit the muscle, so the spasm releases. This means that tight muscles become indicators of joint dysfunction.

There are some instances of muscle dysfunction such as a "pulled" muscle, but mostly muscles are tight because they are recruited to increase the support in the area, due to a joint dysfunction.

When we overextend a joint, the ligaments are often distorted. In this case, we use gentle traction to stimulate the ligaments to recoil back into a length that supports the joints. We also use traction when working with fascia.

Pleasure to Replace Pain

One of the things that often happens when someone has been in pain for a period of time and their level of pain changes during a session of Ortho-Bionomy is that they go searching to find it. So, in order to shift the pattern from looking for pain we have clients feel for comfort and ease of movement. In effect we are asking clients to notice what is working rather than focusing on what isn't working.

Another way that can be useful is to offer feedback from the body that creates pleasure.
One way to do this is with the CT afferent receptors.

CT Afferents

CT afferents are a type of sensory receptor in the haired skin, which, when gently stroked at approximately 5 cm/sec, stimulate the pleasure centres in the brain.[36]

Try this one your own arm.
- Close your eyes.
- Gently stroke up and down your forearm for a 30 seconds, see if you feel more relaxed.
- Then go and experiment on people around you (with permission of course).
- Babies in particular love this on arms and legs.

The moving nature of this stimulus may make it more preferable for people who tend to go into the flee response but in general if people like being touched this will create a pleasant sensation.

When we touch a person's body, we are really touching their brain, and when we connect to a person we are changing the chemical balance of their brain. You can either be creating stress hormones, or helping them to relax.

You can look at pain as the body saying NO.
Conversely comfort or pleasure is the body saying YES.

Another way to change your response to pain is to change your brain. This is what we will be playing with next.

Three Ways to Change Your Brain

There are three ways to change your brain.

Changing your brain chemistry
When we change our thinking, do exercise, or shift out of an emotional pattern, we change the chemical balance of our brain. This is really quick but doesn't lead to long term changes in how the brain works. The behavioural change needs to be repeated to create the shift again. This does however open the possibility for creating a different experience in the moment and can lead to long-term changes. So, for instance, if you are depressed and you can shift out of it for a period of time, this will confirm that you can shift your mood. The period spent feeling lighter and not depressed will also allow you to experience other emotions, which you can recall if you later become depressed again.
In short, being able to create a shift in your emotional state by changing your brain chemistry is an important tool.

Growing new neurons
This is the process of neural plasticity at work. Neurons can take between 3 weeks and 18 months to grow, so daily practice will help upgrade your brain. This is what happens when you practice a new skill. So, if you find that a particular technique is effective for you, then repeating the technique on a daily basis will create a shift in the structure of the brain within as short a period as three weeks. This might be doing a form of exercise, doing breathing exercises or a short meditation, finding something that creates a positive shift in your brain chemistry, and repeating daily till it feels like you are addicted to it.

Changing networks
When we change what we are doing and are consistent, any old patterns that are no longer needed start to change. This is a slower process, but allows the whole system to realign itself. If you have spent a few years being depressed, then you will have set up your brain to do that really well. This might include noticing what isn't right in your life, ignoring all the things that are working, or downplaying their importance, avoiding exercise, eating foods that make you feel bad, etc. So, when you start to collect techniques that offer you some respite from feeling depressed, you can get longer and longer periods where you are not feeling down. You shift your focus to what is functioning well, supportive friends, family, enjoyable activities, etc. The connections that aren't being used daily will start to be reorganised. Constant persistence over time is the crucial part in reorganising your brain networks. But it all starts with the decision to change, and repeatedly reinforcing the new pattern on a daily or weekly basis.

An example of how you can use this:
Let's say you would like to increase your level of exercise. The best way to do this is to make sure whatever you do is pleasurable for the first three weeks. By actively stimulating the pleasure circuit in your brain while exercising, there will be natural tendency to do more. If on the other hand you choose a form of exercise that you hate, your resistance to exercise will increase and you are more likely to stop.

Once you have established that exercise is pleasurable, then starting to push a little bit harder will be a natural extension of the process, who doesn't want to feel more pleasure?

Some people need to exercise with others because the social aspect is what makes it pleasurable, while others need solitude. Get a feel of what works for you, then set aside the time to make it happen.

Even 10 minutes of exercise at the start is beneficial. For me, buying a second-hand kayak and going down to the local river has been a brilliant way to increase my level of exercise. Being able to watch birds, lizards, fish and rays while doing resistance training with a cool breeze is such a great way to shift my internal state and work my body.

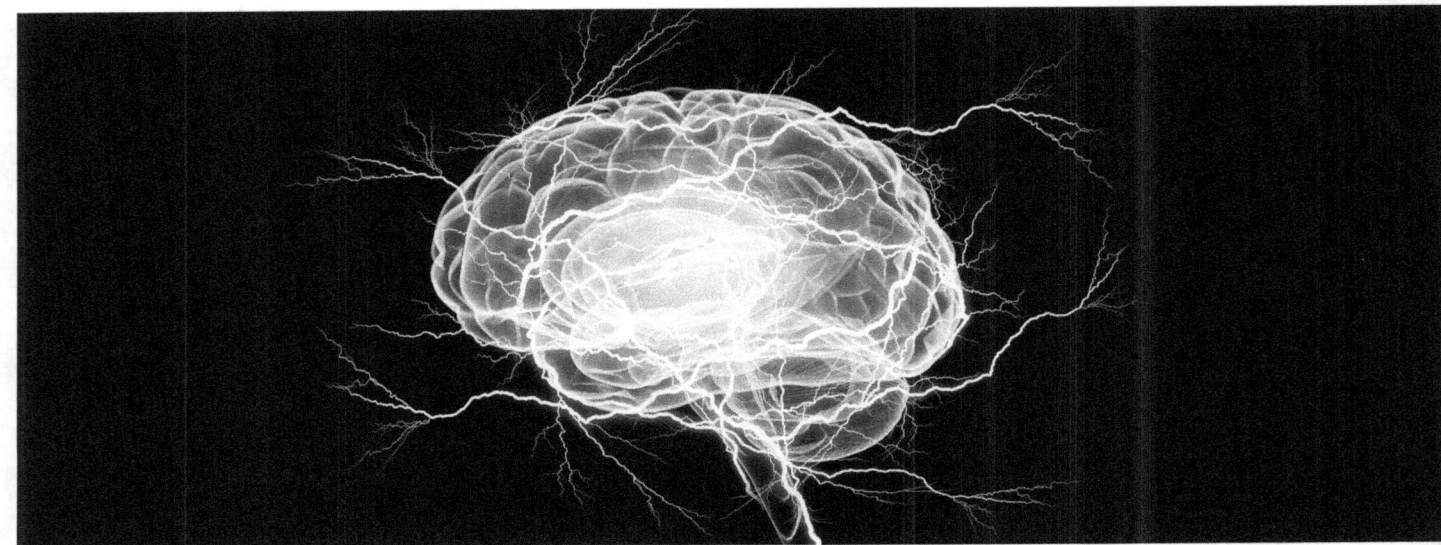

Changing Your Brain to Change Your Life
One of the major factors affecting your life is your general attitude.

Are you a glass half empty or glass half full person?

This actually makes a huge difference when it comes to pain.

When a person has experienced years of chronic pain and nothing has helped, the experience sucks the joy out of their life and becoming a pessimist is very common.

However, this is a positive feedback loop (increasing the pain) as a pessimist will expect the worst and when it comes to chronic pain which, as we have seen above is associated with the emotional parts of the brain, you will create what you expect.

In particular, frustration and anger seem to increase the sensitivity to pain.[37]

By focusing on the pain, the body gets the message to increase the sensitivity in that area, which of course means the signalling can become louder.

When I do a session on a pessimistic person, they will often immediately ignore the change in level of pain in the area I have worked on and point out the pain somewhere else. This is a sign that we need to spend some time on working with the mind as well as the body.
Noticing increases in range and ease of movement — what is working rather than what isn't working — starts the process of changing the automatic focus on the dysfunction.

Spending time noticing the small successes, reduction in the level of pain in a small area, and increased range of movement is an important aspect to shifting the habit of focusing on the dysfunction. This creates hope that the chronic pain maybe temporary and allows the person to look beyond constant pain. The tools to work with emotions are also invaluable for this process.

Understanding pain allows you to work out whether the stimulus is more likely to be from damaged tissue, or chronic pain due more to emotional holding patterns. Sometimes this can be more complex, for instance when there is constant pain in a joint from inflammation or autoimmune issues. There can be both an emotional component and physical damage leading to pain in this case. Our conditioning about what pain means is also important, as it can focus our attention either on the pain as a threat or more as an inconvenience, and our experience of the pain will vary accordingly.

Trying the different tools in this book may help you find the level of your dysfunction and therefore help you find how to work with it.
In the next chapter, we will look at how our thoughts can impact on our health.

CHAPTER 5.
WORKING WITH THE MIND

WORKING WITH THE MIND

Self-care on the Mental Level

Humans are tricky beings, particularly on the mental level, and it is far beyond the scope of this book to deal with all the possibilities and suggest ways of working with them.

Each person is an individual and how your mind and emotions work will reflect that. Finding tools that work for you at this present time is the best thing to do. As you change, the tools that are most effective may change as well. With this in mind, I have included a number of different ways of working. All the tools that I favour are aligned with the principles of Ortho-Bionomy. The focus is on increasing the level of awareness of the underlying dysfunction, because once it is understood, the system will self-correct. This holds true for the mental and emotional aspects of being human as well as the physical.

Just because you think something doesn't make it right

One of the golden rules with thinking is: Just because you think something doesn't make it right, or based in anything more stable than your best guess with the limited information you have at present. Often, the people with the most rigid opinions are those who have NOT looked at research or had personal experience around the topic in question.

This means that the opinion is based on someone else's thoughts or opinions, or specially created to sway public opinion and create a power base or sell a product or idea.

This is often to do with social conditioning and feeling unsafe, so the stress response engages when a particular topic arises/belief is challenged or a particular person is in the conversation. Being in fight, flee or freeze will affect how the mind works, so the tools in chapter 2 can be used to shift out of the stress mode, allowing more flexibility in thought processes.

This is a great place to start exploring and discovering why you think particular things. So, the question, "Why do I think this, who gave me this perspective?" Can lead you on an interesting exploration.

It's amazing when you realise that a simple comment or attitude from your parents (or other person you looked up to) when you were young can act like a concrete weight in your mind. How they approached a subject can be projected down through generations, and unless you challenge it, it will remain there in the background colouring your world and creating judgement, narrow mindedness, and isolation from people who could make a positive impact on your life.

It is fairly common with parents that when they are stressed, they slide back into patterns that their parents used. The statement "Sometimes I open my mouth and my mother comes out" seems to cover it well. This shows the power of conditioning when the stress response is turned on.

Brene Brown, a research professor at the university of Houston, who has spent 20 years studying courage, shame, vulnerability and empathy has suggested a useful technique for avoiding falling for your own conclusions and then reacting to them, by separating the stimulus from your reaction of what that means.

So, for instance if a person you know walks past you without saying hello, rather than being upset, say to them, "The story I told myself when you walked past me without saying hello is that you are angry with me or dislike me for some reason."
This beautifully simple technique creates dialogue that eradicates misunderstandings without making anyone wrong.

There is more on Brene Brown's work below.
Here are a few mental patterns that can keep you stuck in negative thought processes that will then affect your emotional stability.

I KNOW...

The approach taken in this book is about being curious, curious about the relationship between the physical, mental and emotional aspects of whatever dysfunction you are working on. We all have a proclivity, a preferred way we do things. So, some people are tuned into their physical structure but resist on an emotional level, others are thinkers but have very little relationship with their body, or a third option is that people feel deeply on an emotional level but are not grounded in their body. Your pattern will give you some information very clearly, but it is highly likely that this information is not what you need to unwind the dysfunction. If it was, the self-corrective process would have occurred already.

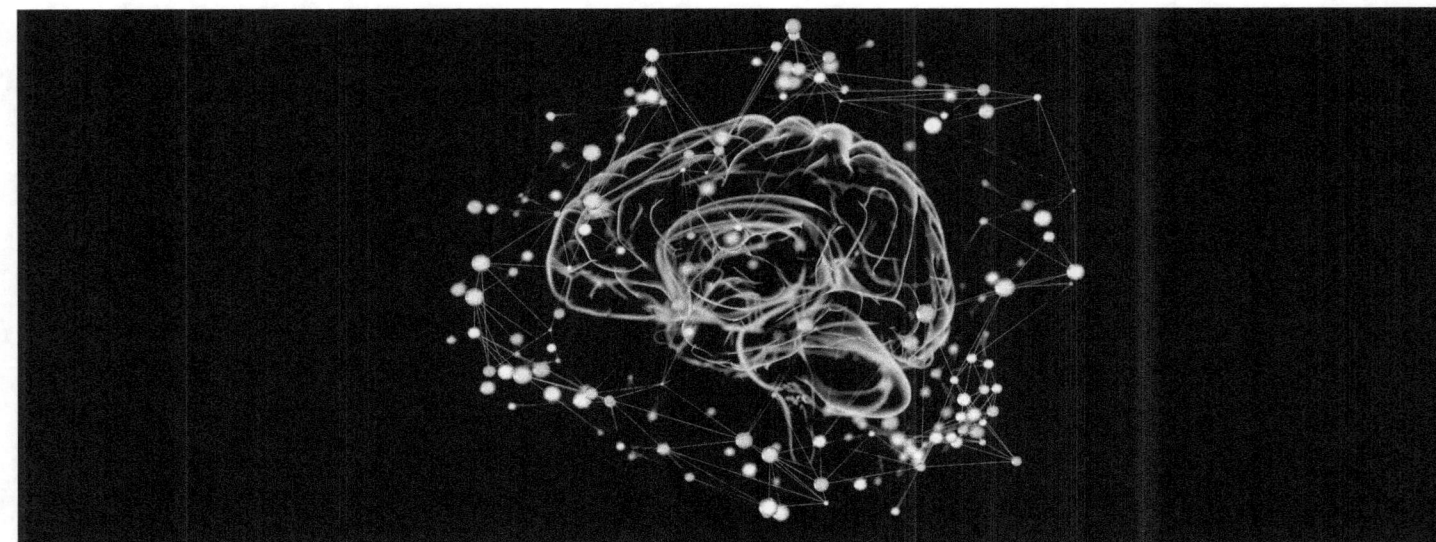

Therefore, you are looking for information that isn't in your customary format for your system. This requires curiosity. One of the fastest ways to kill curiosity is the thought, "I know."

Try this: look at something and get really curious, look at the physical structure, notice the details. Then think to yourself "I know, it's a ..." and label it whatever the object is. So, for instance I'm looking out the window at the plant in front of my house, there are new shoots that are a lighter green, different shaped leaves, stems at different angles: when I get curious I notice all sorts of details. If I then say "I know it's a plant," my attention changes.

Thinking we know ends exploration. You change a new situation into what you already know and there ends the learning process. The "I know" pattern is like a message to your brain to put whatever you are looking at on automatic so you can shift your attention to something else. Becoming aware of when you slip into this pattern will enable you to increase how much you learn from the current moment or from the person you are talking to.

Rumination
The pattern of focusing on a failure or stressful issue/conflict repeatedly is called rumination, which is a great way to crash your self-esteem and mental health. A psychological approach to breaking this habit is to use distraction. If you can distract yourself by focusing on something else for a couple of minutes, and repeat that for a week or so every time you start ruminating, then you will break the habit. Another option is to convert whatever you are ruminating about into a question. So, for instance, if you are ruminating about a negative interaction with someone, shift the monologue from replaying the situation into what can you do to change this.
Write down a few options to either change the tone of the interaction or avoid further interaction and put down a time line. So, it could be "Call X tomorrow and discuss the issue."

Another approach is to observe the story. Watch how the story affects your system. Feel the underlying pattern that motivates you to focus on what is going wrong.
Is there the sense of some pleasure in the pain you are inflicting on yourself?
Do you deserve to feel bad?
If the answer is yes, then track that down. Find where that self-sabotaging aspect of yourself is hiding, and fully experience that feeling. This will shift the whole pattern and free up a lot of attention. There is more on working this way in the next chapter.

Loneliness
One of the bizarre paradoxes of our society is, we are much more able to communicate with people, yet individuals are experiencing more loneliness than ever before. Loneliness has direct physical health impacts such as increasing blood pressure and cholesterol, undermining self-esteem, increasing emotional instability, impacting on sleep, and in some people increasing comfort eating, which impacts on body weight and therefore body image.[38]
This sense of isolation can also increase the sense of being unsafe when around other people.

The cult of the individual, which has eroded the sense of community, has reduced our ability to create real connections with other people.

So, what can you do today to start to change this?
Join a meditation group (or any other group), reach out to a person who lives alone and see if they want to catch up for a coffee. Find a group of people who are doing something that may interest you, and join them.
Recognise that you will not feel like reaching out, there will be some resistance as you are taking the risk of being rejected, but ultimately the only way to change loneliness is to take that risk.

Victimhood

Feeling like a victim creates a sense of helplessness that crashes you into freeze mode. In order to shift this pattern, you have to choose to let go of the trauma — this is the first step. Releasing the effects of the trauma from your body and freeing yourself from it follows on from this.

The sooner you can shift out of blaming another person, the sooner you can recover your sense of wellness. Victimhood costs you far more in terms of ill health and negative mental health. If you have been affected due to either an accidental or intentional damaging act, then take all precautions that it can't happen again — remove yourself from the reach of the perpetrator, then forgive them, not for their sake but to free you from being a victim to the situation. This does not mean you have to let the perpetrator back into your life. Sensible risk management suggests that if someone is willing to hurt you once, they will do it again.

Even if you cannot forgive the person, seek where you could have made different decisions that could have avoided the situation. Or if there was no possibility at the time of the traumatic event, how can you work in this moment to release the past? Trauma is being stuck in confusion in the past. Victimhood is a response to that confusion. Releasing the victim mentality opens the possibility of finding the way out.

I will give you an example. I was in a yoga class doing a seated twist, and an experienced yoga teacher came up behind me and took my shoulders and twisted me further than my body could handle. There were a few pops, though nothing at that point felt painful. However, the next day I picked up a small brick and the pain up my neck just exploded. This was easily the most acute pain I have ever had in my life.

What made the situation worse was when I emailed the teacher, she refused to communicate with me at all. It took me a month of savage pain to work out that the posterior rib attachment of the first and second ribs on my right side were dislocated.
The sense of being a victim and being ignored was part of what made the pain so intense, and it took me a long time to realise that and release it.

The victimhood was held in my body and was in part holding my system out of alignment.

What was my part in the injury?

I know that my thoracic spine and ribcage are not that flexible and that rotation is a dangerous movement for people with rigidity. If that rigidity is due to calcifications, then you can break off an osteophyte and damage ligaments. If it is due to soft tissue tension, then you may get increased movement but you may also over-stretch the areas that can move, leading to damage to those areas rather than an increase in the overall range of movement.

I didn't know the teacher well, and earlier she had done some things that made me not sure that she was really paying attention to the individuals in the class. In short, I should have been wary and protected myself from her rotational movement rather than allow her to move me as if she knew my body better than I did.
Finding a way that you played a part in the situation can allow you to recover your sense of being empowered.

Checking for Victimhood

If you create the feeling of being a victim, does it feel familiar, or do you resist creating that feeling? Focus on whatever the feeling is there and yawn until it clears.

Scepticism Vs. Cynicism

Being sceptical of new information that doesn't fit with what you know about the world is a sensible position to take. It is really an approach where you look at new information and want to test to see if it is valid, how reliable is the source and how does it fit with what you already have found works for you. Can you test the information for yourself?

Being sceptical does include having an open enough mind to be curious and explore to see if what is being presented to you is a better reflection of reality than what you currently believe.

Cynicism is more a lifestyle choice, as no information from new sources is really assessed. You know in advance that it's all wrong. The cost of cynicism apart from a narrow view of reality is that you are rejecting possible solutions to problems that will arise in the future.

Chronic disease is an area with a generally high level of cynicism towards new information. Western medicine regards anything from alternative sources as unlikely to be useful, and change is slow. People who are interested in alternative approaches view western medicine with cynicism and sometimes rejecting the valuable input from science. The solution to chronic disease is likely to come from multiple approaches for different people.

For instance, dealing with stress may be most efficiently done by meditation, getting a massage, or working with the tools in this book; diet maybe a vital piece and for different people and this may include different foods; drugs may offer short term relief in order to help shift pain until other tools can be used to relieve the underlying cause rather than just the symptom.

If you do find yourself being cynical, feel into how closed in and contracted you feel. How you need to protect yourself from change that may happen if you actually get curious about the information presented. Don't get me wrong, there is so much manipulated information where people have started with an agenda and contorted reality to make it sound realistic - usually to sell something. But if you explore how they are doing this you become immune to the scams and dodgy sales pitches by seeing through it.

The Right/Wrong Game

Part of the right/wrong game is that when you are in fight mode, you need to have conflict with someone. Now that you can shift out of that, you don't need the right/wrong game, do you?

Let's further dismantle the right/wrong game. Consider vision. In most people, vision is a dominant sense that we rely on to create our knowledge of the external environment. We receive an image through our eyes that is upside down and mostly in black and white, except for the centre area, where we see colour. We also see only a very small part of the visible spectrum. The picture below demonstrates this limitation. If we had the ability to see in infrared like insects, what flowers looked like would be different. So, the reality our vision creates is very limited, yet the stories we tell ourselves often strongly rely on visual information.

If we had the ability to see infrared as an insect does, the version on the right is what the flower would look like.

Checkout colour pictures of flowers online as the black & white version doesn't show the big difference.

In short, we make up things constantly from a small amount of fairly dodgy information based on limited sensory input, and are then very sure we are right. Our ability to become concrete about how reality is and then defend that view is a great way to create conflict and inhibit learning. This comes down to our brain wanting to make reality predictable, so it can use the automatic patterns it already has created to deal with the external world. It is so much easier to assume "I know..." than to really look at whatever is happening in front of you.

The problem is, you miss the wonder of being alive, because you have already labelled everything and are seeing the current situation as the same as in the past. If you experience boredom, chances are this is what you have done.

> *We see the world not as it is but as we are or as we have been conditioned to see it.*
> Stephen Covey

One of the real limitations of the right/wrong game is how aggressively we attack someone who disagrees with our perspective on reality — even if they have evidence to support their position. A great example of this almost immune-system-like response is the horrific treatment of Ignaz Semmelweis, which led to the death of huge numbers of women.

In the 1840s childbed fever, which was a post-birth bacterial infection, killed up to 40% of women who were giving birth in hospitals in Europe and North America. This condition is now almost unheard of due to improved hygiene and antibiotics.

A doctor named Ignaz Semmelweis, who was working in an obstetrics clinic in Vienna, noticed that when intern doctors were training, there was an increase in deaths from childbed fever compared to when just the midwives were in attendance.

He developed a theory that the doctors who had been doing autopsies in the morning were contaminating the women who were giving birth. He collated the data from the hospital on the timing of deaths and proposed a radical solution — that all staff should wash their hands with chlorinated lime.

Dr Ignaz Semmelweis aged 42 in 1860.

Even though a basic form of germ theory of infection had been around since 1025 when it was written about by a Persian doctor named Ibn Sina and expanded upon by Marcus von Plenciz in 1762 in Europe, it was treated with disdain by European doctors. It wasn't till the end of the 19th century that the germ theory was accepted by the European medical fraternity.

When Semmelweis documented the reduced deaths by hand-washing (from around 18% at the Vienna general hospital to below 1%) and published his data, he was ridiculed by the medical community of the time, and in 1849 lost his job. He was never employed again. In 1865 he was forcibly admitted to a mental asylum after having a "breakdown" and ended up dying after being beaten up by the guards.

We can see the same aggressive bullying happen with politics and religion, both online and in conflict areas around the world. It would be a great achievement to shift this from a standard way for humans to operate to a weird spectacle where everyone would smile like when a 2-year-old spits the dummy and has a major meltdown. This is unfortunately a long way off.

One of the causes of our strong tendency to become rigid in our thinking about what is right is that our brains function by putting things on automatic. The neuroscience descriptor for this is "what fires together wires together." The neurons that are activated at the same time become connected, and this creates our functional patterns, which means it takes less effort/thought to do things. A great example of this is the difference in the amount of concentration it takes to drive now compared to when you were learning.

With ideas, it is easier to decide what is right, then reject everything else.
Whenever that topic comes up, you have your standard position, no need to question but just react.
In today's society, we in fact never really need to worry about even questioning anything as there are always radio personalities, the news or bloggers online to tell us what to think. We can then just defend that position — beautiful, we need never put our minds in gear at all.

The point is that there are always different perspectives on any topic, and if there is no damage to another person then freedom to explore different perspectives should be encouraged. This is not to suggest that some thoughts/hypotheses/theories aren't rubbish. There is a lot of rubbish both in the alternative health world and in the science world.

Our society has many areas where questioning the assumptions underlying a particular area ignites a strong response. The idea that western medicine is evidence-based is one of those.

The closer you get to the pharmaceutical companies, the less the science is challenged. An example of this is Tamiflu. This drug is marketed as an antiviral, and was promoted as reducing the likelihood of complications during a flu epidemic, such as pneumonia, which can be the cause of death. In preparation for a flu epidemic, Australia (as did the UK, Europe and other countries) bought billions of dollars' worth of antivirals including Tamiflu.

The Cochrane group tried for 4 1/2 years to get the raw data from Roche, the company that makes Tamiflu, and once they got it and analysed it, they found that Roche had lied about the effectiveness of Tamiflu. On average, Tamiflu will reduce the time you feel sick from 6 days to 5.5 days and does not prevent complications at all.[39,40] So far, no government has sued Roche for fraud. In fact, I recently wrote to the health department and the response was, there hasn't been anyone interested in the scientific backing of Tamiflu since that paper was published in 2014 and the Australian government continues to keep the stockpile up to date. In other words, we continue to pay Roche for drugs based on inaccurate science, and if there is an epidemic and we have a 20% death rate, who will the politicians blame for the drug not working?

Unfortunately, there are many examples like this. Mind you, many don't have the scale of Roche's fraud. This makes the work of real scientists who are willing to question everything so valuable.

This is desperately needed when there is a billion-dollar company/industry that has funded the science and then controls whether a paper is published or not.

Dr Ben Goldacre does a great TED talk discussing this, see the reference section for the link.

So, there is no doubt that there are some things that need to be exposed. The question is, what happens to your brain chemistry when doing this. If you are going into your stress response, then you have gone into the right/wrong game. If you can stay calm and present why this idea is bad and this is why you have decided on this position, then you can still engage without the emotional angst involved with being right and making the other person wrong. This is an ongoing exercise in awareness, as some topics will shift you into a reactive mindset very rapidly. I guess that's why it takes a lifetime to master being human.

Another perspective on the right/wrong game is that the ego has a lot invested in being right. If you find yourself wanting to be right, look at how that feels — that is what your ego feels like when it is in charge. Notice it, smile and let it go, and see if there is a different way of looking at the issue that encompasses different perspectives.

So, is there another option?
Yes. Instead of a duality where things are divided into right and wrong, try three divisions.
1. Yes, this works for me at my current level of understanding.
2. Maybe there is something to this idea/theory. I need more information to decide.
3. Bullshit — I'm confident that this is crap but I'm interested in why someone would believe this.

And have the possibility that you can misfile things and be willing to reconsider ideas when new evidence arrives, collaborating or presenting the information in a different way that makes more sense.

Another structure is to consider your view of reality to be a model based on data that you have received through your senses. Some of this data is probably flawed, and possibly the conclusions you made based on this data are flawed. Therefore, as new information comes in that conflicts with your model of reality, you can see if there is sufficient evidence that supports revising the model.
What we choose to believe has impacts on many things such as what input we focus on from our senses, what that sensory input means. This information, and the meaning we assign to it, affects the quality of our relationships, how we experience pain, and how adaptable we are when our world suddenly changes. Having the ability to be flexible is a great gift you can give yourself.

> "Education is not the learning of facts, it's rather the training of the mind to think". Einstein

Is education limiting how we think?

One of the common things that happens when you go to university is that the pressure to pass exams and the sheer quantity of information means you don't have time to question the quality of the information being taught.

Decades ago in the 1960s, the Bio-psychosocial model of health was proposed,[41] yet a majority of university courses such as physiotherapy used a biomedical approach, which is reductionist and looks at pain as a result of physical dysfunction (tissue damage) only, ignoring the emotional and mental aspects of the human being.

Slowly as pain research, FMRI and other research has made the biomedical model redundant, there has been a shift to accepting that the physical body is impacted by things such as emotions and thoughts.

Now, many courses pay lip service to the bio-psychosocial model, then teach the same techniques that they were teaching before.

If you have ever had an emotion and felt the physical impact of grief, heartbreak, depression, sadness, etc., you will recognise that emotions have a big impact on the physical body. Therefore, any theory of the body that ignores this aspect is limited in its application.

In order to be effective at releasing pain and improving function, we need to be able to recognise the level of the dysfunction, whether that is physical, mental, emotional or other, and then interact with the system in a way that stimulates the body's ability to self-correct.

To do this, we need to approach the person as a whole and find where the possibility of change is. This requires the practitioner to be flexible, and find where the client is rather than impose standard one size fits all solutions to "fix" the problem.

Difference as a Strength

I'm sure you have noticed that different people think very differently. Some are great at maths, others are more tactile; some can read maps while others can't. Our diversity in ability is a strength when we find what a person does well and empower them to do that job. It becomes a weakness when we expect that everyone should do things the same way we do. This is completely unreasonable, as we all have slightly different ways of wiring up our brain, which leads to different abilities.

Education should be about identifying what a person will excel at and helping them to do that.

The point is that what you think is right is based on what you have assumed. This is based on education, social conditioning and the input from your senses. None of these are reliable sources to be sure about anything.

So, is there another way?

Yes.
A person's perspective/attitude/judgements gives you information about their level of education/social conditioning and whether they are in their stress response or not.

So, is it worth arguing with someone who is trapped in their fight response?
Can you help them feel safe enough in order to help them shift out and then offer different interpretations about some of the things they are basing their opinions on?

So, for instance, a person who lumps all people of one race into a category, e.g., all blacks are criminals, is living in a fear-based reality. The racism is a symptom of that fear, so how can we help them shift out of their fear?
Is it possible to make them feel safe?
Will this change how they view people of different races?

Daryl Davies is a great example of how this can work. Over the last 30 years, Daryl has met many members of the Ku Klux Klan and asked them a simple question. "How can you hate me if you don't even know me?"
He then spends time getting to know them.
This approach has seen many Klan members question the ideology of the Klan and leave the organisation. Check out Accidental Courtesy on Netflix, or Daryl's book, Klan-destine Relationships.

It seems that the increase in racism in Australia has benefited some people such as right-wing politicians and the Murdoch press, because it has made sections of the population predictable and controllable. The level of fear in society is a tool to achieve this, which is why they focus on negative aspects and exaggerate the impact that these threats have while downplaying things that don't suit their political agenda.
I wonder what would happen if as a society we refused to spend our time in our stress response. Would we be able to elect better leaders? It would be worth a try.

Scale of Importance
One of the sources of stress on the mental level is a mismatch between the level of importance of a particular thing and the level of emotional energy we have invested in it.
There are a couple of ways of working with this.
1. In two years, will you look back at this and say, that is when your life changed? If not, and it is creating stress, you are probably investing too much energy in it.
2. On a scale of 0 to 10, what is the level of importance the issue you are dealing with has for you?
3. On the same scale, what is the level of energy you have invested into it?

Suppose, for instance, if you have said something and offended someone and are worried about this to the point it is disturbing your sleep. How important is this relationship to you?
If the relationship is worth 2/10 and your level of invested energy is 8/10, then you probably can just relax. Next time you see the person you can discuss it, or you can give them a call, but you don't need to worry about it in between.

If you have an 8/10 level of investment and the issue has an 8/10 importance, then spend some time looking at what you can control about the situation. Make a list of things you can do that may help create a favourable outcome and then a time-line of when you can do them. Breaking things down into steps can help you shift from being stuck into action.

Emotional energy really should be considered a limited resource. If everything is too emotionally charged, then life is drama-filled and exhausting. Adrenal fatigue is probably the outcome of too much emotional energy invested over too long a period.

Perspective
Whatever we focus on becomes larger and more important. It is like a dog that runs up and down a fence line, barking. A track gets worn in the lawn. When we focus on an issue or cultivate a way of thinking, we create the networks in our brain and make it more likely to repeat the process.

The antidote is to take a larger perspective. What is working in your life?
Are you healthy?
Do you have a few good friends who would be willing to help you if you asked?
Do you have enough food?
Do you have a safe place to live?
Can you find a place to sit in nature, daily or weekly?
Is your family safe?

In a Word document, you can design a pie chart in which you can give each of the questions you choose a score out of 10. You can see that when presented in a chart, the problem area can be placed in a different perspective and life seems more functional. A list of all the things that are going right can also help as when we are feeling stuck in one area we tend to ignore things where we have been successful.

Another way to do this is to list what areas are important to you, for instance;

- Relationship
- Health
- Work/career
- Education
- Personal growth
- Relaxation/social life
- Parenting

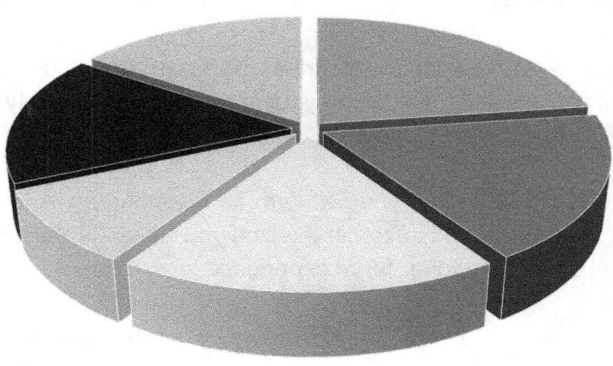

Make a note of what you have done this week in all these areas. Note down successes and ideas for improving the out comes in each section. If one area of your life is suffering this week, invest more time next week.

Review this regularly to see where you can best invest your time.

Perfectionism

The idea that being perfect is possible increases stress dramatically. In fact, in a study of middle aged men, the idea of being perfect was associated with an 18% increase in stress hormones in their systems when exposed to test conditions.[42] Another way of looking at the idea of being perfect is that it is the fear of making a mistake. This is a handicap to learning and therefore growth.

The concept that you can be perfect is also dangerous. It drives people to invest a lot of emotional energy in an unattainable goal. Of course, we can all pretend to be perfect, but that takes a great deal of energy, creates stress and comes across as fake anyway. For instance, the fashion industry and magazines have really distorted our perspective of what is attractive, and the image of perfection. Half-starved models wear overpriced clothes and the photos are Photoshopped to give them a longer neck, flawless skin, leaner, longer body. It is all bullshit to sell you things you don't need to impress people you probably don't like.

I like the idea that perfection is a dynamic process, that if each day you improve by 2%, then in a month you will improve by 60%. This of course leaves the option that you will fail regularly. Whenever you start something new there is a learning process and this requires failure. Of course, ideally you will rapidly learn from those failures, so you will be less likely to repeat the same mistake. It's always better to make different mistakes than the same ones over and over.

The key with learning from a mistake is to identify the error. It is really easy to blame something and move on quickly because it feels uncomfortable to ponder failure. However, if you really don't want to repeat the error, it needs to be explored. This is the same as finding the driver of the dysfunction rather than just treating the pain in a compensation pattern.
If you really don't want to repeat mistakes spending time exploring how you failed is the antidote. The upside is the discomfort from failing disappears when you stop resisting the experience.

Seriousness Vs. Playfulness
Our brain is designed to play, and we learn better when we play, just like animals and children. Seriousness is a form of stress or an absence of playfulness.

From FMRI imaging work, there is evidence that the brain processes and stores memories differently when there is joy in the learning experience. If you can increase the amount of time you play in your life, your memory will improve and you may just enjoy yourself.

Taking the stories you tell yourself seriously creates so much distress because, naturally, no one else is going to take them nearly seriously enough to keep you happy, so conflict about ideas will occur.

The wars over religion are a perfect example of this. If burning a book or a flag or drawing a rude cartoon is worth killing someone over, you are definitely taking your stories far too seriously. I think any form of god who wants you to kill someone who disagrees with you isn't worth following.

Instead of identifying yourself with an idea, find an emotional space you would like to work from, say open-hearted, grateful, compassionate, and question the stuff you currently are serious about. Integrate the serious stuff and put more time and attention on what you would prefer to experience.

> *"When you lose the ability to laugh, you lose the ability to think"*
> Clarence Darrow

Stilling the Mind

If you become curious about a thought, your attention can slow it down or in fact hold it still. Play with this when you are not stressed, or if you are stressed, do one of the exercises for shifting out of your stress response and then watch your thoughts.

The interaction between mind and body runs in both directions: a thought can create an emotional response that can change your body (e.g., release stress hormones and increase muscle tension), and signals from your body can create an emotional response and your mind will seek a reason you are feeling this way. Have you ever felt anxious and then gone looking for what is about to go wrong? This is probably your body signalling and your mind playing catch-up.

Your brain will respond automatically when your body sends internally created warning signals. This is because our system is set up to prioritise threat warnings from our senses. Therefore, if we are not deliberate with our thought processes, we can end up with a fear-based reality.

Becoming Aware of Your Thoughts

Notice what general kinds of thoughts you have. For instance, are they based on fear, scarcity, is there negative self-talk (putting yourself down)? Or are your thoughts more aligned with gratitude or loving kindness?
If you notice a particular thought process occurring on a regular basis, get really interested in it.
Either write down or just track what you notice about the thought process, and when it occurs.
How much charge is around it?
Do you ruminate about it, coming back often to run the same program?
Can you stop the thought and get really curious about what you get from running the program?
Explore it like you were studying it.
Many negative attitudes are protective mechanisms for emotional patterns that you are holding in your body. Cleaning up these patterns will free you of the mental distortion and chatter.

Keep track of fear-based thoughts and what response your body has to them. We shall work with these in the next section.

Modes of Operation

You may have noticed that with some people you behave/think in one way and with others a different side of yourself comes out. This is because we have different modes of operation. For example, when we are stressed, we operate very differently from when we are not.
This difference even runs to what we can remember. It's relatively common for people who are trained in the health field to completely forget how to deal with common complaints for themselves when they are sick.

This has more to do with what level you are operating at rather than any inherent failure of intelligence. When stressed, we are all far less capable than when we are relaxed.

So, rather than judging a person, one option is to recognise what level they are operating on. People in fight mode will be unpleasant to be around but maybe if you can help them recognise where they are, this may change their whole life and how they relate to others.

People in flee response will be unreliable and people in freeze will be unproductive.

Then you have layers of conditioning.

Your primary conditioning is what brings you pleasure and what you are passionate about — in this mode, you will be alive and enjoy yourself. Your secondary conditioning is what has been imposed by society — carrot or stick. When you operate from this level, you will be looking for approval, or resisting punishment. There is also learnt behaviour around how you get what you want/need. What you would like others to think of you. Do you put on a "game face?"

The funny thing with pretence is it sticks out like dogs ****s and makes other people feel wary of you. It also takes such a lot of your energy you will need time alone to recover.

Then there is the state where you can just be present.
Here is an exercise to help you get there (if you haven't found your own way there already).

Still Point in the Heart
We often bounce from desire through to resistance in an emotional rollercoaster.
Imagine that as a continuum

Desire _____ _____ Resistance
                              |

Right where the line is pointing is a still point.

Imagine dropping through that still point into your heart.
Feel your heart beat, feel the breath flow through your nostrils.

Then bring your attention off yourself and onto the outside world. Notice how bright the light and colours are.

Play with this whenever you are waiting in a checkout line or at traffic lights, or for family.
Being present doesn't have to be a big deal. It is just being here rather than in the past or worrying about the future.

So, if you can identify what mode of operation a person is at, then you can fine tune how you communicate with them.

If you can help a person shift out of their stress response, the chance of having a mutually acceptable outcome increases dramatically.

Positive Psychology
One of the great shifts in psychology has been moving from creating labels for different deviant human behaviours (focusing on what's wrong with people) to looking at how we can improve human productivity and mental wellness.

While the list of human mental illnesses/dysfunctions keeps getting longer (I suspect that being alive will soon be listed as a mental illness), there is a growing group of psychologists focused on exploring how to optimise the use of our minds.

Our brain chemistry is affected by the story we tell ourselves. So, let's use this as a tool to create a space we would like to live in. The key with this is, we need to clear the space before we plant new patterns. This is the weakness with positive affirmations. You can say "I love myself" till you're blue in the face, but unless you have cleaned up the underlying belief that you are unlovable, you are creating a fantasy over what you really believe. This will work only until you are upset, then the real belief system will reassert itself. Unwinding the pattern that holds the original belief in place is the essence of what internal work is all about.

So, to use the above example, if you are struggling to love yourself and are doing things to sabotage your own success, then the pattern will have two parts: the resistance to feeling the underlying emotion (being unlovable) and the emotional pattern itself. The resistance to the emotion is what keeps the suppressed emotion held in place, and this suppression takes up a lot of energy and leads to all the avoidance or compensation patterns.

So, first we need to accept the resistance, which can be done by deciding it's OK to feel the resistance. Alternatively, you can feel it and yawn. Once the resistance has melted, the level of charge will be reduced, but you will feel the underlying emotion and any judgements you have about that thought process. This might include shame, which really locks things in, because it is incredibly uncomfortable to feel.

When you can fully experience being unlovable without any resistance, the pattern will shift. This enables the belief that you are unlovable to integrate, and then there is the space and free attention to create a different reality. Into this new created space, you can set up your preferred thought process with a positive affirmation.

Positive emotions have been shown to increase the connection between the emotional regulation centre in the pre-frontal cortex of the brain and the amygdala. This increases the possibility of staying emotionally stable, and therefore improves cognitive function.

Gratitude

Research on gratitude has shown it to be associated with a huge list of positive outcomes such as:[43]

- Improved mindset
- Reduced stress levels
- Improved mental wellbeing
- Lowered risk of psychiatric disorders
- Higher life satisfaction
- Increased resilience
- Reduced aggression
- Lower levels of depression
- Reduced heart rate

If this was a pill, it would be recommended for everyone to take as a preventative. Fortunately, you don't need to buy it, since you can create it yourself.

If you find yourself spending time dwelling on emotions like anger or resentment, start being grateful for small things like the joyful noises of little kids playing, the sunshine or rain, bird song, the wind moving through trees. Go for a walk and pat all the (friendly) dogs you can find. Most dogs have a spiritual master level of being present in the moment and loving their pet human unconditionally. They are just waiting for us to catch up.

If you have a history of being abused, then eventually you will need to deal with the emotional trauma. This should be done with the support of a person or people you trust. In the meantime, become grateful for something to help shift the networks of fear and stress in your brain.

Forgiveness

Forgiving is not an act to benefit a perpetrator, but for freeing yourself from the impact of the events of the past and therefore allows you to change your brain chemistry. There is no need to communicate your forgiveness with the perpetrator, and definitely no need to allow them back into your life, unless you would like that to happen.

Forgiveness has been shown to reduce the physical pain of fibromyalgia in some people.[44] Forgiveness also reduces stress, hostility, anger, resentment and maybe even inflammation.[45]

How to forgive:

- Take a gradient approach.
- It will be easier to forgive small breaches of trust and betrayals than major events, so be gentle on yourself. Work slowly through a list of people who have negatively impacted your world. Free up your attention, notice what your part was in the interaction. Could you have done something differently?
- Forgive them for their part in the event, and feel the relief of not holding onto the resentment.
- Next, appreciate the courage you have shown by looking back at something that isn't pleasant. Feel a sense of achievement. This stimulates a dopamine release — enjoy.

Happiness

Happiness on the surface seems to be something to aim for, but it may be a two-edged sword. In one study, researchers found that people who value happiness too much were prone to bipolar disorder.[46] This may be a chicken/egg thing, but it makes sense that if you value something highly and you are not able to experience it, then you may send yourself on a downward spiral.

Serotonin, the neurotransmitter thought to be associated with the emotion of happiness, is mostly produced in the gut by our gut bacteria. This is one of the most obvious connections between diet, inflammation and depression.

As I mentioned before, most grains are desiccated (sprayed 7-10 days before harvest to dry them out) with glyphosate (Roundup). Glyphosate is a biocide, which kills all organisms that have the shikimate pathway, such as plants and microorganisms. Glyphosate has also been associated with increased inflammation of the gut wall of pigs. There is growing evidence that inflammation is strongly correlated with depression.

In his book, Why Isn't My Brain Working, Datis Kharrazian[83] presents a theory of how gut inflammation can also impair the blood-brain barrier and lead to inflammation of the brain. This creates foggy-headedness and impairs the ability to think clearly. Inflammation in the brain has also been associated with brain-degenerative diseases.

So, looking at diet is important when considering happiness. But there is also the ability to create the internal state deliberately. And the impact of happiness on your biochemistry can be quite incredible. Laughter was found to decrease pro-inflammatory cytokines (the chemicals that create inflammation).

Jump on YouTube and look up some funny videos and track how you feel before vs after.

The balance of neurotransmitters in your brain is determined by you. So, you can deliberately do it again without an external trigger.

Happiness exercise
Smile until you feel the emotion of happiness

Unreasonable Happiness

It would be completely reasonable to be unhappy, it is a human emotion after all. However, our species seems to have chosen unhappiness as our society's chosen emotion, which we create by focusing on what is not going well. One just needs to watch the news in order to understand exactly how bad reality is (or is the news just a collection of the most negative stories from around the world blended into a narrative to sell a particular perspective?), so, being unreasonably happy is an act of rebellion. If everyone was happy, the consumer index would plummet. You don't need to buy stuff, you don't need to impress people you don't like if you create happiness within yourself. So, let's rebel together!

Unreasonable happiness is yours to create simply by focusing your attention on creating it. The neurotransmitters such as serotonin are yours to release if you put your mind to it. This isn't to suggest that you ignore what is happening around you and become a bliss bunny pretending that all is rosy while living with abuse.

This is more a tool for creating happiness when you otherwise may have had your focus on what someone else is doing wrong, or waiting in traffic. Try it when you have a few minutes spare. It might change your reality.

To change your brain chemistry, you can choose to create periods of happiness. To create new connections based around happiness, you can make time to do things you find enjoyable, or alternatively start doing things you don't like while creating the feelings of happiness and a liberal sprinkle of dopamine as a reward for doing the chore. This will encourage the brain to rewire the connections from negative emotions to positive emotions.

Exercise is a great example of this. If you have previously found exercise to be a struggle and really hate it, then take a gradient approach. Choose a form of exercise that doesn't make your body hurt afterward, and do it for as long as you can keep a positive attitude. As soon as it becomes unpleasant, stop.
The aim is to slowly increase the period of time you are enjoying the process.
If this means you walk around the block while listening to a TED talk, and over a month build up to walking while listening to two

TED talks, then that is great. The recommended time for daily exercise to improve mood is 30 min/day.
The important point is the emotional rather than the physical aspect of the exercise.

Creating an emotional state is like any other skill. Practising it intentionally makes it stronger, and easier to do. You create the networks in the brain to do what you most often do.
So, play with creating happiness as often as possible until it becomes automatic.

Happiness or Pleasure?
One of the traps with happiness is confusing happiness and pleasure. A piece of chocolate doesn't create happiness, it creates pleasure (if you're that way inclined). Pleasure is a short-term rush. So, the pursuit of pleasure is a process of getting repeated short-term rewards for your brain. This is not a way to create happiness as the first piece of chocolate gives a bigger reward than the tenth. Happiness therefore can be associated with pleasurable experiences but is not pleasure.

In fact, the pursuit of pleasure will often create unhappiness as it depends on an external factor (person, food item, holiday, activity) to create the sensation. This is not to suggest that pleasure should be avoided, but enjoyed with the knowledge that this too shall end. In contrast, if happiness is created as a background mindset, it will be more stable and be present even when you are challenged by life.

Contentment
One alternative to trying (and failing) to be happy is to focus on contentment. How much of your life is actually pretty good? Can you create the sense of contentment based on those areas and put the areas that need fine tuning to one side to analyse and work on?

Exercise
Focus on something that you have achieved until you feel content or state "I am content" and feel for the emotional response to that idea.

Creating a Stable Internal Sense of Wellbeing
Now that you have the internal recognition of both happiness and contentment, we can work on using them to create a more stable internal state.
- Smile until you feel happiness
- Then place your attention on being content
- Then add in some gratitude
- And finally add the sense of being safe and secure within yourself.

Suffering
Although we don't like it, suffering is a part of life. If we resist suffering, we increase our sensitivity to pain associated with what we are experiencing. People who can fully experience whatever they are experiencing, particularly their suffering, can move through the pain and return to a sense of wellbeing sooner. Acceptance of suffering as part of being human helps with that, thanks Buddha.

Being Your Own Best Friend
Even though you know all the shitty thoughts you have, you notice all your imperfections and can recall every time you have been out of integrity, you are still the best person to be your best friend. After all, you are allowed to have the shits at your best friend or think they acted badly once in a while and yet see that on average they are a pretty great human. So, why not extend that to yourself?
The core of this is accepting yourself, warts and all.

Create the feeling of deep acceptance for things you like about yourself, then slowly spread the feeling out to things you don't like about yourself.

Meditation
One of the most beneficial activities you can add to your day is meditation of some sort.

There is so much evidence that some form of meditation is useful for your health that it has become well accepted. This can be some form of mindfulness training, or a more traditional spiritual practice, or if you can't sit still, try a moving meditation such as tai chi.

Meditation has been found to change the default mode network — the parts of the brain that you use when your mind wanders before coming to be preoccupied with what's going wrong in your life.[47]

Recently a client of mine, following a year of emotional hell, was diagnosed with a rapidly worsening case of psoriatic arthritis with inflammatory markers up at 128 (most people are at 6). She was in intense pain in all her joints, and was very worried about the likelihood of permanent joint damage. She cleaned up her diet (which was fairly good anyway), and started meditating twice a day. After a few weeks, before she got in to see the rheumatoid specialist, she got a new blood test and her inflammatory markers had dropped to 8.

I don't know if the difference was the change in diet or the meditation, but allowing the body to self-correct can create amazing changes in all sorts of health conditions.

Meditation doesn't need to be taken seriously, in fact having a playful mindset will help you become more mindful.

Here are some things you can play with either before you go to sleep or when you wake up:
- Tune into your body.
- Slowly scan from your feet up to your head, noticing where you come in contact with whatever you are sitting or lying on.
- Notice the air moving through your nose for a while.
- Start to breathe slower and gentler with a focus on extending your exhalation.
- Bring your attention to your breath and then your heartbeat.
- Now shift your attention to what you notice just out beyond your skin: see if you can get some perception from outside your body.

You can include all of these steps or some of them, make a voice recording of the parts you want to include on your phone, and talk yourself through it.

Even 5 minutes of relaxation, mindfulness or meditation on a daily basis will have a beneficial impact on your life, especially if you are going through a tough time.

In the reference section is a TED Talk from Sarah Lazar, looking at some of the evidence of how beneficial meditation is. Check it out, it's amazing.

CHAPTER 6.
EMOTIONAL SELF-CARE

EMOTIONAL SELF-CARE

Do Emotions Really Have an Impact on the Physical Body?
If you have ever had an emotion, you may notice that your physical body is strongly impacted. Think of the tight neck, shoulders and jaw that goes with anger, the heaviness that goes with depression etc.

However, the western medical model often ignores the role of emotions, and it is hard to scientifically measure the relationship between a chronic disease and an emotional state. There is however a growing body of evidence that the impact of emotions on physical health is large.

As more research on emotions and the connection between physical dysfunction is being done, there is no question that the emotional aspect of being human is very important for physical function and health in general. One example of the impact an emotion can have on the physical body is Takotsudo cardiomyopathy.

Takotsubo Cardiomyopathy
One of the physical changes that has been associated with a strong emotional response is the effect of heartbreak or grief on the physical heart.[49] This condition is named after a Japanese pot used for catching octopus.

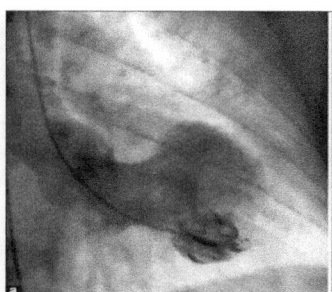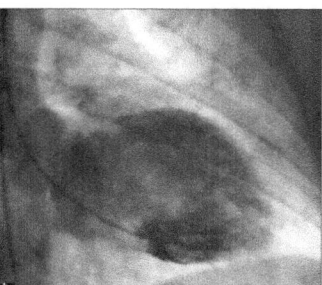

During a period of acute grief or heartbreak, the heart can change shape as the left ventricle balloons. In the image below (a) is a heart during a bout of takotsubo cardiomyopathy compared to (b) which is an image of a normal heart.

The image below is a takotsubo pot.

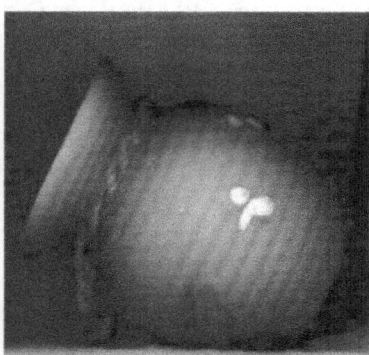

In the reference section is a TED Talk by Sandeep Jauhar, a cardiologist, who looks at takotsubo cardiomyopathy in more detail.

There is also a relationship between our immune system and our emotions.
The neurotransmitters that are thought to create our emotional states have a direct impact on our immune system.[50] Evidence for this is that our immune cells have receptor sites for neurotransmitters, so cortisol, oxytocin and other transmitters do impact your ability to deal with microbes. You may have noticed this when you have had a stressful time and either during that time or afterward, you end up with the flu.

On a physical level, stress hormones like adrenaline use up Vitamin C and the B vitamins, which impacts on the other systems in the body including the immune system.

Working With the Emotions
If there is any area of human health that needs better tools, it's emotional work. Many people have had limbs removed due to diabetes, and want to live on, and then we have people who are perfectly healthy on a physical level who commit suicide because they cannot deal with how they feel within themselves. This is tragic as it comes down to a misunderstanding of what they are feeling and how to work with it effectively.

Our nervous system is designed to rebound after periods of distress. We are genetically programmed to do this, but we have systematically changed our culture to exclude the components that actually help the nervous system release the built-up charge and move on from the trauma.

One of the challenges of working with emotions is the current level of the tools on offer. As we saw in the section on sleep, the emotional regulation area in the brain is impaired by stress and broken sleep. One of the common things when you are struggling with emotional issues is to resist sleeping. As soon as you stop, up come the feelings you are trying to avoid. So, any way of working with emotions must include a way of shifting out of the stress response and creating enough relaxation that drug-free sleep is possible.

The next step is to have tools that work on the different levels affected by suppressing an emotion. This includes the mind, which creates the narrative, the charge that creates the sensations, and the underlying holding pattern in the body, which is part of our resistance to fully experiencing the emotion.

There is a difference between a suppressed emotion that is triggered by an external stimulus, and a current event that triggers an emotional response. For instance, if there is a death in the family, it is completely natural to expect an emotional response. If, however you don't fully grieve, whatever that means for you, and resist being dysfunctional for an extended period of time, then at some stage it is highly likely that this resisted emotional charge is going to erupt. Or that suppressing the emotion will take so much effort, you will become ill in some way.

It makes sense to resist emotions for some period of time, to allow you to create the space to release them while maintaining enough function to earn an income and keep up with your responsibilities. It is also important to recognise the value of working to release these suppressed emotions before they impact on your relationships or health.

If you have a pattern of going into freeze mode when stressed, then it is likely that when you feel resisted emotions coming up, you will feel overwhelmed and slide effortlessly into freeze mode. The pathway out of freeze mode, a deactivated state, will often include becoming angry (fight response) or feeling like you have to move/being agitated or frustrated (flee response). A higher level of activation is a great thing as you can create some action that will help the emotions to move.

Once you are in an activated state, you can use the exercise from chapter 2 (see box below) to shift up and activate the emotional regulation centre in your neocortex.

Objective: To Overload the Senses Until You Shift Out of Your Stress Response.

Think about a stressful situation until you notice you have shifted into one of the modes of your stress response — unless you are already there.
- Close your eyes.
- Bring your attention to a sound in your environment.
- Now while listening to that, include a second sound.
- Now a third sound.
- While you are listening to the sounds, become aware of the feeling of you clothes on your body.
- Now while maintaining your attention on the sounds and you feeling of the contact with your clothes, feel the air passing in and out of your nostrils.
- Now wriggle your toes.
- Finally open your eyes and notice something shiny.

Once you are back in a more functional mode, you can feel into the body and release the holding pattern either with awareness (just being present without reaction), or by yawning.

There is a difference between the external trigger and the emotional response, although sometimes the speed of the response makes it seem as if it was the same thing. This is where blaming others for your emotions comes from. Of course, if you believe the other person created your response, then you have no power to change the situation. But if you acknowledge that the emotional response is yours and therefore you can change how you react, this is taking back your power. Not taking it from the other person, as they didn't take it, but you just deciding not to give it away.

As I mentioned before, there are three components to an emotional response.
1. The story.
2. The charge.
3. The underlying physical holding pattern in the body.

In this section, I will be focusing on resisted emotions. An emotion that isn't resisted flows through us and is gone, like a temper tantrum of a two-year-old: it happens then it's over. This doesn't mean we need to behave like a two-year-old, as hopefully our emotional regulation centre in the pre-frontal cortex of your brain will allow us to watch the emotional charge surge through our system without getting swept away. It's the difference between watching the train go past vs. jumping on it.

1. **The story** — the current story is irrelevant when you are experiencing an emotional reaction based on resisted past experience. For instance, if you have been abused as a child and someone says something that makes you feel unsafe and you become dysfunctional, what was said isn't the real issue. In general, I don't spend much time with the story. Having a person talk about their trauma is more likely to re-traumatise the person unless you are a skilled practitioner in EMDR or something similar (which I am not). There are many ways of working on this level, and for some issues, it's beneficial having a chat with someone you trust. Sometimes talking about things doesn't improve things. If in fact you seem to go around in circles with a similar emotional patterns showing up at different times, making you dysfunctional, this is a sign you need to work differently.
2. **The charge** — the charge is mostly your resistance to feeling the original emotion.
   This can feel like anxiety, make you feel fatigued, make you feel incredibly tense and stressed or have you comfort eat, but it's all just resistance. The charge often feels much larger than we are, which is why it is so easy to be overwhelmed. Making the decision that you are safe to feel through the resistance and accept that it is OK will start the process of feeling the underlying resisted emotion.
3. **The physical holding pattern in the body.** This is where we resist the emotions.
   Imagine you have a strong emotion. Your body is tight, and then you hold on to that tension and don't release it. Over time, some of the tension releases, but the core area stays tight. The tension constantly sends stimuli up to the brain, which are interpreted as a threat, or something to be stressed about. This constant messaging of threat from the body pushes the nervous system into overwhelm that makes you unable to be fully present. The stronger the stimuli, the more it feels like you will be swept away by the constant flood of threat if we don't resist it.

There are many ways of working with emotional content, but they can be grouped according to which of the three components they focus on.

Talk therapies predominantly focus on the story as the trigger for the emotion which is then experienced in a safe situation. The success of these techniques will be whether you feel safe enough to be completely vulnerable and re-experience your trauma. If there is not that sense of safety then there is the possibility that talking through your trauma time and again will actually re-traumatise you, leaving you more dysfunctional after a session.

To me there seems to be a weakness in this approach as the emotional parts of the brain (the limbic system) are non-verbal. So, working in a verbal way to affect more primitive parts of the brain may not be the most efficient way of working.

Processes that do work involve engaging other areas of the brain that can release the charge and the physical holding patterns in the body.

If you have worked through a trauma yet it still comes up and makes you dysfunctional, then you may need to use a different approach. The endpoint for a successful trauma resolution should be that you are able to be emotionally neutral when something reminds you of the situation. One area to look at is often whether the patterns in the body have released.

Breathwork and Rebirthing

Breathwork and rebirthing can be used to release the charge and create the calm space to feel into what else is beneath it. One negative aspect to this approach is that the charge is often released in a catharsis, which is a state that is incoherent — you are not in control of the release process and you may end up so tired from the process that you don't push deeper to unwind the underlying pattern. If this is the case many sessions may be needed to clear the space and integrate the trauma.

From my perspective, the most effective ways of working with emotions are focused on unwinding the underlying holding pattern through accessing the body. This can be done in a number of ways, but all of them need to be simple, as complexity is a requirement of the higher processes of the mind, which become dysfunctional when you hit strong emotions. The key piece is that you should remain as coherent and functional as possible. This creates safety and makes it easier for you to process resisted emotions in the future. This means, you are more likely to jump right in and integrate what is coming up for you by yourself and be less reliant on someone else for support.

The Difference Between Resisted Emotions and Being Traumatised

You can have resisted emotions and not be traumatised. We all have experienced things that we would have preferred not to, and for a short period have been dysfunctional. However, trauma is a much more extreme experience that doesn't necessarily change with time but can be unwound with effective tools and support.

Experiencing trauma fundamentally changes how your brain works. FMRI scans of people who have been traumatised show changes in the brain structure and function.[51,52] The trauma shifts the person's ability to function down into the more primitive areas of the brain. This leads to the array of symptoms and can lead to the person self-medicating with alcohol or drugs to try and change how they feel.

Different people experiencing the same event may have completely different reactions, and some maybe traumatised and dysfunctional while others are not. Trauma is such an individual pattern that comparisons to others who experienced a similar event should be avoided.

Research in the US on adverse childhood events (ACEs) found that a childhood exposure to traumatic events makes PTSD more likely.[61] Often, the individuals did not actually consider the events such as witnessing physical or verbal abuse to be a big deal, yet the research clearly shows the impacts can change how well they deal with a potentially traumatic event later in life.

Trauma work needs to be done within a supported, safe environment with someone you can trust, so you can unwind the resisted emotional patterns while remaining coherent and safe.

> Bessel van der Kolk, a psychiatrist and research scientist who has researched PTSD for decades, explains the experience of trauma in his book, The Body Keeps the Score[84] as follows, "Traumatized people chronically feel unsafe inside their bodies: The past is alive in the form of gnawing interior discomfort. Their bodies are constantly bombarded by visceral warning signs, and, in an attempt to control these processes, they often become expert at ignoring their gut feelings and in numbing awareness of what is played out inside. They learn to hide from their selves." (p 97)
>
> Another person who works with trauma in a body-based way is Peter Levine. His view of what happens when we are faced with a traumatic event is, "In response to threat and injury, animals, including humans, execute biologically based, non-conscious action patterns that prepare them to meet the threat and defend themselves. The very structure of trauma, including activation, dissociation and freezing are based on the evolution of survival behaviours. When threatened or injured, all animals draw from a 'library' of possible responses. We orient, dodge, duck, stiffen, brace, retract, fight, flee, freeze, collapse, etc. All of these coordinated responses are somatically based — they are things that the body does to protect and defend itself. It is when these orienting and defending responses are overwhelmed that we see trauma.
>
> "The bodies of traumatized people portray 'snapshots' of their unsuccessful attempts to defend themselves in the face of threat and injury. Trauma is a highly activated incomplete biological response to threat, frozen in time. For example, when we prepare to fight or to flee, muscles throughout our entire body are tensed in specific patterns of high energy readiness. When we are unable to complete the appropriate actions, we fail to discharge the tremendous energy generated by our survival preparations. This energy becomes fixed in specific patterns of neuromuscular readiness. The person then stays in a state of acute and then chronic arousal and dysfunction in the central nervous system. Traumatized people are not suffering from a disease in the normal sense of the word — they have become stuck in an aroused state. It is difficult if not impossible to function normally under these circumstances."
>
> While the tools in this book will be useful to someone who is traumatised, it is highly likely they will need more support, and so I recommend working with a practitioner who can include some form of body-based trauma work. Alternatively, work with a bodywork practitioner and someone to work with the trauma.

If experiencing strong emotions feels unsafe, we are more likely to resist the experience.

I suspect that when we are already in our stress response and we are challenged with a strong emotion, that is when we are likely to resist experiencing it. Of course, if you have never been taught how to process strong emotions, or when you have been punished or humiliated for expressing them (e.g., "Stop crying or I'll smack you," or "Big boys don't cry"), then there is a good reason to choke it off and resist the experience.

When we resist strong emotions, we use the body to do it, either muscles or fascia. For example, is there an area of rigidity in your upper back? This could be structural (in response to gravity), or it could be emotional, or both. Releasing emotions trapped in the body is one of the most freeing things you can do. The energy used to hold down/resist the emotion frees up, as does your body. This gives you much more spring in your step, improves your posture, immune system function and sleep, and allows you to experience positive emotions with much greater depth.

The first step in working with emotions is being able to recognise when you are about to "hit it." So, if you comfort eat or shop or whatever you do when you are resisting emotions, flag those behaviours and when they show up set aside time just for cleaning up your emotional space. This should be a high priority, as avoiding it will affect your health, sleep and close human relationships.

Another step is to track your emotional state. You can use a scale from 0-10, with 10 feeling light, calm, peaceful and invigorated, keen to learn new things and with a bounce in your step. Where would you put yourself at this moment?

Track yourself for a week or so. What are you doing when you are higher on the scale, e.g., hanging out with friends, doing exercise or something you enjoy should lift you up.

If you always feel heavy, have tension or chronic pain in your body, are short tempered or angry, or if you don't feel any difference (everything feels the same) or if you have what is unkindly called a resting bitch face, then make it a priority to learn how to deal with emotions. It will change your life.

Emotions normally flash through your system and are gone. It is our resistance to having the full experience of the emotion that makes us feel heavy, rigid, numb and distressed. Changing emotional states is a bit like changing your shirt: you need to decide to do it and take some effective action.

So, if you are habitually sitting in an uncomfortable emotional state, or visit one on a regular basis, then it is time to upskill and decide to do the work to change your life.

The main point is that we tend to feel the charge of our own resistance, and resist feeling any further. It takes courage to feel through that, but no one has ever suffered permanent damage from feeling through their resistance and integrating the emotion underneath. The same can't be said for continuing to resist the emotional baggage you have — that can kill you.

Once you have practised working this way, the discomfort does reduce and it becomes shorter-lived and you can integrate the layers quicker.

Years ago, I resisted everything, used a couple of drinks to make the resistance disappear, and soldiered on with my repressed emotions safely tucked away till they re-emerged. Once I found out how to work with emotions, I still resisted them, but this reduced significantly as I have done more work with the tools. The level of charge now is usually 10% of what it felt like before. Doing internal work daily is an investment that enables you to upskill in dealing with emotions and empowers you to govern your emotions rather than be ruled by them.

The relationship between the mind and emotions is tricky and subtle. What I mean by this is that you can become overwhelmed without warning if a thought triggers an emotion with a strong charge.

This is what happens with trauma. You can either be barely functional and something small shifts you to dysfunctional, or you might be functional in 80% of your life and then get triggered and it all falls apart. The transition can seem instantaneous, but if you can quieten your mind, you can "rewind" what happened and feel the different parts of the process (the thought, then the emotional response). One of the ways of stilling the mind is exercise 4 of working with the stress response. I have repeated it in the box below.
The key with digging yourself out of a highly changed emotional state is to completely accept being where you are — don't resist it.
Bring a tiny amount of attention out laterally and just hold the intention. It's like stretching your attention outwards. You will notice that there is a change in the amount of charge and then you will "pop" out of the emotion.

Objective: To Focus on Peripheral Part of Your Vision to Shift Out of Your Stress Response.

This is a great, quick way to shift out of your stress response while talking with someone in a potentially stressful situation.
- Bring your awareness to the edges of your peripheral vision on both sides.
- Hold your attention there until you feel a shift in your stress levels.

Once you have more space, are not overwhelmed, then take a gentle approach to releasing the rest of the angst. This involves starting to yawn. If you are in an emotionally charged discussion with another person, then stay with the exercise above to remain in neutral, then when you have some space you can release your emotional charge by yawning.

If you can yawn, then feel into the body, looking for where the tension is. Keep following the tension, yawning often to release the charge. When you have cleaned the area up, it should feel like the issue is no longer interesting, there isn't any charge left. If you then focus on what triggered the response, it should feel like there is no emotion.

With life-threatening trauma, when you feel like committing suicide to escape what you are feeling, get help from someone who can support you while you process your trauma. Emotional states can feel incredibly powerful when you are in them, so make sure you feel safe and supported, and take a gradual approach to working with the emotions.

So, start with small things like why you get angry at bad drivers, and release the charge and underlying pattern (and similar-sized triggers), until you feel confident with your ability to release in this way, before you tackle anything big, like a traumatic event that changed your life.

Some people struggle to yawn. This can be because they are already in a state of elevated charge. If this is the case, start off with the exercises for working with the stress response. Then fake a yawn until you trigger a real one. Making the action of yawning will stimulate the vagus nerve and activate the parasympathetic nervous system.

Because yawning is contagious, doing this with other people is actually a good thing. The added advantage of working this way is that you don't need to wade through your story. The focus is on the underlying tension in the body, and to get to that you have to be able to release the charge. The choice is to suffer this stuff for a lifetime, or acutely for a few seconds.

Resistance, Control and Judgement

When we are working with resisted emotions, resistance, control and judgement all get in the way of fully integrating the underlying emotion. However, it is not that these ways of operating are inherently bad, we have just used a tool for the wrong job.

Resistance training for the body is a great way to safely exercise, if you have a large dog on a lead and there is a curious little kid it is perfect for you to be controlling and if you are looking out the window at a bleak cold winter day, it is wise to use you best judgement to select suitable clothing for the day.

So, it therefore in the right circumstances these ways of operating are useful but just not when it comes to emotions. It might be very helpful to upgrade your response and get more efficient at cleaning stuff up.

When you can slow your mind down enough you will notice that what actual happens is that a sensation happens in your body, that you have connected to an emotion, this triggers a memory that you resist so you resist the sensation. Within that process is a judgement that the sensation threatens you and the use of contraction within the body to try and control the sensation.

So, if you can make yourself feel safe, and ignore the story and tune into the sensation in the body this will help feeling through the resistance and help you integrate the underlying pattern.

Internal Work — Investing in Your Own Self-Development

Your body has within it patterns that are associated with unresolved emotional issues.

Once you get the hang of releasing the charge from your resistance, you can start to clean up these patterns.
The key thing is to start yawning before you tune into the tension pattern. This is a bit like opening a tap before you start the pump, letting the pressure dissipate rather than build up.

Some common hiding places for emotional baggage include the digestive system, thoracic spine, ribcage, psoas, lower back. I'm not a big fan of the one size fits all prescriptions that this part of your body is where you store that emotion. I think we are all unique, so what you find in different places will be unique to you. This creates more of a sense of exploring rather than having expectations — expectations limit what you find.

When you intentionally look for repressed emotion to release, you may find your resistance patterns show up. Examples are comfort eating, getting really busy, feeling too tired or having to do exercise, whatever you do when you are resisting feeling something.

This is great as you can fully experience this behaviour and then ignore it and return your focus to the part of your body you were going to release.

When you find something, don't stop till it is released and you feel relaxed and have more energy. If you do find yourself "stuck" in something, ignore the story, release the charge of your resistance and bring your attention to the underlying tension patterns in your body. Yawn, or fake it till you make it.

Psoas Release

The psoas (Psoas major in the diagram) is one of the muscles we contract when we have stress hormones circulate through our system. The psoas also turns on to stabilise the lower back if there is a misalignment, so muscular tension can be due to a number of different issues. This exercise works on the emotional/stress response of the psoas muscle. If tension persists, then a more structural approach is most likely needed.

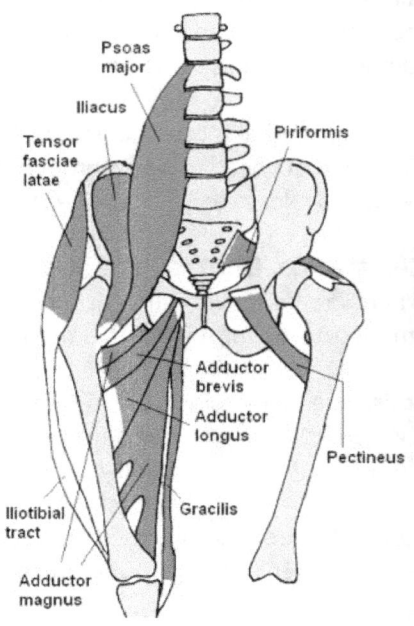

If your psoas is tight you may experience stiffness in your lower back, a deepened lumbar curve or being bent over to one side in the lower back. As the psoas attaches to the femur (thigh bone), it also externally rotates the femur so your foot may point outwards (a few other factors can create this too).

- Lie on your back with your knees bent.
- Feel into your lower back.
- Feel the tension the back muscles, and then feel on the inside of your spine for tension in the psoas muscles.
- With your attention on any tension on the inside of the lower back yawn extending the exhalation. Continue yawning till you feel the psoas relax.
- Then bring your attention to any tension in your back muscles. Yawn till they release.
- Go between the back muscles and psoas, releasing tension until the back feels nice and relaxed.
- If there is some residual tension or when you stand up the tension reoccurs that may mean your lower back has a misaligned vertebrae that requires muscular tension to create more support.

Digestive System Release

Your digestive function is run by your parasympathetic nervous system, and digestive problems often involve stress. This is one way to release this stress on a regular basis and improve your digestive function

- Bring your attention to the inside of your mouth and yawn.
- This should release some saliva in your mouth.
- As you swallow the saliva, feel it go down your oesophagus.
- Bring your awareness to any tension in your oesophagus and yawn.
- Next move your hand around your abdomen, feeling for tension.
- When you find tension, feel into the area and yawn.
- Keep palpating to find areas of tension, and release them.
- Feel any emotions or stress you may have in your digestive system, and yawn to release it.

If you have digestive issues, you may not feel this area at all. It may seem frozen, and this is a sign you need to repeat this daily until the whole area feels relaxed and you can be present there.

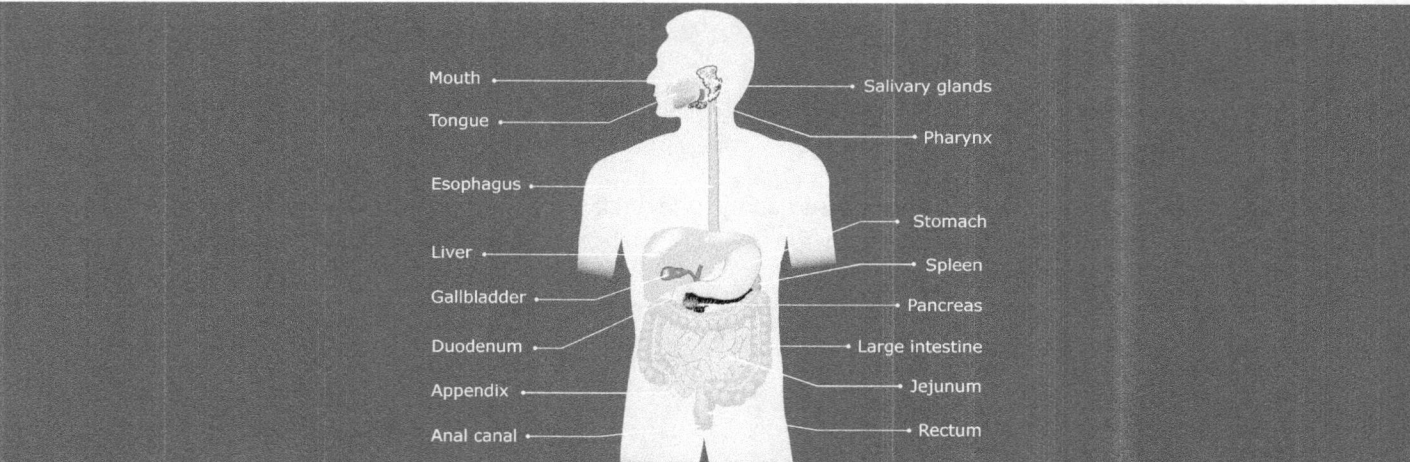

Upper back release

This exercise can be done standing, sitting or lying down.

- Place your fingers on your sternum (breast bone).
- Feel the movement as you breathe.
- Feel the connection from the sternum to the thoracic spine.
- With each breath, your upper back should change shape.
- Notice what areas move and what areas are rigid.
- Bring your attention to the areas that are rigid, and yawn.
- Continue yawning until you feel the area release.
- When there is more movement in the spine, bring your attention to the area around the heart, take your time and yawn lots to release any tension on the physical or emotional level.

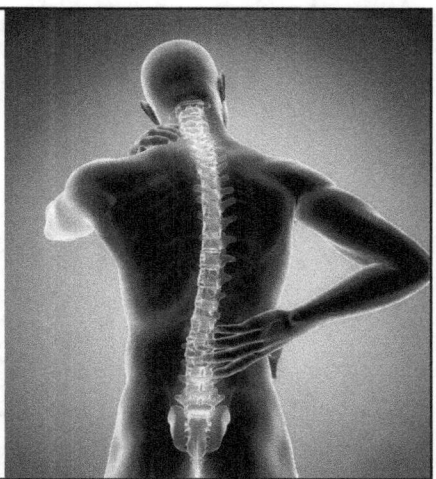

The top down approach of using the rational mind to analyse and change how your mind works is one of the most common approaches to personal growth work. One of the problems with this is it can become academic — just because you have thought about an emotional issue doesn't mean it is going to change. In fact, you are more likely to be in denial once you have fed an issue to your intellect. "I've worked out what the problem is — It's you" could be the rational mind's basic go to for solving emotional problems. Of course, the rational mind is a valuable tool but it's not the only tool and it needs to be used for solving suitable problems. It is great for recognising reoccurring patterns of behaviour and then you need to explore, using your felt sense to find the other parts of the pattern.

Some of the limiting emotional patterns that maybe suppressed include emotions like shame.

Brene Brown, who has studied the relationship between shame and vulnerability, looking for how people can live in a wholehearted way, defines shame as the fear of disconnection.

Shame — the fear of disconnection — is there something about me that if people know or see, that I won't be worthy of connection?
Brene Brown

Her TED Talks in the references section are worth a watch if you haven't seen them already.

One connection that made a lot of sense to me is the link between shame and addiction. My experience of shame was of intense discomfort that was hard to experience in the present moment. So, I can understand that if intense shame haunts you each day, you may want to numb it. Working around shame has been very freeing for me, and I highly recommend it. Your ability to become vulnerable will have a huge influence on the quality of your interactions with others.

"Vulnerability is emotional risk, exposure and uncertainty, and the most accurate measure of courage."
Brene Brown

According to Brene, in order to become emotionally fit, you need to be able to identify close to 30 different emotions, and that most people have the ability to identify three. These three tend to be angry, sad, and frustrated. If you only have three flavours, there is not a lot of space for subtlety, or discussion about what is going on.

One interesting overlap between emotions and neuroscience is with the work of Candice Pert, a neuroscientist who did a lot of work on neuropeptides, which she identified as the molecules of emotion.[53] Areas of the brain associated with emotion, for instance the amygdala, have up to 40 times the number of receptor sites for neuropeptides than areas that are not associated with emotions. Another interesting connection that Pert mentions in one of her talks is that the areas identified as the energy centres or chakras in the body have a larger number of neuropeptide receptor sites than other areas.

Another area that has been found to have receptor sites for neuropeptides is the immune system. So, how you feel will have an impact on whether you fight off a cold or end up sick.

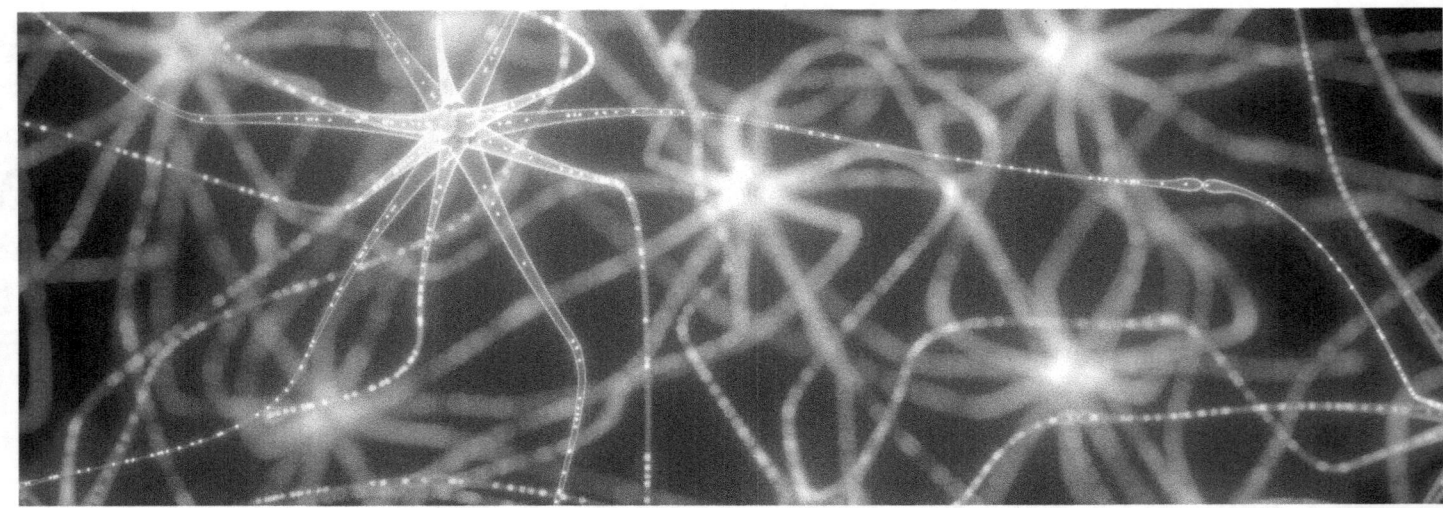

Neurotransmitters as a Model for how Emotions Work.

The work of neuroscientists such as Dr Candice Pert have established that there is a link between neurotransmitters and what we experience as emotions. However, this is not causal that is they can't prove the neurotransmitter creates the specific emotion. It is far more likely that we each have an individual blend of neurotransmitters that we identify as a particular emotion. However, in this book I have used an individual neuropeptide and linked it with a behaviour or emotion, this is common in papers by neuroscientists such as Dr Sue Carter, who did a lot of work on oxytocin. This is a useful simplification that allows us to discuss how to stimulate the body to self-correct.

Neuroscientists have identified between 50-60 different neuropeptides that may be connected to emotional states. The relationship between neuropeptides and emotions is likely to be complex. An example of this is that Oxytocin, the neuropeptide that helps us create attachment to others, resilience, love and contractions during birth, is also involved in emotions such as envy and gloating. This suggests that there is a blending effect of different neuropeptides that creates emotions.

One of the challenges with identifying new emotions is to distinguish the subtle feedback from what you consider to be you, and to identify this sensation as something new. This is easy if the stimulus is physical, say someone stroking the back of your neck.

However, you have billions of receptors sending feedback to your brain every second, and a very small capacity to actually pay attention to that feedback. This means that in any one second, there is a huge amount of data flowing into the brain that is subconscious. So, there is a lot of background noise from your sensory receptors.

All this information could be essential for survival at some point, but often is just ignored. So, in this huge mix of feedback hides the subtle flow of information that will increase your emotional vocabulary. In order to find it you have two options:
1. To intentionally create the emotional state so you get the feel for what it feels like, and
2. Pay attention to the emotions you experience and try to identify/recognise what they are.

So, become an emotional detective, feel with curiosity, and label different feelings as you recognise them.

The reward for doing this is a more emotionally colourful world and the ability to have a broader discussion about what/how you feel, and in the process being able to free yourself from limiting emotional patterns that are interfering with your ability to experience positive emotional states.

Recognising emotions exercise
With anything you would like to find more information on, it is important to recognise what you already know. Exploring emotions is no different.
- On a piece of paper, write down what emotions you can recognise and which ones you feel the most.
- Next, have a look at the list of emotions below and see if you can get a sense of how they feel, and spend a few minutes

on each to really identify the experience. Make the emotions as big as you can so you will really recognise them. Have the emotion fully flood your system and notice any change in body language that goes with these emotions.

- After each negative activated state, yawn until you feel you are back in a neutral state.
- The list is organised into contrasting pairs so you can really feel the difference.
- So, you will yourself to be angry and feel what your body feels like when that emotion is present. Then yawn to release it and go to joy.
- If you have a predisposition to being a particular negative emotion for instance being anxious, then skip over it, you are familiar with that one. You can explore what is underlying that emotion later on.
- Rather than trying to complete this list in one go take a few different emotions and experience them then yawn to release them. Finish on a positive emotion.
- If you feel numb, dead inside or are stuck in your head and feel nothing these are all signs that you are resisting feeling something. It may feel unsafe to feel your body or feel the emotions that you are resisting. Doing internal work will free this up and make life a lot more pleasant.

Emotional states to play with (not a complete list):

- Anger
- Joy
- Anxiety
- Grace
- Frustration
- Calmness
- Jealousy
- Excitement

- Fear
- Curiosity
- Disgust
- Attraction
- Repulsion
- Love
- Judgement
- Acceptance

- Wariness
- Forgiveness
- Hate
- Love
- Contraction
- Peacefulness
- Deceitfulness
- Playfulness

- Regret
- Caring
- Spite
- Relaxation
- Vengefulness
- Flexibility
- Rigidity
- Openness
- Gratitude

Notice if you have any resistance to experiencing any of the states, or if something feels familiar. Both are signs that you have some stuff to clean up in this area.

Another interesting thing is to track where you go to check how you are feeling.

- If someone asks you "how are you feeling?"
- Where in your mind/body do you go to check?

Once you can create positive emotional states at will, then the question is, why don't you do so more often rather than wait and see what arises from the mixture of repressed emotional patterns and your social conditioning?

The key is to accept whatever you are feeling, because denial is a form of resistance. Release the emotion if it isn't how you would choose to feel, and in its place, create something else.

Nature doesn't do vacuums, so you can either create something positive, or watch as your attention sticks to the next negative emotion.

The Importance of Your Story

Your brain sits in the dark cavern of your skull and relies 100% on the constant flow of information from your senses. The brain's job is to make sense of this information, but as I mentioned, it can only process a small amount of data in any one period of time. Therefore, a lot of information is ignored. This is why we put things on automatic as fast as we can, so we can shift our attention to something else.

In essence, our brain assigns meaning to the data we get from the outside world, and this becomes our story. This is how we remember our past and create our future.
What you pay attention to will depend on what story you are telling yourself about reality.
Things that trigger the stress/survival response will get more attention than things that create pleasure, unless we are deliberate about how we invest our attention. People who write the news are well aware of this.

The story we tell ourselves about what we are experiencing is very important for finding solutions to pain. What you think affects what feedback you pay attention to.
Imagine for instance that the story you are telling yourself includes the idea that your pain is getting worse. Your nervous system will sensitise to the pain and you will feel it more. This can be due to a growth in the number of nociceptive receptors in the area, or inflammation of the nervous system increasing the activation of the existing nerves, which increases the sensitivity to the feedback from the area, or that you are fearful of acute pain returning.
On a larger scale, this may be due to more stress hormones tightening muscles, putting more pressure on the lower back where the pain is coming from, or it could be that the emotional charge about being in pain could increase and a sense of "this is going to last forever" could lock in a sense of being trapped.
Compare that to the idea that this pain is temporary and you just need to find the right piece of information to help your body self-correct. This may help you take a break from stressing and start looking in areas where you haven't tried before.

The body/mind has an amazingly strong ability to heal itself when people radically shift their perspectives on life and the stories they tell themselves.

The other type of story, the one about why you feel the way you do, is actually part of the problem. The way you feel is being created in the present moment, holding on to a reason from the past that locks you into the current experience can be a big part of what is holding you in the "stuck" place.
This is why forgiving people is an act of release for you, not a "get out of jail free" for them.

So, the story you tell yourself is very important as it focuses your attention on specific data that supports your narrative as being real, but its details don't matter.

Forward-leaning Beliefs

One of the important uses for creating a story is to create a forward-leaning belief that is positive. For instance, "I get better every day" is a better option than "I'm never going to get better." Even if you struggle to believe your narrative, some days it is better to be positive and wrong than negative and right because there are benefits outside of your physical health to having a positive outlook. There is a catch with this: if you refuse to acknowledge a load of information that your forward leaning belief is just fantasy, then you will eventually run into reality in a big way. So, "I can fly" is fantasy and if you throw yourself off a 40 storey building, you will have experiential clarity on that when you reach the ground. However, "I will continue to do my own research and with this persistence I will find my own solutions to what is affecting my health" is a good forward-leaning belief. You then look for evidence to support this belief.

The Default Mode Network

Part of how you use your brain when you are not focused on a task at hand is to slip back into what has been called the default mode network (DMN).[55] If your mind wanders, this is where you end up. Rumination about what is wrong in your life is the output from the default mode network. As our brain has a tendency to focus on the negative aspects, which is where a potential threat is more likely to come from, we will tend to spend more time dwelling on the small number of things that are going wrong. This focus makes it seem that this is more important than it often is if you look at the larger picture. It is no wonder that the DMN has been found to be connected to major depression.[56]

In fact, the DMN should come with a flashing warning sign saying "all characters in this thought process are there for entertainment only and do not reflect any the thoughts or actions of people either living or dead". How many times have you been chewing over a situation in your head about an interaction and found that it was not what you thought it was?

It is interesting that in a survival situation, you fully use your brain's capacity, or it shuts down, as you go into your stress response, so you don't spend time ruminating about the small issues that don't really matter. So, if you are ruminating, you can actually use that as a benchmark that you are safe. You will survive, and when you have finished wanting to feel crap and feel through the emotional heaviness/resistance and find the core of what you are resisting, then integrate it, you will rapidly shift out of the emotional trough.

The next part is to start to reprogram the default mode network. As I mentioned earlier, changing networks takes time, and as you start to reduce the time you spend using the current pattern, the brain will re-purpose the unused parts of the network. The new network connections form as you invest your time in a new pattern.

So, are there ways of making this more efficient?
Yes, if you link positive feelings like those of achievement or pleasure with the process, then you are going to pay more attention to it and return more often. As was suggested with the process of making exercise pleasurable, do this in a way that maximises enjoyment.

Reprogramming the Default Mode Network (DMN)

- Become aware of when you are ruminating about small negative crap.
- Smile, because you have caught yourself indulging in a naughty pleasure. Create a "got you" moment when you become aware of what you are doing. This can give you a dopamine hit.
- Completely accept what you are feeling. Feel through it. This will help still the mind, clear the resistance and shift the underlying emotional aspect and shift you back into your body.
- Alternatively when you notice that mind racing feeling name it " I'm in my DMN again" this will help you shift out of those parts of the brain into the areas that create self awareness.
- When you have created a bit of space, create the feeling of contentment.
- When you feel content, then create a positive thought process that will help focus your attention on what you would prefer to experience.
- The process is then one of persistence. Enjoy catching yourself playing in your DMN. It means you have spare capacity to create a new experience of your reality.

Another way to work with the DMN is to look at the overall theme: is the story running about being a victim or fighting back, being anxious?
You can then treat this as an invitation to explore this whole theme in more depth and integrate the underlying emotional patterns.

The Importance of Awareness

Awareness training is really a process of finding different inputs and starting to listen to and identify what these receptors are communicating and what you can learn from that.

For example, feel your body. Your experience is probably a mix of the stimuli from your body going up to the brain and the projection from your limbic system coming from your brain into your body. This mix of information is why we often don't recognise when we have an emotional holding pattern tightening up muscles until we become deliberate and feel into the area.

In a much subtler way, there is a flow of information whenever we are in contact with others. We usually look at this in terms of body language, but our mirror neurons track people around us, giving information on a whole range of things such as how another person feels. This information is not objective data, but rather a combination of information through the visceral nervous system (the nervous system in our gut), visual and other sensory information picked up from the other person, and our interpretation of what this means. So there is often plenty of room for misunderstanding.[57]

However, we can use this information-gathering ability to put subtle information into another person's nervous system. This is a way to convey information that may be more powerful than verbal communication. For instance, you can inform a person's nervous system that they are safe. Your presence and how you connect to a person will do this more efficiently than anything you can say to them. This can make a huge difference with releasing trauma from the body. This therapeutic presence improves the likelihood of a client deeply relaxing and unwinding both physical and emotional dysfunctional patterns.[58]

In Ortho-Bionomy, we work with this form of felt communication to put information into the nervous system of our clients to help them notice behavioural patterns, emotional holding patterns, attitudes, and resistance.

Once you can recognise the feel of an emotional/mental state, you can start to recognise when a person goes into that mode of operating. For instance, feeling like a victim is fairly common for people who have experienced chronic pain for a long period of time.
A person who is in that space is more sensitive to pain and more focused on the intensity of the pain, so helping someone integrate victimhood is part of moving out of chronic pain.

Tracking when a person slides into that mode and either asking them verbally to recognise that state or just holding the space so they get to recognise it can often help them shift. Once a person can identify the feeling of being a victim, they can track it and, with awareness, integrate it.

The next important step is to have a positive goal to focus on when you have cleared up your space. One trap is that as something negative clears, you look for the next problem or thing that is wrong instead of a positive aspect of your situation. If you are working toward a big goal, investing your free attention there will enable you to feel better longer. The idea of personal growth is to become more productive and enjoy your life more, not just to spend endless hours navel-gazing or focussing on how you are broken and need to focus on yourself.

Intentionally Creating a More Positive Space to Live In

The body is amazing with its intricate interrelated systems that work so beautifully, most of the time.

For instance, your immune system is integrated with the parts of the brain that produce and release oxytocin. Oxytocin has been nicknamed the love hormone, but also plays an essential role in stimulating and strengthening the immune system's ability to recognise new bacteria, as well as strengthening the response to dealing with bacterial outbreaks.

This makes sense, because when you get close to another person, the risk of being exposed to new microbes dramatically increases. This is particularly important as a woman selects a partner subconsciously based on how different their genetic make-up is, in particular their immune system, as I explain below.

An Interesting Tangent

Women choose a mate, taking into account whether the man's genes and immune system are different from their own, so that any offspring will have a diverse gene pool. This is done on a subconscious level in response to the odour of the man. Interestingly, when a woman is on the birth control pill, the hormonal changes seem to disrupt the hypothalamus/pituitary/ovarian system responsible for this mate selection. This disruption then leads women to be attracted to men who have a similar genes and immune system.[59]

This is thought to be because the pill tricks the body into thinking it is already pregnant and there is a tendency for pregnant women to feel comfortable being surrounded by family when they have a belly full of arms and legs. (This of course depends on the family, but as a genetic proclivity it seems to be so.)

This can mean that if a relationship has started when the woman is on the pill, then goes off the pill to breed, her choice of mate may change, leading to relationship wobbles.

Imagine you have just fallen in love. You have a cocktail of neurotransmitters surging through your system, and feel amazing.
So, just as you swap spit with your new love for the first time and expose yourself to a whole new world of bacteria, your immune system gets an upgrade to recognise and kill the new bacteria — how cool is that!

So, let's hack this system by intentionally creating the feeling of being in love and see if we can improve immune function.
- Do you remember how it felt when you fell in love?

- Or when you held a baby?
- Or maybe when you held a puppy?

Recreate that feeling of love.
Imagine you are filling your body from your toes up with that emotional feeling, like pouring love into an empty vessel shaped like your body.

Fill all your cells with that love.

Feel it flowing through your pelvis, flowing into your digestive system, pouring into your lungs and heart. Feel it flowing down your arms to your hands and finally filling your head with love. Then bring your focus to your cerebrospinal fluid around your spinal cord and brain and really flood that with love.

If you have an pain in an area, flow the love into that area.

How does your body feel?

The great thing with this is you have removed an external source from the process which enables you to be content whether you are in an relationship or single.

> Babies are experts at manipulating everyone around them with generous doses of oxytocin. Their lives depend on it.
>
> Mother nature really wanted to make sure this worked because there is a monosynaptic nerve (a nerve with no joins) linking the nipple with the hypothalamus, meaning that when a baby breastfeeds, the mother gets a dose of oxytocin to help her connect and stay still long enough for the baby to feed.
>
> If you are bottle feeding a baby, you can improve attachment by having skin on skin contact, making eye contact and interacting with the baby both verbally and with touching. All of this increases the oxytocin released.

Another thing to play with is the relationship of different emotions. So, for instance compare jealousy and love.

Jealousy may be associated with the neurotransmitter vasopressin. Vasopressin is the sister molecule to oxytocin and fits into the same receptor sites in the body/brain. Because of this close connection between vasopressin and oxytocin, it has been hard to differentiate the response of each neurotransmitter. However, we can just play with this in our own nervous system.

Imagine a situation where you have been jealous. Once the feeling has been created, stop with the story. Now love the feeling of jealousy. This may seem hard at the start, especially if you have recently experienced a betrayal of trust in a relationship, but stay with it. As you love the sensation of jealousy, oxytocin will replace the vasopressin and you will be left with the feeling of love.

Then check back in to see if the story recreates the same level of jealousy. If there is still some charge repeat until it all melts.

> If you are overwhelmed by the emotions stirred up by this, then use the exercise below to pull yourself out.
> - Bring your awareness to edges of your peripheral vision on both sides.
> - Hold your attention there until you feel a shift in how you feel.

The cool thing is, you can change the flavour of your positive created emotional state to gratitude, kindness, grace, and in this way change your whole experience of your body. The more you practice intentionally loading an emotional state into your body, the quicker it will become until you can just decide and it will happen. So why not make this part of your waiting in a checkout queue, waiting for a red-light or as part of your breaking a default mode network reprogramming mindfulness practice?

You can set up some form of physical or verbal trigger that goes with the emotional state. For instance, my father uses the word "click" to shift into an internal state of inner peace and contentment.

How Do We Experience what Another Person is Feeling?

There is a survival advantage to being able to predict what people around you are going to do. This is both on a physical level such recognising a threatening movement, and on an emotional level. The emotional areas of our brain are thought to have developed to enable greater socialisation and the ability to work together. This has been the key to humans being a successful species. The discovery of mirror neurons in the brain has enabled neuroscientists to fill in the blanks as to how we track another person's movements and get a sense of how they feel.60 In this summary, I'm going to focus on tracking another person's emotional state as that is relevant to our discussion in this chapter. This is based around a great book called The Empathic Brain by Christian Keysers.[85]

The research looked at the emotion of disgust.
Imagine standing in dog shit with your bare feet. As you think about this experience, notice the facial expression you pull and feel the emotion of disgust.

Researchers had subjects in FMRI machines look at photos of someone else experiencing disgust and the areas of the brain that became active were recorded.

They found that information from the visceral network is combined with the information from the visual cortex. This is synthesised, and the premotor area of the brain is stimulated, which stimulates the primary motor area of the brain, causing you to move your facial muscles into an approximation of what the other person is experiencing.

Your emotional centres in the brain then get a reading of the what the recruitment pattern is of your facial muscles and create the appropriate emotion. This is then our best guess at what the other person is experiencing. So, there is an interpretation aspect to feeling what someone else is feeling. This creates the possibility of misunderstandings, or misreading the emotion. It is also highly likely that some people are going to have this ability stronger than others, so identifying what another person is feeling comes a lot easier to them. Of course, people who have worked as counsellors for many years would also be more skilful and have developed those connections in the brain to improve this ability.

As I think having different ways to approach dealing with emotions is a high priority, I have asked Lisa Tyree, someone who specialises in unwinding emotional trauma, to write about what she does in the next chapter.

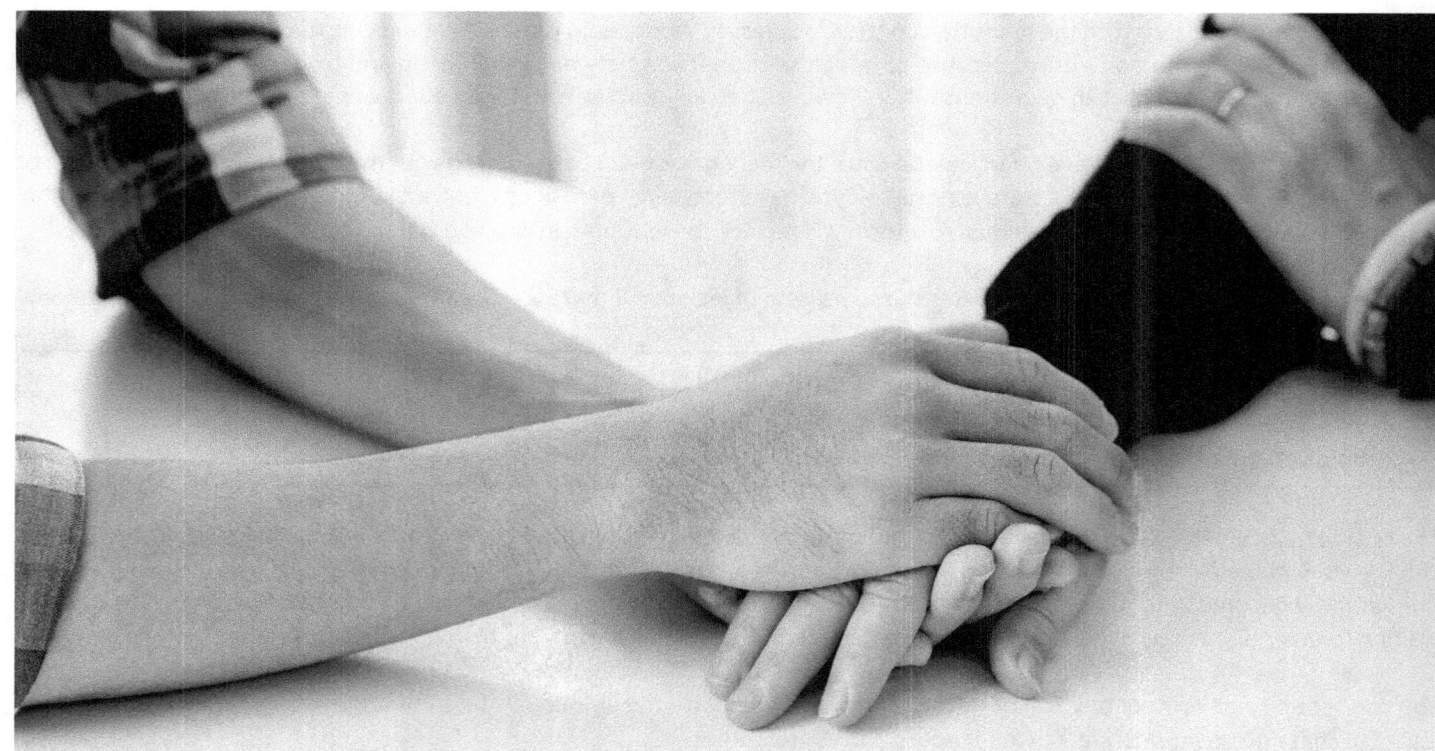

CHAPTER 7.
SOUL WISDOM ARRIVES IN THE SPACE WHEN WE LISTEN

CLEAR YOUR EMOTIONS AT SUPERSONIC SPEED

by Lisa Tyree

SOUL WISDOM ARRIVES IN THE SPACE WHEN WE LISTEN

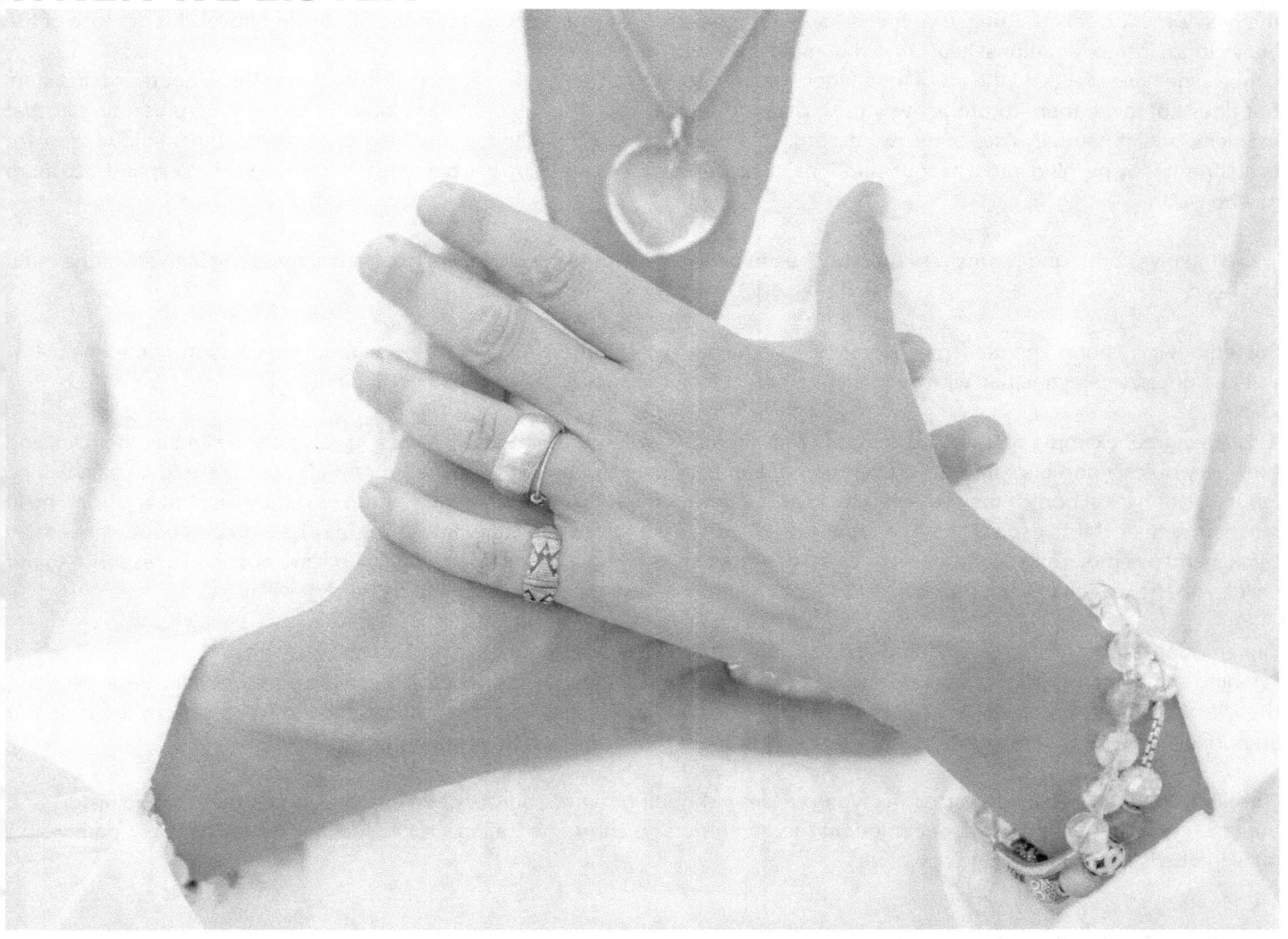

As Rob mentioned earlier, doing internal work daily is an investment that enables us to deal with emotions, empowering us to govern our own emotions rather than held hostage by them. My area of passion rests in this area. I would love to activate in you a very powerful gift all humans are born with — the ability to travel or go into and through all feelings, emotions and controls at super-sonic top speeds. I call this 'travelling.'

The purpose of travelling is to duplicate the exact tone your emotional heart contains from either past upsets and experiences or from present time reactions to life's circumstances without resistance. A 'tone' is a collection of feelings. Travelling is listening with your felt sense to a feeling or tone and pro-actively moving into and through it, until it naturally rises. By doing so, it will change. There may be tears, there may not be. Feeling the feeling, embracing the feeling, loving the feeling — understanding you within, without words.

Golden Guidelines of Where Travelling is Useful

If you are aware of any low feeling in yourself, you wake up in the morning at resting point with no external stimuli to justify a low tone — this is your base tone. By gently sinking into or gently pushing deeply into it with recognition that it is not your most expanded happy self, the feeling will literally start melting. By doing that exact base tone, you will never wake up with that again. It will be a different base tone, lighter or perhaps heavier, whatever your heart has recorded. This is true for everything in life. Anything that is not joyful, hopeful, expanded and loving is something to travel. The reason for learning this is, as you travel every low feeling and tone that rests in your emotional heart, you will never react to that feeling or tone again — not from you or anyone else.

There are many types of meditation. Lots of people choose to learn it to quieten the mind. Some people find this a baffling exercise as they struggle with their thoughts. The reason for this is they are not listening with awareness to the correct field. If this has been your difficulty, instead of warring with the head and listening to your brain's thoughts, bring your attention to your heart's tone:

the heavy, murky feeling sitting in your chest and gut screaming for your attention to notice, listen and travel. It is because of the heavy tones in your emotional heart that your mind is noisy.

Others who have practiced the art of meditation quietly observe the feeling by allowing it to be there. This is good as a first step, but does not invite them to pro-actively push deeper to experience the full depth and breadth of the tone presenting at that moment, until it naturally rises of its own accord. The result is, you will be limiting the heights of your potential growth. So, for everyone, it is by pushing into what our emotional heart contains that the mind will become quieter and we can expand into more of who we are.

Travelling gives profound results very quickly. The deeper we go within, the higher we rise in awareness and stillness of the mind and heart.

Sometimes it is a button pressed from experiences of the past, whilst other times we are low without explanation. Sometimes a low will be from an interaction had with another, or we react to a small upset, like our child getting hurt.

Kids are a great example of travelling things in present time. They hurt themselves, have a massive cry, feeling all the pain, and then very quickly pop back into the playground of life. They may end up with a graze superficially, but no residual pain will be left in their physical body if they felt everything at the time. A parent will be there for them as best they can, but will often be in reaction to their child's experience. They suppress it and carry it for longer. Sometimes they may be worried about what others think, perhaps embarrassed, or they want to tell the other child off for hurting their child. By noticing our heart's response to our child's experience, whatever it may be, gently pushing into the feeling and allowing it to be there, it will melt.

Our emotional hearts record everything in detail, making tiny little adaptations — shutting off bit by bit and suppressing by not listening and being there for oneself throughout daily life. Unfortunately, by suppressing the millions of small and large reactions, the average human becomes very full from an early age. The good news is, by travelling some big troughs from the past, our emotional hearts become significantly cleaner, making space to become far less reactive in the present.

Travelling within is useful right across life. When we enter shopping centres, houses or different countries, they all hold history and their own tonal frequency, which our emotional heart registers on entry. The feeling you pick up may be dull or heavy, perhaps set off alarm bells to exit as quickly as possible.

Reading the newspaper and watching the news also provokes reactions within us. By letting the tone come through us when watching the news — there is the visual picture, words, the intention behind the story and your reactions or response to what you see and feel — all coming into your living room. We may judge and have staunch opinions, both of which are our own reactions. To be more conscious in our TV watching or reading the newspaper, we can learn to observe our reaction and travel it instead of being in a constant state of reaction, which fuels significance to the story presented, and this is often the intent of the media.

This allows freedom to be wherever we are, without the influence of external sources. As the world and what we see is a reflection of what we have within us, we can use the news to observe global leaders and their behaviours to find the same behaviours and tones inside us and gain awareness by travelling what we do not like in them. This is a quiet way of changing the world and what we see.

In our relationships with one another, behind every behaviour or communication there is a tone, a feeling, and therefore an energy. This is what we react to with one another. By travelling our reactions first, we create space within to fine tune our own communications, preventing the very predictable outcome of ping-pong blame parties demanding understanding from another.

When a relationship couple master this together, they cease seeing the other as separate to them, and become two human beings mastering anything in their space that is not love. One might say, "Hey, I'm having trouble travelling this heaviness in me, can you travel it with me?" In this action together, they become united in their choice to love and understand all that is not their purest of selves.

With practice and clearing a few primary areas, we are able to observe our own reactions and that of others with the absence of fear, right or wrong, judgement, criticism of what has happened or is happening. We are learning to embrace all that exists and travel everything that is not love. It is all pure energy. This very natural gift is a primary key to living life with awareness and ease, so I want to pass onto you the joy I have experienced in how to navigate the quagmire of human thoughts, emotions, controls and tones. Be free to explore yourself, because you are truly extraordinary.

Step By Step Travelling Within…

Read the following a few times in full, including the troubleshooting to understand the concept first, and then the remainder of the chapter for further insight.

1. Choose an upset with a person, or an incident that happened for you. (Perhaps a small incident for learning purposes, for example your family member left the wet towel on the floor for the 9 millionth time). Alternatively, consider a singular feeling from the emotional chart, or if you are aware of heaviness in your heart right now, choose this first.
2. Start by recalling the experience. The feelings will come into your awareness and heart space. Your thoughts of the story will amplify, and perhaps you may have visuals with it.
3. Notice any thoughts, but do not pay attention to them. The purpose is to notice and listen to the full tone your heart presents. A tone is a collection of feelings.
4. Gently let yourself sink into it, allowing it to expand to its fullest and heaviest tone. Gently push deeper.
5. Now pause in here and observe the feeling. It may be a singular emotion or a collection of feelings. Allow it to be here. How deep is it? How heavy is it?
6. Open and relax your heart toward the tone, gently scanning to the left and to the right... how broad does it go? Can you gently push deeper and get under it with your love? It may feel like your heart has surrounded the feeling or tone. This is good.
7. Relax your mind and continue to listen to the feeling. No forcing, just allowing. It will start moving. The tone may go lighter and disperse naturally. Perfect, it will be complete. If it goes heavier, it means you need to gently push deeper. You are following one of your heart's threads. This is proactive travelling. Small feelings often link to a larger pool. Go for it and allow the full heaviness to be there. We want to explore the entire heaviness — to understand you in exactly how you feel or how you have felt.
8. Continue for as long as it feels heavy. Stay present in your observing. There is no time limit on a thread. With some of them, it may take minutes, hours or even a few days when doing it by yourself until you gain experience. There will be a lot of backlog. Just remain aware that you chose to travel it and will come out the other side into lightness. Let your partner or kids know you are in session. With practice, you will be able to speed through things in minutes. The difference is, your relationship to your story will change. Your awareness will start recognizing things as pure energy, neither positive nor negative, with far less significance or resistance to experiencing what rests in your emotional heart.
9. You may have memories float in, different incidents. This is your brain lining up the files that relate to this tone. Excellent. Notice the files or flash incidents without letting your brain munch on the story. Continue for as long as it is heavy, until it naturally becomes lighter. The emotional heart is an energetic muscle. Just like all muscles, the more you use it, the stronger it gets.
10. For some of you, body aches or pains may switch on whilst travelling. This is perfectly normal. Often, that body part is holding the tone you are feeling. Allow it to be there without significance. Some people only notice the body parts in pain. This distracts them, taking their attention away from the emotional feeling or tone. If you are a person who feels only the body response, try turning up your awareness on what the feeling is. It is like switching radio frequencies. What switches on in the body will switch off on completing the tone.
11. As the feeling or tone becomes lighter, it rises in the body. You may notice a bulge in your thymus or throat area. This is the energy heading up toward a porthole above your head called the crown chakra, which is a wheel located roughly one foot directly above your head. This is a gateway to your higher, more awake self. (If you are cynical toward things you are not yet aware of, travel the tone of cynicism until it melts.) There are several portholes around the head. If you use your hand now and scan around the head, you may notice the density change in the various chakras or portholes. If there is heaviness anywhere, place your hand there and listen to the tone, observe it change into lightness. For travelling purposes, we use the crown to listen to the last tentacles of the thread you are experiencing.
12. Gently bring your heart's awareness up into your crown and continue observing the feeling in the throat as it rises. At this point, notice any feeling of stress or pressure in your head and brain. This is the residue of brain stress from improper thoughts generated from the thread you are currently travelling. Say you had an upset with a person and the thoughts whirled around in your head for days or weeks. This created a stress tone in your head. Do not buy into it, it is all just energy caught inside your brain.
13. As an alternative to placing your heart's awareness in your crown, place your hand in the crown chakra instead. As your hand is an extension of your heart, your hand will feel the exact tone in the chakra. Using your hand, from the top of your head, scan upward until you feel a change of density in the air. It will feel heavier when you run into the wheel of the crown.

When you find it — congratulations by the way — pause here and listen with your hand. Again, by listening with your hand you are getting the exact tone in your crown. Relax your thoughts. Your hand will notice the heaviness, and by feeling it through your hand, it will start to become lighter. Stay here until it feels beautifully light. This is an excellent tool to use at the end of every day to quieten the mind, and very handy for draining out headaches.

14. If another low presents from the heart space whilst feeling the brain tone, bring your awareness back to your heart space and begin the process again. Be thorough.

15. On completion, allow yourself to pause and expand into your own peace and enjoy the quietness within. Well done!

Troubleshooting

1. **Your brain says, 'I can't do it!' This is doubt creeping in.**
   Doubt is the first place I start with clients. Throughout your life, you will have been generating quite a large pool of suppression and invalidation. Your heart and brain will present three distinctive ways of looking at any one of these files. The first; where others have invalidated or suppressed you. This is the victim flow. The second; where you have doubted or suppressed yourself. This is self towards self. And the third; where you have been invalidating and suppressing others. This is your contribution to causing another to feel less than what they are. I would like to highlight these three ways of looking at things and for you to start programming your brain in understanding that each are equally as important as the other but ultimately we are heading towards full awareness as a powerful human being. In this state there is no victim, only full comprehension of your own heavy pools of negativity that contributes to your world and others.

   When doubting yourself or allowing others to doubt you, you are suppressing all of your awareness, gifts, communications and the pure essence of you. By travelling the pools of doubt, (which is not you) you begin to reclaim the freedom and expansiveness that is you.

   Key files to investigate thoroughly are; as a family member, at school, towards yourself or your body, at work, with friendships or towards areas you are passionate about.

2. **Overthinking with the mind** This is not travelling the heart's tones. Notice when you do this, and gently return to the feeling in your heart space. You can place your hand on your heart to remind yourself to keep your attention in the correct area. Remember, you are not your mind. You are the soul that notices when your brain is talking and thinking all the time. This produces the stress tones, the anxiety tones. Begin to discipline your mind by listening to the heart space instead of the headspace. When doing this process for the first few times, the heart space is always heavy, often because it is full of millions of your own reactions, resistance toward life and unfelt feelings and emotions. Most people have no true reference inside themselves for a clean, peaceful heart. Be patient and trust you will become extraordinary at this gift. Do it daily and learn to be there for yourself like never before.

3. **Distractions.** Your mind wonders off. Gently bring yourself back and discipline your mind to finish what it started. Remind yourself why you want to do this. For me, my decision to understand all feelings and tones that were not me catapulted me into activating and growing into many extraordinary abilities I could never have imagined possible. I have grown and am still growing into all that I am. I also know that by understanding all that is not who we are, I am raising the consciousness of humanity, one human at a time. This creates a beautiful ripple effect. Travelling is pure understanding, and by each of us choosing to master this natural gift and demonstrate to our children and those we love, you too are lifting the consciousness of humanity into a far greater state of self-responsibility and true freedom in your heart to love, grow and thrive daily.

4. **Create your own bigger picture** so you have a guiding post to pull you back on track, something that really matters to you. Many **parents** choose to learn to do this for the love of their children. Often, before having kids we are aware of family traits or generational patterns. Knowing this, we want to avoid passing negative patterns on to our kids. Here is the secret: As a parent, travel your reaction to your child's behaviour first, then recall the feel and exact tone coming out of your child. This is pure understanding towards someone you love. Let the tone come right through you and it will melt in the child like magic. By bridging and strengthening your connection with them, starting from the beginning of your lives and continuing all the way through using both communication and listening with awareness, invites them to share with you always.

   This is true for every human being you wish to understand. The very best gift you can give to your children is to clean up your own emotional history and your present time reactions, so you have first-hand experience on how to navigate life, love and relationships. When we lead by demonstration and honesty with emotional maturity, our children have a spectacular reference point on how to navigate the quagmire of human emotions, controls and behaviours.

   Therapists choose to learn this for themselves, so their space is free of their own case and therefore are able to be there for their clients, reaching much greater depths in sessions. This technique is not an 'us over here' and 'them over there' — it is a 'we travel together to extraordinary depths.' I feel everything in full detail another human is experiencing in the session room. I do not wear their case as I/we are clearing it by understanding the exactness of it.

   Relationship partners notice eventually that their emotional cases are creating a ping-pong effect with one another when both individuals lack willingness to be responsible for what energetically and behaviourally is coming out of them. This generates stalemate situations with a disconnection of themselves and their chosen other. This is symptomatic of each individual not clearing their past and having it play out in present time in patterns and behaviours. Master this skill in your own reactions, and you will both have an extraordinary capacity to love with clean open hearts and true mutual understanding.

5. **Forcing the feeling.** To move fast with force and impatience will stop the thread in its tracks. Imagine putting a twig in the wheel of your bike. Remove the twig and the wheels start turning again. Travel the tone of impatience and force, as that is the tone presenting in you in the now, then return to your original thread.

6. **"I don't want to go there."** This is resistance. It is OK not to travel something until you are ready. Come back to it a little further down the track when you are. If it is fear that rises in you, travel the fear. Master the fear. Your heart will understand that past experience when you are ready.
We cannot change the past, but we can change how we feel about it. There may be areas you need a helping hand with from a therapist.

7. **You hit a blank feeling.** Gently push deeper, and expand your awareness out to the edges of the blankness. There may be blankness, nothingness or numbness — these are all tonal threads to travel and explore. Everyone has these tones in their emotional heart space. I promise you will come out the other side.

8. **On completing a tone, ensure you rise to full expansiveness.** It has been my observation that most people have as much difficulty in expanding out to 'all that they are' as they do in confronting the heavy tones. Almost everyone remembers moments when everything just is; when they felt an extraordinary moment of peace and connectivity to everything. This is home ground for us all. Both ends of the spectrum — the highs and the lows — can be unfamiliar territory, which makes it difficult to expand into all that you are. The other piece of the jigsaw puzzle is that if you cannot go deep within yourself, you cannot rise into all that you are. Nor will you be able to be there for others to the depth of what's available in each of us. So, one of my favourite catchphrases is, "the deeper you go, the higher you flow."

9. **Got stuck in a feeling?** Try gathering the tone in full, and push or project the feeling away from you instead of going into it. Ask your helpers for help. If you are unaware you have helpers, which you do, it is high time you invited their help in. Ask for the helpers who are most attuned to real love. Stay present and gather the tone in full, then gently push it outward. Observe as it lifts out of you. Note: as most of the threads you do are part of your soul's learning, this particular move is reserved for backup only. If it does not lift out, your helpers are inviting you to travel the full thread as there will be soul learning in it for you.

10. **The thread becomes too intense, and stops moving.** Pause, and allow it to be as it is. This sometimes happens when the brain and heart are very full with the area you are travelling. Treat the feeling like a tight rubber band and decide to release the whole thing. I call this 'pinging.' Drop the tone, shake it off, get up, walk around and have some water. Go to the toilet and connect with the things you love like nature. When you come back, place your hand on your heart and pick up the felt tone you have there. Relax your mind and sink into the feeling with fresh determination. It will start moving again. Remember, some of the more loaded parts of your case will feel very heavy, so be patient with the tones and trust you can travel it comfortably, even if it takes a few days. The tones that last a few days are always in the beginning of your learning. Go for it, press pause on the feeling or tone when you need a break, then return to it a few hours later.

11. **The feeling or tone is too dark and heavy.** It seemingly feels too hard to shift or too full on. No energy is bigger or stronger than you are — if we can feel it, you are ready for it. Sheer will and determination at that very moment to understand the tone is the one thing that shifts it, no matter what. Never, ever doubt you can travel and understand anything. A cardinal rule of being human is, never ever give up on yourself. There have been times for me when travelling a tone with another, that I have the thought 'this is not shifting, I don't know if I can do it.' This I spotted as my own doubt, so with sheer will and determination I pushed deeply into that tone and it has always cleared.

12. **Patterns we use for avoidance.** All our avoidance tactics play out unless we as individuals are driving our own ship. Looking at the phone, contemplating our navel, TV, the list of incomplete projects put off for months. Have a laugh! You know when you do it. If I notice any low tones in myself,, I travel them when cleaning, meditating, doing jobs around the house or driving. We are all very good at multi-tasking. Be free to attend to your heart. It is waiting for you to be there for it.

13. **Using colour is a spectacular way to melt the cement tones fast.** Each colour has its own intelligence and purpose. Willing a golden yellow colour in through the crown chakra trickles down like a beautiful waterfall, melting anything that is not love. Open yourself to the heavens with this one. It will make all your cells sparkle with life. Electric violet also works beautifully as it has its own intelligence and knows where to go without you having to direct it. Play with both these colours to notice what they do.

(Many wonderful modalities are available to help amplify your gifts when investigating the chakras and the field around our bodies: Pranic Healing, Ortho-bionomy, Horstman technique and Hexagonal Diametric technique are just a few — there are many more.)

14. **Grudges.** A grudge is an actively held decision, therefore requires an active decision to let it go.

    When we hold a grudge, it closes down a part of our emotional heart, shutting us off from further harm. Unfortunately, the hardness is loaded with self-righteousness, feeling hard-done-by and narrow mindedness. We view only what we want to see. It is cold cement. By holding a grudge, we prevent full awareness of our contribution to the situation and therefore inhibit our learning. Even though that grudge might be specifically toward someone or something, the hardness actually prevents all loved ones from coming all the way in right across your life. So, the first person who misses out on feeling loved all the way in and loving others to your greatest capacity is you.

Example of a Grudge Well Held

Adam came to me for sessions because he wanted to get his daughter back. His ex-wife had declared on her departure that he would never see his daughter again. They had been divorced five years, speaking via phone only twice in that period. Doctors had found a benign tumour the size of his middle finger in the frontal lobe of his brain. This section of the brain controls emotions, higher intellect, inhibitions, and self-control. Discovering the tumour urged him toward wanting his daughter back in his life. Halfway through his first session, I asked him about his relationship with his ex-wife. His response was, "Each day I wake up, I see her photo on the mantle-piece and wish her dead. She deserves to die, she took my baby away."

We spoke about grudges being an energetic attack on a person and what we put out invariably returns tenfold. I then told him, no more sessions until he lets go of the grudge. We cannot access the hurt until the grudge is no longer there. I called him a week later to see how he was going, "No way am I letting it go, she deserves it!" The week after — he was still hanging on but laughing at me down the phone. By the third week, he called to say his grudge was gone. The very next day, his ex-wife called for the first time in three years to see if he would like to see his daughter. Blown away by the direct and immediate result of letting the grudge go, he rang me to share the news and begin our sessions again. He turned up an already changed man. We travelled the remaining upsets with his wife and his relationship with his parents. Adam went on to forge a brand new relationship with his ex-wife and daughter with exceptional willingness to do things differently. We ran into one another a year later. They were back together.

Life is made of energy. It is an unseen world, but very felt. Through this example, I took extreme measures in holding him accountable for holding the grudge with all his gleeful justifications for hanging on to it. It was an extreme grudge. For most who are holding a grudge, I highlight it in a session and invite the person to willingly let it go, which they do. We are then able to proceed easily to the upset under the grudge and travel it in full.

You Will Know When Things are Clear...

When you choose to adventure into your heart's backlog with the intention of clearing it, you will know when it is clear after you have experienced the entire depth and breadth and come out the other side into lightness. A higher level of understanding your contribution to the situation will become present in your awareness. You will feel liberated. You will view the upset quite differently. There will be no blame or resistance, only a lighter, happier and hopeful heart and therefore a higher frequency from understanding yourself. If you do not feel lighter, do not view the situation differently or there is blame or guilt toward others or yourself, more depth is required. As you read in the grudge story, there was direct change in the physical world from his decision to let it go. Direct change in the physical world does not always happen so do not expect it, but when it does, it means you went to a spectacular depth.

I will also say that when you travel any primary areas like Mum, Dad, siblings or relationship partners of the past or present with excellent results, and revisited the same area of choice three months later, you will get a completely different depth with very different data. This is because as we clear layers, we become more aware and more awake to other tones we did not notice the first time. This is progressive unravelling. As you rise in awareness, so too does your ability to travel stronger tones inside you.

As for the outside world... it only reflects what you have inside you. The world will highlight the buttons you still have within to help you in evolving into the very best human being you can be. So, when you notice the tones and behaviours or react to them, they are yours to understand. It is all pure energy.

Resistance

What if nine-tenths of any one experience was simply our resistance to feeling a feeling — our own.

Just the word 'resistance' will bring up the feeling of resistance. It is just a feeling. Have a giggle with this one. Before you read on, I invite you to do one thing. For the next three hours, three days or three weeks if that is how much resistance you have in you, I would like you to stand in your resistance. Really notice it, roll around in it, laugh at it or have a big fat moan about it.

Our resistance can be towards looking at past upsets or towards feeling how we feel. Our resistance can be towards being responsible for understanding our own learning in situations or events that have happened. What about when people tell us what to do or we do not get what we want. There may be resistance to deadlines, going to work — to life's collective stresses. Resistance may be parents', children's or our partner's behaviours.

There are many points of resistance in our lives. Notice the feelings that rise in you as you read these words. This is the tone of resistance. Write them all down or stomp around and say them out loud with an intention to be free of them by exploring what comes up. Our resistance to life can be very funny, especially when we exaggerate the truth of what is there.

The curious thing about resistance is, when we resist someone's behaviour or the tones in how they deliver it, we eventually become the very thing we don't like in another. We become what we do not understand. For example, you hated your parent for certain behaviours, now you may find yourself doing the same thing. Even if we consciously choose not to become a certain way, the tone from our parent still sits in our field waiting for us to understand it in its raw form. This happens throughout our lives. We could say it is a universal guideline, inviting each of us to understand everything in ourselves and in others from all angles. All humans have the same energies within. The only difference is a choice to do or not to do a certain behaviour. This is sometimes a challenging concept, because we are exposed to many behaviours that we often cannot comprehend. We all know with full awareness that they are not love. We all have the love gene and we all feel when this becomes distorted. By travelling the tones under those behaviours, we can find freedom and peace within and a genuine compassion for what another has chosen for themselves or been exposed to in their lives. Life is full of potential understandings on multiple levels.

Emotional Tone Scale

Here is an emotional tone scale for your brain's education. Just like a musical scale, each feeling has its own resonance or frequency. Everyone has each of these feelings and tones within, provoked by different experiences — even all the control feelings at the bottom of the list. Each feeling or collective tone can be travelled in full, leaving us lighter and more expanded with a greater sense of self. Practice this gift to its fullest potential and many other gifts will switch on and grow in you. We truly are spectacular beings playing very small. Lighten your load and watch your lights turn on!

Bliss	Excitement	Withdrawal	Self-blaming
Wakefulness/present/ awareness	Boredom	Sadness	Deep disappointment in self or others
Joy	Frustration	Loneliness	Powerlessness
Empathy	Anger	Grief	Shame
Love	Fear	Anguish	Apathy
Gratitude	Anxiety (there are many flavours: high toned, low toned)	Overwhelm	Numbness
Compassion		Helplessness	Nothingness
Acceptance	Doubt / Uncertainty	Hopelessness	Blank
Determination	Invalidation / "I am not enough"	Giving-up	Barely existing
Trust		Remorse	Spiritual death
Courage	Suppression	Undeserving / guilt / unworthiness	

Then there are the more defensive feelings and emotions, which are controls designed to push others away, keep us separate and stop us from being honest, vulnerable and able to handle relationships with emotional maturity. They are in no order of frequency.

Superiority / Arrogance	Distrust	Resentment /Grudges	Manipulation
Stonewalling	Envy / jealousy — comparing self with others from invalidating self	Vengefulness	Neediness
Covertness		Rage	Expectations
Cynicism		Hatred	Significance
Sarcasm	Righteousness	Blaming others	Attachment

I have used the word 'significance' in the above list to highlight it as a form of control. There are healthy controls and then there are controls that typically shut both ourselves and others down. If for example you are a book editor, it is your job to have significance on attention to detail with the positive intention of ensuring all readers will be able to understand the content of a book. This is a healthy significance that enhances the writer's content.

An example of an unhealthy significance might be: a friend comes to you with emotional difficulties, speaking only of what their husband is doing or not doing. You as the listener engage with the story from your 'own reactions' to what you are hearing. This in turn fuels the significance of the story, only adding to the drama and blame.

This action has no positive intent or result. Your friend is not understanding their contribution to what has occurred and will walk away still confused and upset because you as the listener has not been there for what is really happening for them inside. You will also walk away with all the same feelings your friend just shared with you.

You are now wearing energetically what you did not understand by travelling the feelings they presented with. There is no intention to clear from either parties, and by default only added to the drama.

The potential for change in a positive direction dramatically improves if you can stay neutral within when listening to a friend's difficulties, and holding a positive intention that your friend will learn from their experience, and travelling the feelings they are experiencing with them. If you notice you are reacting, travel your reaction on the spot and return to your friend's heart tones. Another example of an unhealthy significance is: everyone has experienced times when a problem has presented and we whirled around in our brain about the problem with a whole lot of significance in not knowing the best solution. We may experience tunnel-vision and generate feelings of stress, anxiety and over-active thinking. We might be attached to a specific outcome. By deciding to let go of the problem and hand it over to our highest of selves and changing the direction of our thoughts and actions to something entirely different, the solution will float in when we least expect it.

The terms significance, expectations and attachment are all feelings and controls we have within us, which deserve thoughtful consideration when we are doing them to ourselves or another. All three have a polarity: an effect in both the positive and the negative.
How do the controls affect us on the receiving end? For example, how do you feel when someone has expectations on you? How do you feel when someone has an attachment to you?

Travelling the way you are affected on the receiving end will give insight as to how others feel when you do it to them. Then you will be free to travel the actual tone of expectation, with the awareness that you are energetically pushing this control out on another.

With the emotional tone scale or travelling different areas of difficulty, it is not always important to know what feeling you are in, but rather to become fluid in experiencing all that is in there. This is the primary objective: experiencing the exactness of what rests within you. Some of you will be very comfortable doing this without having to intellectually know. You will simply be able to locate any heaviness and zoom through it at supersonic speeds.

For others, experiencing what has happened from both an intellectual and heart-felt comprehension provides insight across all areas as they understand recurring patterns, ways affected and ways others have been affected by their own behaviour and unawareness. This for most is where we all start from when we begin to understand ourselves.

There are many lists of emotions available, along with statements or catchphrases that may resonate with you that highlight specific patterns or threads you may have noticed about yourself.

Some examples of threads: 'Needing approval,' 'having to get things right,' 'not feeling seen or recognized for who I am' all fall under the umbrella of invalidation and suppression of self — though the statement reflects more specifically the pattern played out throughout one's life.

When doing a session on yourself, hold your mind and heart to just that one statement and travel the thread all the way back to when you first noticed the pattern. Again, remember the files and memories will naturally float in when you are travelling the feelings and tones. There is no need to hunt with your mind. All the answers will float in as if on angel's wings. Push deeply and gently, following it all the way through to completion.

An Exercise: Heart Boot-camp
Pick a feeling from the emotional tone scale above and amplify it without using a story from your past to access it.

Option one: Travel it and notice if any files float in. Follow the instructions as usual.

Option two: If you pick for example 'anger,' gather the tone in full by letting it get as big as it gets. When it is in its fullest state, push the feeling outward until it disperses in full. Don't aim it at a person. This style will train you to become more aware of what is coming out of you energetically. Mostly people project their feelings and tones from autopilot without being consciously aware that is what is flowing out of them.

The intention of both these options is to increase your felt sensory perception on what is in your emotional heart, and the sub-tones of your communications felt by others around you. You perhaps might get some 'ah-ha' moments where you have received feedback from others in the past but at other times not understood what they were talking about.

Both options will disperse the feelings.
If you pick a lighter, more expanded feeling from the list, for example love, amplify it in full but notice if any lower tones rise in your heart. These will be feelings of suppression, which need to clear in order to rise and expand into a purer form of love. Gently push down into the suppression, travel it and then you will be able to expand into love more than before. Keep playing with it until travelling becomes like breathing.

One day, I instructed a man to 'project the feeling of love' toward another person standing three metres from him. He did as he was instructed. We paused after a minute and I asked the receiver what she felt on the receiving end of his love tones. Her feedback much to his surprise was, his love didn't feel like love at all. It felt manipulative and needy, wanting her to like him.

I asked him to relate that to his life with women, to see if there was any correlation. He was offended at first, but then laughed as he told us the feedback he often got from women he was wanting to date was the same. This gave him good insight and a true ah-ha moment of honesty, enabling him to become more aware of the tones he was unconsciously projecting.

All Our Relationships Reflect what is Happening Inside Us
If there is a button within that has not been understood in full, life will keep pressing that button until it is clear and understood, and the lesson is learnt and complete.

For example, if for your whole life, you have stayed small, invalidating and doubting yourself with the feeling of uncertainty, you will perhaps notice that many of your upsets have been from others doing that very same thing to you. They are reflecting what you already are doing to yourself. Pause and ponder this statement: They are reflecting what you already are doing to yourself. When you have progressively or completely understood this, (within your family, at school, work, how you feel toward yourself or your body, or in intimate relationships) and have travelled that deep pool of 'I am not enough,' you will notice miraculously that the outside world will cease doing it to you.

If you have 'Kick me!' on your forehead, people will kick you. If you wrote on your forehead, 'Respect me,' but still have the undercurrent feeling of kick me, then no matter what your intellect conjures up by way of positive thinking, life will always listen to the frequency tones coming out of you. Travel the tone of 'kick me,' and it will clear for good. After travelling the tone, we naturally rise to the feeling of confidence, which generates a feeling of respect towards self, first and most importantly. Others will follow suit.

You move first, and your reality will move, too. This is a progressive unravelling as you unwind out of the history your heart holds.

What you perhaps are not aware of yet, but soon will be after travelling the troughs, is that by any of us choosing to stay small, we are actually fuelling and encouraging those controls and negative traits in others and ourselves. There is always a cause and effect — action and reaction in every relationship from both parties. There is no blame, just each individual and our own contribution to a downward or upward spiral. By understanding the depths of 'I am not enough,' we discover the multi-layered truths available to all who want to understand themselves. We are creating these realities in our relationships in both behaviour and the frequency tones we emanate. It is we as individuals who are suppressing the very essence of who we are and in turn allowing others to do the same thing.

Everyone is at different stages of recognizing and understanding their contribution to their relationships. Everyone is suppressing and invalidating themselves, has been suppressed and invalidated by others and is invalidating and suppressing others. Interestingly enough, the people who play the dominating suppressor in your life will also have a big pool of not good enough, uncertainty and a bunch of other heavy tones that rest in their hearts, just like you. They unconsciously project and hide behind the tones of arrogance and superiority. Say you travel the tone of arrogance in yourself. After a couple of minutes, you will notice it slides into the undercurrents of uncertainty within, with perhaps hardness or upsets from the past underneath, but it presented as arrogance first. The files in your brain that are related to the uncertainty/doubt or not good enough will float into your awareness as you travel the feelings. The arrogance is hot air, and something to understand.

You will begin to learn what real love looks and feels like when you travel your own threads with determination and the desire to be responsible for all that is inside you. This will give others space to willingly explore their own backlog and reactions. Until then, two people have been playing a game. Now that you are no longer playing, the game stops. Either the other person will also choose to grow in emotional maturity, or will move on and attract someone else to engage in the negative pattern you have just understood within you. Mind you, this happening may also be a reflection of insufficient movement inside of yourself.

As I have stated previously, you travel your own reactions first, and then your abilities to feel the exact tones coming out of another will amplify to supersonic speeds, so you can help them to move too. Ideally, you do this together, but there will be many times your heart notices that another is still strongly buying into something negative as their real self. That inside negativity is not who we are in a purist form. If your heart notices the tone in another, let it come all the way through you until it rises. From here you will no longer be triggered by it as you have understood the tone in its exact form.

You choose what is right for you, and allow others to do the same. When we align our thoughts and actions with the purest part of ourselves, we cannot go wrong.

Life, love and relationships have a curious way of repeating until we each understand the lessons in full. The bigger picture is that each of us, starting with our relationship towards ourselves, can bloom into all that we are. This is through seeing, feeling and hearing ourselves. As you do this for yourself, you naturally will do the same for others. All our relationships flourish from here.

Utilizing This Gift As a Parent

Our children guide us perfectly when we know what to look for. Becoming a parent brought on spectacular learning for me as a person. There are two portions to this tale to learn from.

My daughter, at the age of 2 months old, right on 5 pm daily, would have agonizing tummy pains and had done so for five weeks. She had colic, which as any parent has experienced, can be very distressing for the parents as much as for the child. (Typically, colic peaks between 6-8 weeks, and ends for 50% of cases around 3 months, and in 90% by 9 months of age.) We did everything we could to ease her pain. We danced, walked, rocked, flopped her over our laps, massaged, removed everything from my diet that may have made my breast milk an allergen. We gave her colic relief herbs, and the doctors simply said she'll grow out of it as her intestines developed. I was not content with this answer and became curious as to what I was doing energetically/emotionally that may have contributed to her colic. I genuinely felt love for her, and she for me, but I was aware in the background of my heart's awareness that since she was born, I was confronting all the parts of me that was selfish.

I began travelling all the tones in me that related to my loss of freedom and independence that came with my choice to bring this little human into my life.

There was exhaustion and loss of freedom: the grief for all the things I had to give up for her so I could be the best mum possible. It was a pivotal moment when one afternoon just after I'd put her down in her crib, I could finally rest after non-stop mummy activities. We had a 5 am start on top of night feeds and I was exhausted. She began crying. I heard my brain say, "Oh my God! What do you want from me! I give you everything you need, just give me a little peace and space — what do you want, my blood? If I give you this last little bit of me, there will be nothing left of me."

It was right at this moment I stopped dead in my tracks and heard those words in my head. There it was, a belief in the bottom of my heart's awareness and in my brain. It was stopping not just my baby from coming all the way into my heart, but everyone. I walked slowly toward her room, went in and sat her on my lap face to face. I looked her in the eyes and opened my heart. I let her all the way in, every little crevice of my entire soul. Tears welled up in me and I said to her, "From now on, little one, I will give you

the whole of my heart, nothing less."

That afternoon, we waited for the usual 5 pm colic activities to begin. It never came — not that day nor any day after that. All my resistance had dropped away in that moment of decision to be there for her 100%, embracing my new life with a whole heart. Given I had eliminated all the physical possibilities of the cause first before inspecting the emotional cause and effect on her, my decision to give her the whole of me created immediate change in her physical reality.

The second portion of this story happened when she was 8 months old. Bella and I had been doing beautifully together with all the magical things you experience as a parent watching your child develop and expand. I had started noticing a shadow hanging over her head. She did not glow as a sparkly baby does. She was quiet and content mostly, but had started doing these long cries that baffled me as to the cause. The more she cried, the more anxious I felt in the not knowing. I rounded up five of my nearest friends, all of whom where therapists, and asked what they observed. Within a minute of us all sitting together, Bella began crying, deeply and soulfully. With the others assisting I travelled my anxiety until it lifted out of me. It was like changing radio stations from one channel to another: my heart's frequency to hers. Finally, I could feel what she was saying through her tears. As a group, our hearts listened to the feelings of a tale she had been trying to share with me. The more I felt, the more I realised she was sharing feelings about the feelings I had felt during the pregnancy. She had recorded all of my feelings, emotions and tones and had been trying to clear them with me but I could not feel her through my own anxious reactions to her crying.

The session for her lasted exactly 12 minutes with full detail. As suddenly as she started, she stopped. All feelings experienced, she was complete. The shadow was completely gone from her head area and she looked a little stunned when finished. A big smile followed, and that was that.

These two examples closely related to one another, where I had to move my emotions and feelings by travelling them, followed by me expanding into more of me for the love of her. The second example was the residue of my emotions and turmoil during our pregnancy together, which she had recorded whilst in utero.

I share these examples to invite you to become more aware in your observations of possible solutions found not just in the physical world but in the emotional field for both you and the children around you.

One of the best observations you can make in working with your child as they move through each expansion phase in their development is that under the behaviour, there will be a tone. It is both the behaviour and tone that parents react to, and therefore two major points to travel. Travel your reactions first to gain clarity and understanding for self, then do the ones they presented. It is multiple layers of understanding that will illuminate and eliminate many family patterns as they present.

Your children will only press the buttons you still have inside you. For this, they are your greatest gift. They will advance you in extraordinary ways. You move first, and they will move too.

A child goes through many key expansion phases during development. At many of these junctions, a mild war can build up to a loud crescendo between the two parties. Essentially, the controls amplify in them as they spread their little wings, requiring more space for independence in their actions but needing your love to continue. Parenting is a dance between allowing and guiding. It is a war within self that requires us to step into emotional maturity and tidy up our own reactions and controls when they are provoked or rise in our responses. Our children challenge us to rise into the best versions we can be. Notice these expansion phases and recognise and acknowledge using two-way communications with them. They will glow with happiness when you ask all the things they notice and observe.

Awareness changes within your children. How they view life can change in the blink of an eye. When we miss it, it's a little piece of them we did not get. Multiply that by five- hundred, and by early teens your communications with them will have no foundations to freely talk with each other and your connection will be ho-hum. Your precious child, now a young adult, has become a normal part of your heart's furniture without truly knowing one-another, just like your partner or yourself. If this has already happened in your family, start now, because it is never too late. The connection with you will be the very thing they yearn for, and many behaviours are as a result of disconnection from you.

As they become more and more independent in their thoughts and actions, we encourage them to have their own experiences — a little chat here, a little nudge there when they head off track. This creates a relationship between one another that also helps them help us when we as parents are off track in our actions. Our love is just as strong if not stronger, because as they have expanded, so too have we expanded by travelling our own controls and theirs as they present. This is about you gaining mastery within yourself of every feeling and control all humans have within. Your children are trying to speed up your development as a human being. This is a spectacular gift from them to you.

You may need to travel many of your own tones. Go for it and melt them all as they present along the way.
Consider 'You will do as your told' — the feeling that seeks to dominate, suppress and dictate the how and the when and the what they can and can't do. What about micro managing? Feel the tone coming out of you when doing it to loved ones.

What if they drag their feet with unwillingness? Your resistance to theirs will be equal to theirs toward you. A stalemate that will only worsen with time. Have fun with this one. Role-play your own resistance in front of them by exaggerating your behaviour and tone, till you lighten. It's very funny for all.

If your child is particularly strong in character, they are training you to be equally as strong as them, to stand up to them with love and firmness. If it is your habit to collapse or stay small and dominated in life, your child/teen is helping you with one of your key lessons in life. They are empowering you by training you to not be a pushover, and fine tuning your communications and to create clean, clear boundaries.

If you are prone to being overprotective, feel the tone you come from when doing this. Observe what it does to the child. Some will push back because you are energetically squashing them into a tiny safety box, limiting their growth and potential. This inhibits their expansion phases and stops their development in social circumstances. Other kids will feel your own fears and anxieties, again shrinking them into feeling life isn't safe to try new things or stretch their abilities.

A note to all tech lovers who use computer and TV as babysitters: no matter what age, too much of any one thing brings each of us out of balance. As a therapist, I see more and more clients are rolling in with teen boys in particular who as a consequence of too much gaming have fallen behind in the natural development of social skills. They are withdrawn, behave three to four years younger than their peers and are resistant to any form of contribution in action, communication and willingness towards life. In more severe cases, the merging of reality with the game world (for example with war games), it becomes normal to cause harm to another without conscious thought to the physical harm done. This is desensitization to violence. An older client gave gaming up because when he was driving his car, his brain-flicked to game world, losing the importance of care for self or others in a physical car that can crash. In the game world we hit reset. In real life, a much larger clean-up is required.

Teen girls lean more towards phones and social media. This amplifies comparing self with others in their looks, and invalidating themselves. As with everything in life, balance is needed.

Your children will present many flavours throughout your lives together. I invite each of you to choose love with your heart open, receptive and above all connected to those you love.

Utilizing This Gift As a Therapist
Case study of 10-year-old Ophelia

Often in session, a person is unaware of what I am actually feeling in them. After a few times of my asking them to pause and let themselves drop into the feeling present at the time, they notice I am amplifying the feeling or tone to its fullest, with them also being present and aware. The tones fill up the room, so to speak.

In session, Ophelia hit a point of hardness which I noticed was not melting, so I asked her what this feeling was. She replied, "This is the place I go to in myself when I don't feel included at school with my friends. Also, if Dad isn't noticing me." The feeling was sullen, withdrawn, with a dash of 10-year-old resentment. I asked her, "Does holding this hardness and silence work for you?" She said "Not really, I sit and stare at the ground or the wall for an hour, sometimes two, and still no one will come." I asked her what does she choose to have for herself with her daddy and friends. She said, "I just want to be loved and included and noticed." I asked her, "Does this feeling of hardness feel like love coming out of you?" She shook her head. Then I asked, "Do you want to melt it now and never have this feeling in you again?" "Yes!" was her answer. "I am going to get you to push down into this hardness. I am with you every step of the way." She squinted her little eyes, pushed down into the hardness and it popped within twenty seconds. Her eyes welled up with tears as her love and essence came back in. She came in — pure open love.

By duplicating the exactness of the feeling in her present, and giving her freedom of choice to either continue doing the same thing with the same results or change how she feels within, I empowered her to choose love over potential patterns of long lasting suffering in future relationships.

As therapists, whatever our formal training, we learn to listen with our ears, have compassion with our hearts and in some modalities train solely to come from the intellect. As we are all human with emotions, feelings, controls and tones, which are all energy, it has been my experience that extraordinary change happens permanently when the heart is felt and married with thoughtful logic. With travelling as a skill in your toolbox, we are listening to the words but primarily I'm inviting you to learn to amplify the tones you notice when a person shares their story and trust that with practice, you can turn the volume up, push down deeper for them/with them until you get underneath it whilst sitting in front of them or via phone consult.

I'll say that again: as the practitioner, you and the client become one. We lead them into the heaviest of tones presenting via their story. We are honing in pushing deeply and gently, within you — which is them.

We allow the feeling to be there, noticing all the variations, observing any files that float in your client's awareness when in the trough, and inviting them to communicate the files as they present if need be. You, the practitioner, without resistance or judgement or even the intellect assessing this or that, are letting all the tones come through you at supersonic speeds, which speeds them through the process too. Together as one, you continue until the heaviness rises of its own accord. You will feel everything your client feels in full. You will notice any decoys and be able to gently pull them back on tone because you are holding that tone for them and travelling the thread and its variations as they learn to feel what is within. They learn how to safely experience a feeling, and come all the way through the heaviness and out into lightness.

You are teaching them a skill they can use for life.

Trauma Session

There are many types of trauma. Some are short in nature, whilst others are long and drawn out throughout a person's life. Both can have long-lasting effects on a person and their wellbeing. Rob has described what happens for someone in the body/brain relationship when trauma happens. Here I am going to show you a simple way of dispersing trauma from a specific incident to alleviate the multiple layers that can happen from any one trauma.

Using the travelling technique, we do exactly the same thing, step by step, but with short trauma experiences, for example an accident or birthing process, we repeat the process up to three times in the one sitting. With short trauma experiences, this is particularly effective given the average session can be an hour to an hour and a half. Therefore, you will be able to travel all the layers. By travelling the experience together up to three times in the one sitting, at the end the person will remain bright and present as all systems come into alignment without any physical or emotional responses.'

For longer trauma with multiple experiences of the same thing, multiple sessions (possibly up to 20 times pending the severity) will present many tones as the person shares and travels similar experiences allowing access to different layers. You will know it is complete when the client is able to view the upsets with a completely neutral heart space.

For all trauma, be sure to travel in full any tones of freeze, fear, shock, shame, blankness, rage, dissociation, and very importantly ensure the client communicates to you anything suppressed at the time of the incidences.

Dissociation can look different in many people. They can fall asleep as you go into thick, dark heavy tones. As a therapist, we stay present on their behalf and continue feeling in full what they are feeling, even when they are absent. A great fog can descend, blanking their thoughts, rendering them unable to speak, or they can exit their body in full. Their body may start shaking uncontrollably. These are all trauma responses that require you as the therapist to stay present as they learn to stay present.

Travelling the Tones in Your Body When Pain is Present

Whether you are a therapist or a curious reader wanting to investigate the very natural healing abilities all humans are born with, this technique is a spectacular tool to add to your toolkit.

There are informative books on the market that help increase the awareness as to the possible origins of a person's dis-ease or body malfunctions. As we are all uniquely different with many possible influencing factors — genetic, emotional, dietary, environmental, or a cocktail of several of these, it is up to an individual to use wisdom and thoughtful logic to investigate what our body needs at different times with different ailments.

As your hands are an extension of your heart's awareness, one of your abilities is the skill to be able to place your hand on an organ or body part and feel the exact tone it holds.

Some books have given general guidelines as to the emotional origins. For example, liver is often associated with anger. However, often a person will read this and then go hunting with their brain to discover all the possible points in time where they may have suppressed anger. This sends them on a wild goose chase leaving them with the liver pain at the end of the hunt.

If, however, you place your hand on your liver or in the field directly above it, and pause here until you can feel the exact tone that your liver holds, you can create change very quickly. You may at first notice stress tones. Continue feeling with your hand just like you do when running a session on an emotional thread. The stress tones will come through your hand up through your heart's awareness, enabling your emotional heart to register the familiarity of each feeling. It clears by you feeling the exactness of what is there. You are now listening through your felt sensors and understanding your liver and how it feels. Continue and the tone may fully clear into lightness, or it may show you other tones under the stress like anger, resentment or whatever it has in there for you as an individual.
Know that this is your liver sharing with you, not your brain's stories of what it may or may not be.

Travel the tones in full. By doing so, you are clearing the emotional aspect of the liver. It will feel perfectly light after it has run its story for you. If your liver was just emotionally loaded, the pain will dissipate within minutes. If it doesn't fully clear, changing your diet by eliminating all the inflammatory foods and drinks and/or doing a liver/gallbladder cleanse will be perfectly complimentary to rehabbing your liver back to physical happiness and full function. As always, investigating your liver through orthodox medicine for diagnostics to eliminate more serious problems is a wise course of action if pain persists.

Have fun with this ability of yours. You can apply this same technique to every part of the body. This skill will deepen and expand with practice and curiosity, perhaps waken other abilities you have within — we all are truly spectacular in our gifts.

Creating The High Tones From Within Yourself

Practising the art of expanding into the feelings of joy, happiness, gratitude or love is equally as important as acknowledging and travelling the low tones. Like all things in life, it is a choice to expand or contract. We decide to hold onto our backlog or choose to understand it and grow into the spectacular human being we can be when all of life's lessons understood in full. Mostly, people are unconscious in this action and dictated by life's circumstances. We feel happy when things are moving along nicely in our world, but if it is not, we react. Notice the reaction and travel it. Choosing to expand outward and upward as a daily practice trains us to rise in frequency, regardless of what life looks like. In session, I will expand with a person to show how big they can get. We often run into layers of the tone 'suppression.' We travel it, and then find they can continue expanding outward into a purer part of themselves.

Often for the first time, they become familiar with their true soul essence. Learn to do this for yourself, and you will find locating the soul essence of another much easier. It is a beautiful thing.

Locating the true essence of those we love makes it much easier to not buy into the behaviours, controls, tones and emotions they play out and are affected by through their own current lack of awareness.

Expanding into the feeling of joy restores quietness to the mind, relaxing the very cells in your body from stress and over-active thinking. In these higher states of being, we can hear fresh ideas, see things from an outside perspective, and receive guidance from helpers, our higher self or 'all that is' — call it what you wish. It is the part of us all that sees and feels infinite potentials, allowing each of us to gain access to universal wisdom and emotional intelligence in every circumstance.

Divine intelligence has encoded love through the very fabric of our soul. All we need do is listen.

Master this gift in quiet or chaos, and you will truly live an extraordinary life. To speed your growth in travelling at supersonic speeds in yourself or others —for one on one sessions, training for all therapists to deepen and expand your abilities in helping others, parenting and general enquiries, feel free to email me at latyree@gmail.com.

CHAPTER 8.
EXPLORING YOUR ABILITY TO SELF-CORRECT

EXPLORING YOUR ABILITY TO SELF-CORRECT

Playing With Your Self-Corrective Process
The next section will include some theory, but mostly we will be exploring how to work with your body from an Ortho-Bionomy perspective.

Limitations of Self-Care
We often don't recognise our own patterns, which is why we have the dysfunction in the first place, and our pain often occurs in the patterns we have used to adapt to an initial dysfunction. Therefore, when we use self-care exercises, we are often dealing with the pain originating from the compensation patterns rather than the underlying postural or functional pattern that is creating the need for the body to adapt.

In this case, self-care exercises can be used to deal with the symptom (reduce pain), and sometimes this is enough for the body to self-correct the underlying dysfunction. But if you need to repeatedly do the same self-care exercise to relieve pain, then find an Ortho-Bionomy practitioner to assist you in unwinding the whole pattern.

Imagine you have lower back pain. You do the Psoas release demonstrated below, and the pain goes away. Every time you get pain, you use the technique, then you lift something at an odd angle, and the pain is excruciating and you end up in massive pain for a week or two. If you had got help when your lower back pain was manageable, it would have taken fewer sessions to change the stability of your system, and been cheaper than missing work and paying for sessions. Also, when you have low grade pain, your body is more likely to change faster as it feels safe to do so, while if you have severe pain, the body will equate movement to pain and so your body will be more cautious about allowing change to occur.

With Ortho-Bionomy, we initially work to relieve pain, but also lead the body to be more effective at dealing with gravity, which is called postural work. When your posture is more efficient, your body will be more stable and resilient, so you are less likely to get the acute pain in the above scenario when the system was challenged by lifting the weight.

So, if you find that some of the self-care exercises work well for you see if you can work out why. Why does your body recruit the psoas muscle? What can this tell you about how your body is functioning in relationship to gravity? Can you work out the underlying pattern and assist your body to self-correct it? If not don't panic that is what an Ortho-Bionomy practitioner can help you with.

The Only Rule of Self-Care
When you are doing self-care designed to stimulate the self-corrective process, you should not be creating pain. So, if what you are doing creates pain, STOP. See if fine tuning the position makes the exercise more comfortable. If you can't find a comfortable position, then the exercise is not right for your body at this point in time.

Ortho-Bionomy self-care
Increasing your awareness of your patterns

- Lie on a yoga mat or other soft surface.
- Notice where your body comes in contact with the ground.
- Is there even pressure on your heels?
- The back of your thighs?
- Your pelvis?
- Your thoracic spine?
- Your shoulder blades?
- Notice if your head is lying straight, or does it have a tendency to tilt to one side?
- Where you notice your body isn't sitting on the ground evenly, place a small folded-up hand towel or pillow under the side that has the least pressure on it. This exaggerates the pattern you have noticed.
- Allow yourself to relax with the towel(s) under your body for a few minutes, then pull the towels/pillow out slowly while relaxing the body.
- Does your body now contact the floor in a more even way?

Lower Back Pain

There are many potential causes of lower back pain. The self-care exercises below are aimed at helping your back relax so it can reorganise itself. If pain persists, seek help.

Psoas

The psoas major is a very important muscle. It stabilises the lumbar spine, and is the only muscle connecting the lower back to the legs. The psoas is also one of the first muscles to respond when you get stressed. This is felt as tightening up of the lower back.

The psoas is also involved in raising your thigh (hip flexion) so if you need to run away, you will also need to contract your psoas.

This relationship with your fight/flee response allows us to use the Psoas to help the body relax in a general way, and the lower back in particular.

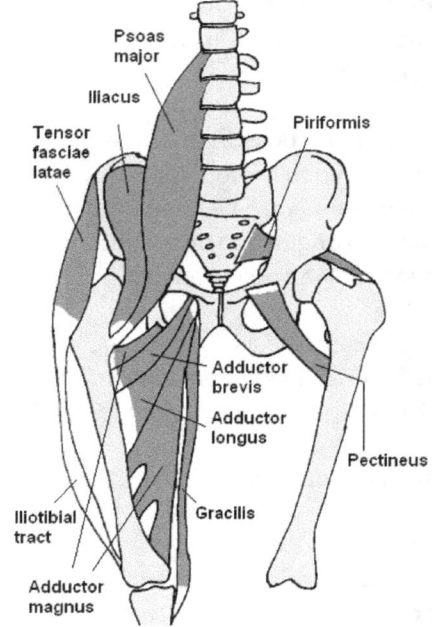

Psoas Release

When to do it?
When you are stressed or have a tight or sore lower back.

- Lie on your back on a soft surface with your legs up on a chair so your calves are fully supported. Ideally, your knees are bent at 90 degrees.
- Slowly bend your torso to one side (lateral flexion), feeling for a position of comfort where your lower back can relax.
- Feel into your lower back for your psoas muscle. If you feel any tension, yawn to release it.
- Fine tune your position to maximise your comfort.
- As your psoas releases, you can fine tune the position further.

If you have acute lower back pain, this position may offer some relief, but you will need to access professional help to assess and assist with your recovery.

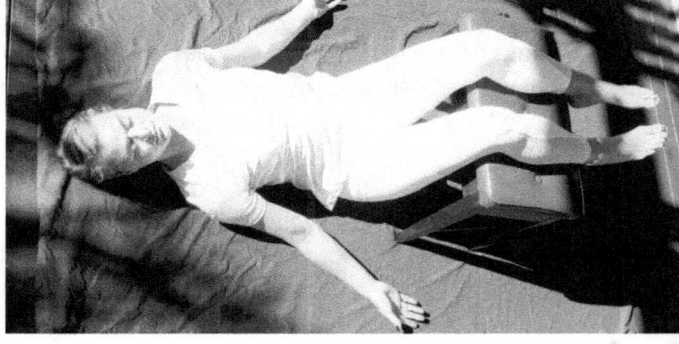

Psoas Release 2

Lie on your back with your knees bent.

- Alternate between contracting the front of your thighs (quads) and your butt muscles (glutes) for 5 seconds each.
- Notice if your lower back relaxes.
- This can also be done seated as well.

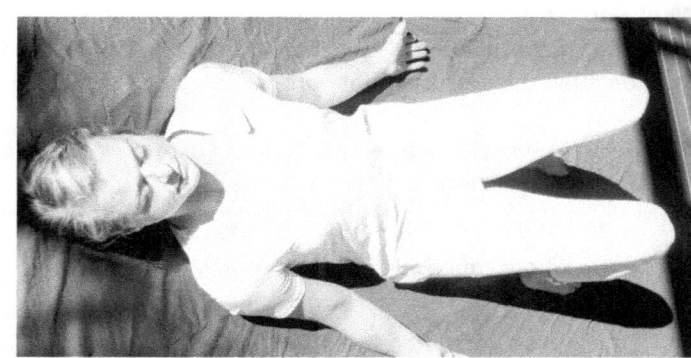

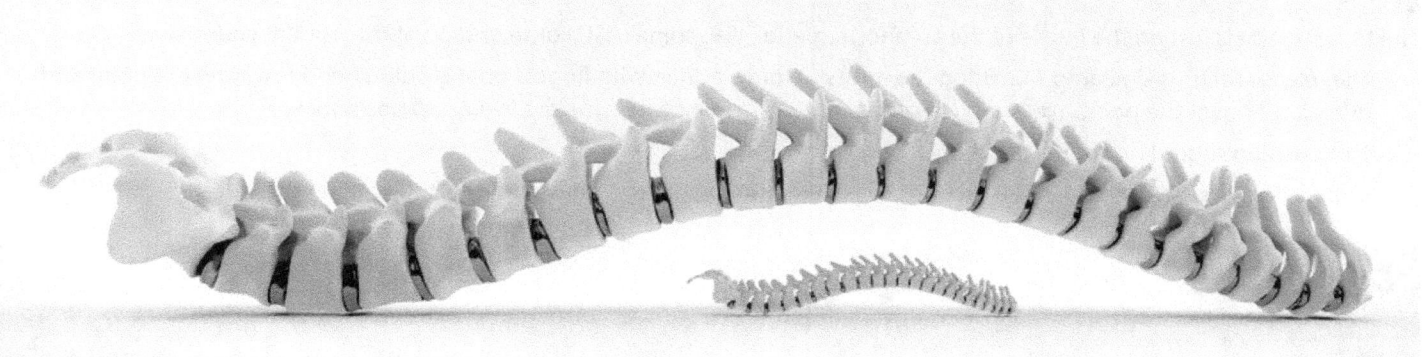

Lumbar Spine Releases

The lumbar spine extends from the base of your ribcage (T12) to your sacrum (S1).

Most people have 5 lumbar vertebrae (some people have 6).

The lumbar spine is designed for flexion and extension (bending forward and backward).

One of the weaknesses of the lumbar spine is in rotation. There is approximately 5 degrees of rotation in the whole of the lumbar spine. Therefore, one source of lower back pain is a combination of lifting a weight, bending forward and rotating to one side without moving your feet.

The following exercises are designed to release tension through the lumbar spine from a rotational dysfunction.

In Ortho-Bionomy, we use referred pain points to assess the tension around a particular vertebra. Check out the diagrams below and test these points on yourself and try the release positions to unwind the affected areas.

T12 is really the base of the ribcage, but it is included here as it is an area that's often involved in chronic back pain.

T12

The test point for T12 is on the lateral side of the iliac crest (if you place your hands on your hips you will be touching your iliac crest).

- The release position is lying on your back on something soft with your knees bent, and legs up on a chair, bend towards the sore point* and drop you knees towards the sore point* (rotation). Your knees should end up above the point you wish to release (or be as close as comfortable to that location).
- Relax in the release position for 30 seconds. This should feel comfortable.
- Then bring your legs down and retest the point for tenderness.
- Bending towards the sore point does not mean engaging the abs and bending forward. It means bending to the side (lateral flexion)

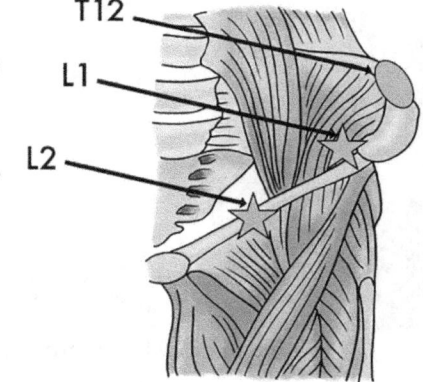

Front view of left side of pelvis showing referred pain points for the last thoracic vertebrae (T12) and the first two lumbar vertebrae (L1 & L2)

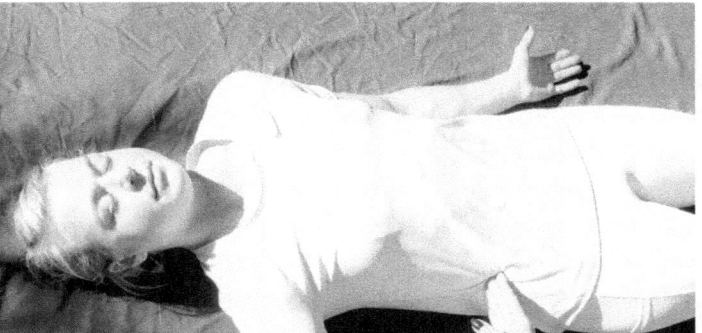

Location of referred pain point for T12

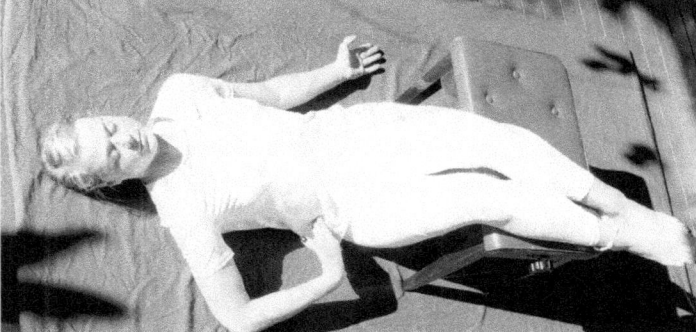

Release position for T12 point

* Bending towards the sore point does not mean engaging the abs and bending forward. It means bending to the side (lateral flexion)

L1

The L1 test point is just on the inside of the anterior, superior, iliac spine (ASIS) or the bump at the front of your pelvis.

- The release for L1 is similar to T12. Bring the knees up on the chair with fingers on the point, bend towards sore point and bring knees over the point. You should feel the sore point relax when you are in a good position.
- This position should be comfortable.
- Relax in the release position for 30 seconds, and then bring your legs down and retest the point for tenderness.

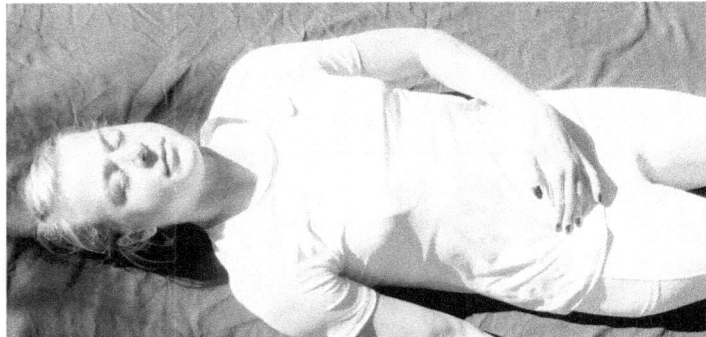
Location of L1 referred pain point

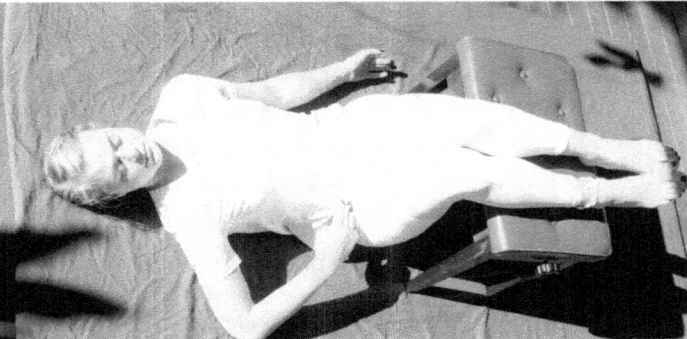
Release position for L1 point

L2

The test point for the L2 vertebra is on either side of the inguinal ligament in the diagram above.

- The L2 release position is similar to L1, fine tune to get the sore point to soften by moving legs above the point.
- Relax in the release position for 30 seconds and then bring your legs down and retest the point for tenderness.

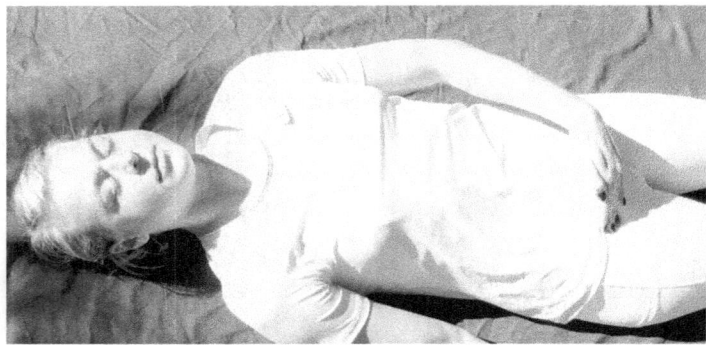
Location of L2 referred pain point

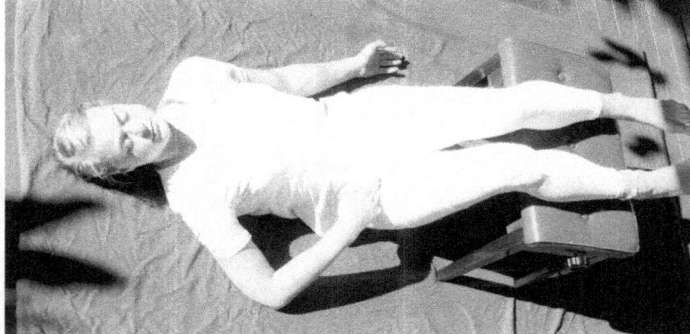
Release position for L2

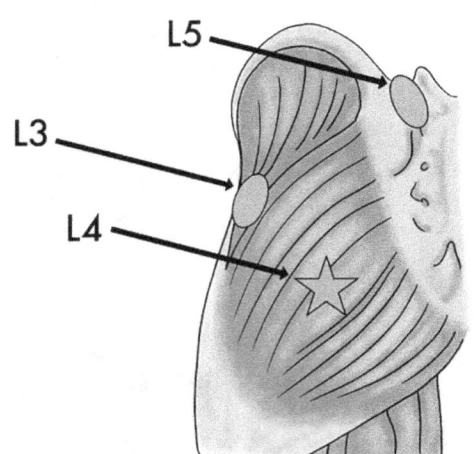
Referred pain points for posterior lumbar vertebrae (L3, L4 & L5)

L3

The referred pain point for L3 is at the lateral edge of your gluteus maximus muscle, just above where you can feel your thigh bone.

- The release position for the L3 is lying face down with a rolled-up towel under your opposite hip. This should tip your pelvis toward the referred pain point. You can fine tune the position and height of the towel by checking if the tender point is softened.
- Relax in the release position for 30 seconds, this should be comfortable, then remove the towel slowly and retest the point for tenderness.

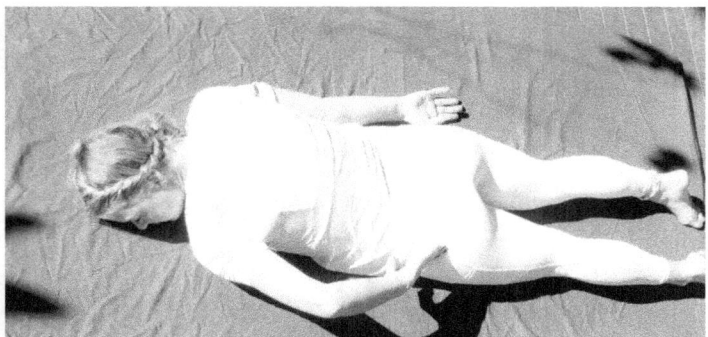

Location of L3 referred pain point

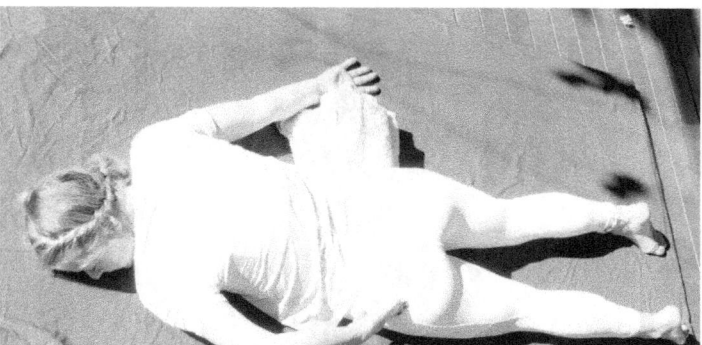

Release position for L3 point

L4

The test point for L4 is in the middle of your gluteus maximus muscle.

- The release position is similar as for L3, but the towel is placed under the opposite side of your pelvis level with the ASIS – the bony bump on the front of your pelvis.
- Relax in the release position for 30 seconds and then remove the towel and retest the point for tenderness.

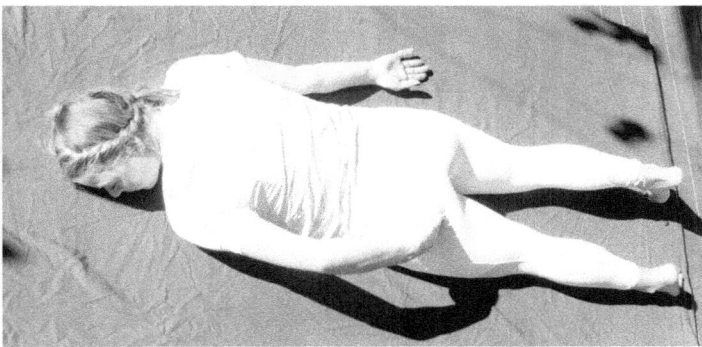

Location of L4 referred pain point

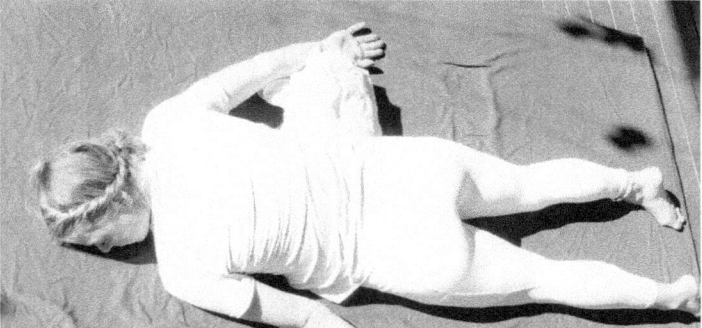

Release position for L4 point

L5

The referred pain point for L5 is on the medial side (inside edge) of the posterior, superior, iliac crest (PSIS) pushing laterally. Another test for L5 is if you have trouble going from sitting to standing.

- The release position for L5 is to lie face down on a massage table/bed/couch and drop the leg on the sore side off the edge. If this is the right position for your body it should feel comfortable. Make sure the top of the foot is on the floor and have the knee off the floor so the weight of the leg draws gently down on the lower back.
- Relax in the release position for 30 seconds and then push your other leg off the table/bed and stand up slowly. Retest the point for tenderness.

L5

The referred pain point for L5 is on the medial side (inside edge) of the posterior, superior, iliac crest (PSIS) pushing laterally. Another test for L5 is if you have trouble going from sitting to standing.

- The release position for L5 is to lie face down on a massage table/bed/ couch and drop the leg on the sore side off the edge. If this is the right position for your body it should feel comfortable. Make sure the top of the foot is on the floor and have the knee off the floor so the weight of the leg draws gently down on the lower back.
- Relax in the release position for 30 seconds and then push your other leg off the table/bed and stand up slowly. Retest the point for tenderness.

Location of L5 referred pain points

Release position for L5 point

If you are in acute pain, get help from an experienced professional. Self-care exercises support the process, but are not intended to replace competent professional care.

If a position or self-care exercise does not feel right for your body, don't do it. Listen to your inner knowing and if there is an increase in the level of pain, STOP.

Apparent Leg Length Difference

If you lie on your back with your ankles together, are the inner bumps of your ankles level?

Often you need someone else to check this for you, but if you go to a chiropractor they may have mentioned that one of your legs is shorter than the other.

Often people will have up to a 5 mm difference in leg length as normal variation, but if your lower back has been sore, one of the common compensation patterns is for the pelvis to be rotated either anterior or posterior, and held there to prevent movement that would aggravate the lower back pain. This is how the body creates more support and tries to prevent movement aggravating the area of pain.

If you have used the Psoas and the Lumbar releases, then the pelvis might be ready to release the holding pattern that creates the apparent leg length difference.

View from above of what an apparent leg length difference may look like. Notice the bumps on the inside of the ankle (medial malleolus) are not level?

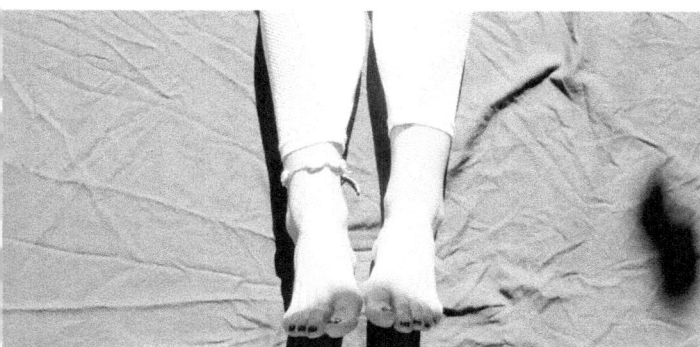

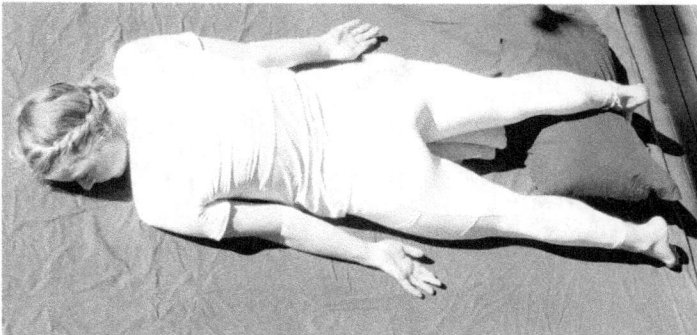

Long leg release – long leg with towels and pillow under it.

Release for a long leg

- Lie face down and place a rolled-up towel or a pillow under the thigh of the long leg side. You can either have the knee bent or leg straight with another pillow under the lower leg to support it.
- Turn head to one side and find a position of comfort.
- Relax in the release position for 30 seconds.
- Recheck leg length.

Release for a Short Leg

- Lie face down and frog your short leg out.
- Turn head to one side and find a position of comfort.
- Relax in the release position for 30 seconds.
- Recheck leg length.

If the body has not readjusted the leg length, your lower back may need more fine tuning.

Finding an Ortho-Bionomy practitioner could be very helpful for this.

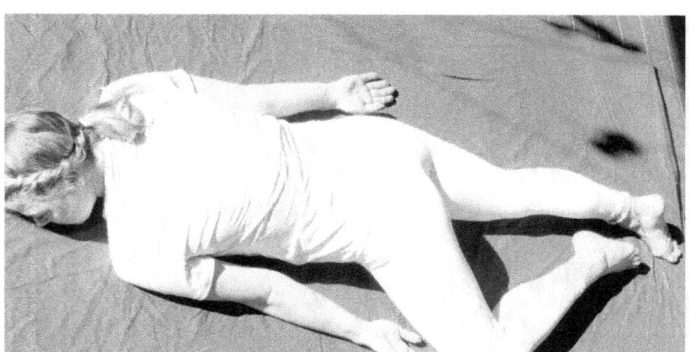

Short leg release – short leg is frogged out to side

Releasing Tension from the Back Muscles

A frequent response to lower back pain is a general holding pattern through the muscles that supports the lumbar spine. This exercise can help release that tension.

- Lie on your back.
- Place hands on the sides of your pelvis.
- Push your hands down toward your feet while you pull your ribcage and spine toward your head.
- Hold for a few seconds.
- Release the tension and let your back relax.
- Push down on your pelvis again. You should feel the stretch in different layers of the muscles in your back.
- If the stretching sensation is not changing, then try once more. If there is no change, stop.
- When your lower back feels relaxed, bend your knees and place your hands on your thighs.
- Push your thighs toward your feet while drawing your spine up toward your head. You should feel the stretch on the inside of the spine.
- Relax and repeat until your back feels loose and relaxed.

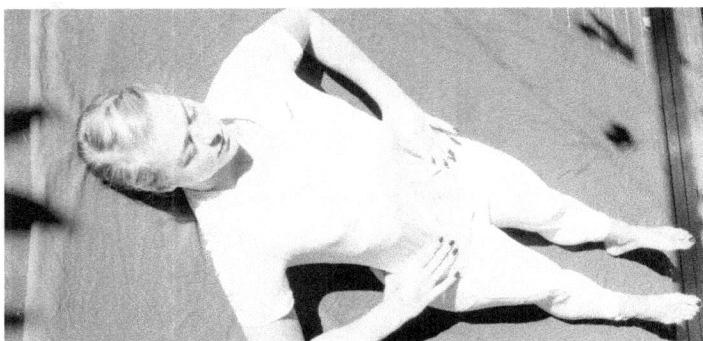

Lower back release position 1

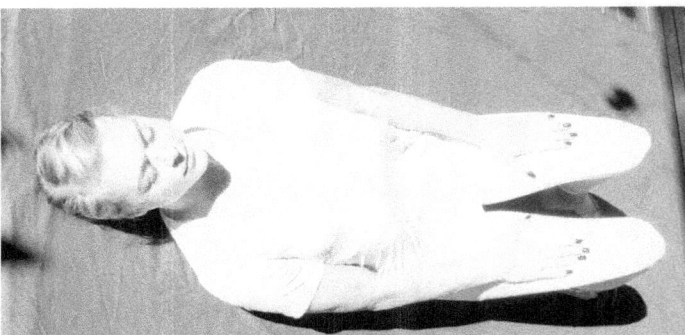

Position 2

Sacrum

Pain in the sacroiliac joints (SIJ) maybe due to a pelvic imbalance. In order to work with this, make sure you have released the psoas, worked with the lumbar points and ilium rotation. This will free up the area before working with the sacrum.

This can either be done lying down or standing against a wall.

- Place a soft ball under the sacrum and gently allow your body weight to drop onto the ball.

- Slowly move your weight around, feeling for positions of comfort.
- Stop where the position feels comfortable and relax for a few seconds.
- Continue exploring how the pressure on the sacrum feels.

If you have a hard ball such as a tennis ball, then place it in a sock and only use it against a wall, because lying on it may put too much pressure on the sacrum and lead to bruising.

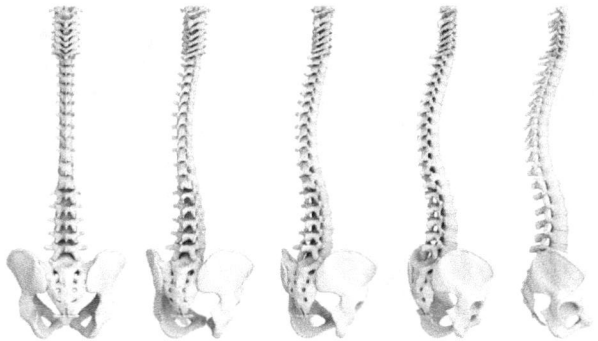

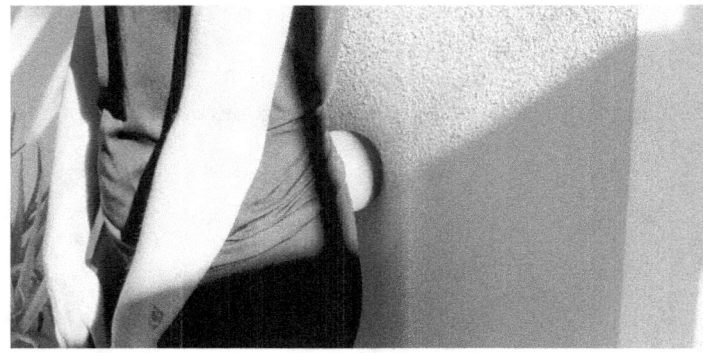

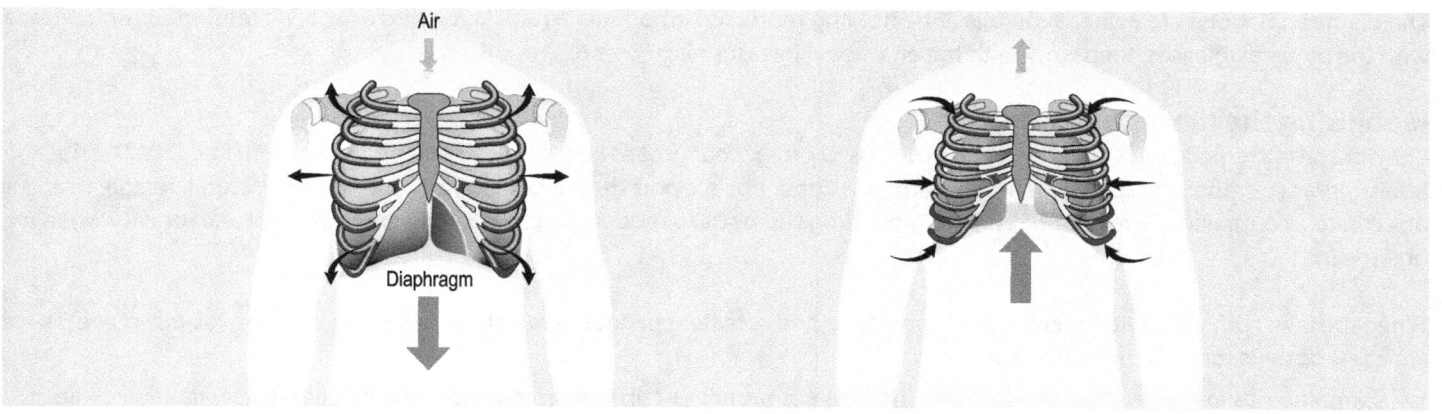

Self-Care to Assist With Breathing

The following self-care exercises can relax the diaphragm, the intercostal muscles and therefore increase the space for your lungs to expand into, which can make breathing easier. These can either be done lying down, sitting or standing, whatever feels more comfortable for you.

- Place your hands on either side of your ribcage and take a deep breath in.
- Did you notice the movement of the ribs coming up and forward on the inhalation?
- And down and backwards on the exhalation?

As you take another breath, feel for any tension in your ribcage.

Run your hands down your ribcage, noticing any ribs that stick out or are lower that the surrounding ribs.

Diaphragm

The diaphragm is an amazing structure that connects from your spine around the lower ribs and forms an arch. It flattens as it contracts. This creates a vacuum that sucks air into your lungs.

Diaphragm release

- Place your hands over your lower ribs.
- Take a deep breath in, then fully exhale through your mouth.
- Hold your ribcage in when you inhale.
- As you exhale, increase the pressure on your ribs.
- Inhale and hold the pressure on until you feel pressure of your breath reach a maximum, then release the pressure on the ribs quickly.

1st Inhalation

1st exhale, hold for next inhalation

2nd exhale, hold for next inhalation

Last inhalation wait till pressure builds up then spring off ribcage

The diaphragm is one area where you might be holding repressed emotional "stuff." If you find a lot of its tension doesn't release with the physical releases, then work with the emotional releases in chapter 6.

Mobilising the Ribcage

The ribcage is a remarkable structure. We use our ribs to protect our organs like the liver, heart and lungs from impacts. The ribcage also supports our thoracic spine when we rotate. The upper ribs support the shoulder girdle, and from a postural perspective, our ribs create a container where the pressure from our lungs helps us to rebound up against the downward force of gravity when we breathe in.

When the lower or upper back needs more support the body creates changes in the ribcage that change how you can move. There are a few options for how this can happen.

1. Jamming ribs in the position of inhalation. This creates prominent ribs. Jamming ribs in the position of exhalation creates depressed ribs. You can explore the rib movement by placing your hands on the ribcage and take a deep breath in to check how they move.
2. Jamming the ribs in rotation. This will create raised and depressed ribs, but there will be more of a rotation to one side. This is often balanced with a rotation of one of the ribs on the other side. You can often feel this as an area of your ribcage that is restricted in movement when you take a deep breath.
3. Pushing forward through the base of the ribcage, which pushes the lower ribs forward. This gives the lower ribs a prominent look when you lie on your back, and you can often feel stiff in the lower thoracic/upper lumbar spine.

As you do the exercises below, see if you can notice any of these patterns

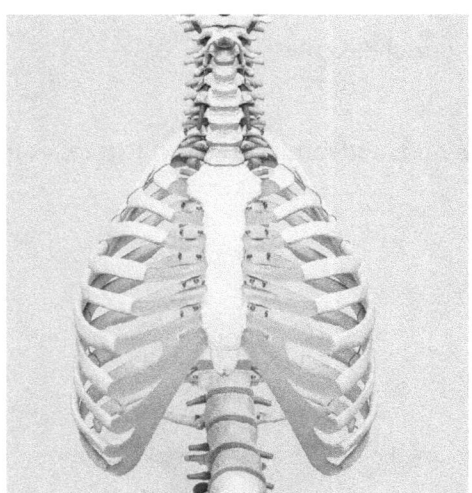

Lateral flexion around base or ribcage

Lateral flexion around mid ribcage

Releasing the Ribcage with Rotation

- Place your hands so your thumb is on the 10th rib.
- Gently rotate the ribcage forward on one side then the other, feeling for what is most comfortable.
- Hold in the comfortable position for 10-30 seconds.
- Recheck movement.
- Move up and repeat with the other ribs.

Rotation with base of ribcage forward

If you have noticed that your lower ribs are thrust forward, use this exercise:

Releasing the Lower Ribcage from Pushing Forward
- Place hands on lower ribs (thumbs to the back) and compress with both hands backward toward your spine for 10 seconds.
- Then bring the lower ribs forward in an exaggeration of the position of your lower thoracic.
- Relax in that position then explore how it feels to move the area.

Once you have gone through the ribcage releases above, go back to any individual ribs that are still restricted, and see if you can find a position where those ribs are comfortable combining the rotation, side bending and if needed moving forward or backward.

Mobilising the Thoracic Spine
Once the psoas, lower back and ribcage are loosened, we can move onto the thoracic spine.
- Sit with your back straight.
- Exhale fully, bending forward with your arms between your legs.
- Hold your breath out until you really feel the need to inhale.
- Inhale strongly as you arch your back, looking up at the ceiling and with arms open wide.
- Hold your breath in, then fully exhale bending forward again.
- Repeat slowly 6 times.
- STOP if there is any pain at any stage of the movement.
- Repeating this daily can increase the range of movement in the thoracic spine. If the tension is due to tight muscles, this should start to create more movement. If there are calcifications present, the thoracic will remain stiff. Fine tune the movement to work with your body, don't push further than is comfortable.

Release for pushing forwards at the base of the ribcage

Exhale

Inhale

S out on full inhalation. Then fully exhale to start position

Neck Pain
Middle neck
- Find a sore point along the side of your mid neck, level with your Adams apple with a finger.
- Once you have found a sore point, lighten up the pressure.
- Bring your ear toward the point, creating a cave around the point. Fine-tune the position until the point softens under your finger.
- Hold for 10 seconds, then straighten up.
- Retest the point.
- If there is still some pain, you can repeat, or move into position and yawn.

Mid neck release – combination of rotation and lateral flexion around the sore point

Lower neck
- Find a point down toward where your neck joins your shoulders.
- In order to access the lower neck, we need to lock up the mid neck by rotating the head away from the sore point. That is, your nose points toward opposite shoulder.
- Then tip the head back toward the sore point, your nose coming up.
- Finally, rotate your head back toward the sore point, your nose moving toward the sore point. Bring the ear on the effected side toward the shoulder on the same side as the sore point. Fine-tune until the area around the point softens.
- Hold for 10 seconds, then straighten up and retest point.

Rotate away from sore point | Tip head backwards | De-rotate towards mid line – you should feel the sore point soften

Upper neck

- Check to see if there is a tender spot up under the ear, between the mastoid process (red in the image) and the jaw.
- To access up under there, we need to laterally slide away from the point (this is a really small movement) before creating a cave around the point by bending ear to shoulder on the same side as the sore point.
- Hold for 10 seconds and straighten up, then retest the point.
- Check for tender points on both sides a bit lower in the neck.
- Fine tune the position to soften around the point.
- You can either add a yawn to the above positional release or just place your finger on the sore point and yawn with an extended exhalation.

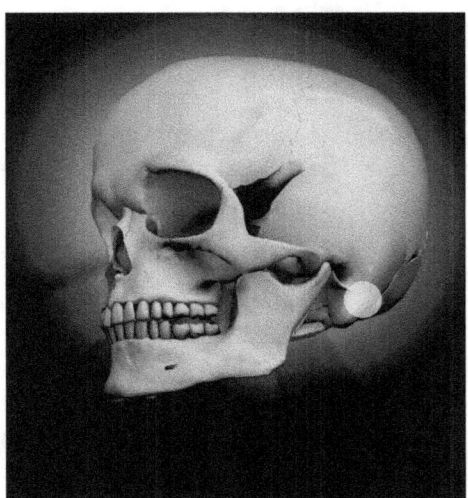

Polygon data are from BodyParts3D[1], CC BY-SA 2.1

Lateral slide away from the sore point then rotate and lateral flex towards the point

Creating more fluid movement in the neck
Using complex little movements to release the small muscles through the neck

Pencil in the ear
- Imagine you have a pencil in your ear.
- Write the word Ortho-Bionomy with that pencil.
- Then repeat with your other ear.

Pencil on the nose
- Repeat the above exercise with the pencil on your nose.

Pencil on the top of the head
- Repeat the above exercise with the pencil coming out of the top of the head.

Pencil on the back of your head
- Repeat the exercise with the pencil coming out of the back of the head.

Pins & Needles in hands

Pins and needles are a sign that there is pressure on a nerve.
One of the common causes of pins and needles in the hands is an elevated first rib.
The nerve supply to the arms exits the neck between the anterior scalene and the mid scalene. When these muscles are recruited to elevate the first rib, there can be pressure applied to the brachial plexus (the bundle of nerves that innervates the arm).
If you work in a trade (hairdressing, welding etc.) that requires you to work for long hours with your arms outstretched without support, then you are more likely to elevate your first rib to create more support for your shoulder girdle if your upper ribs are not supporting the shoulder girdle properly.
The first rib release will help with relieving the pins and needles short term, but an Ortho-Bionomy session on your ribcage and posture is likely to lead to long term relief by creating more support through your whole system.

First rib release

On the affected side, bend your arm with your hand across your abdomen.
Cup your other hand under your elbow and lift up, hunching your shoulder.
Imagine pushing down with your shoulder into your supporting hand. Do not allow arm to move. (You can push down with gentle pressure if you like, but your nervous system should be able to get the message by just imagining the movement).

- Hold for 5 seconds, then relax.
- With your supporting hand, move the shoulder around, exploring how the movement feels.
- Repeat a couple of times.
- Recheck to see if the pins and needles has lessened.
- There a few other options that may create pins & needles so if there is no change find an Ortho-Bionomy practitioner.

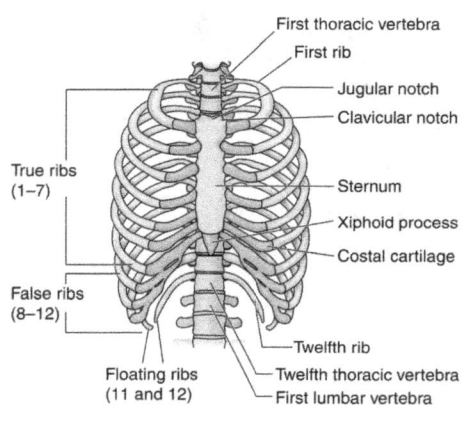

Hunch effected shoulder up, hold with other hand under elbow.
Think about pushing down into your hand.
After 5 seconds move shoulder around check to see if anything has changed

Creating and Programming Your Virtual Self

Your brain has functional patterns, which allows it to put functions on automatic so you use minimal effort to do things repeatedly. Think for instance the amount of effort required when you first learned to drive a car vs. how easy driving is now. The ability to put things on automatic is great, but also means you are less likely to be able to notice the details that would enable your body to self-correct your own musculoskeletal system.

Your awareness of your body currently is a mix of stimuli from your senses, as well as information projected from your brain, consisting of both emotional patterns and thought patterns. This is where beliefs and resisted emotions affect how you experience your body.

What we experience is actually a virtual body. If we can make this interaction a bit more deliberate, we can create changes to our experience of our body.
By working with the virtual body, we can put information into the system without trying to force the system to change.
How can you change a virtual system?
By changing the inputs into that system, which is really what this book is about. Changing your thoughts, judgments of self and the emotional states that you spend most of your time in starts this process. However, we can make this more deliberate. Choose an aspect of how you feel that you would like to work with. Let's say for instance vitality.

On a scale of 1-10 what is your level of vitality currently?
Tune into your vitality and notice any sense of holding, resistance or suppression.
As you notice something yawn to release it.
Return again to your sense of vitality and repeat.

Notice that we are not trying to force our vitality to increase, but rather just integrating what is in the way. When your body is working efficiently, you should have a high level of vitality. Finding a diet that suits your body is also essential for how well your body works. Hannah Moore will write about this aspect in chapter 9.

What if you could alter how old you feel by putting different information into your system?
This sounds a bit too good to be true, but we are constantly renewing our body from the cells that line the gut, which are replaced every 8 days, to our sensory receptors, which are replaced every 3-4 days. We constantly grow new connections in the brain and delete connections that are no longer used.
So, what would happen if we started to experiment with installing a younger pattern in our virtual body?

At what age did you feel your most healthy?

Can you recreate the feeling of that?

Alternatively, can you create the feeling of being incredibly fit, healthy and energetic?

How would that feel?

Or how did you feel when you fell in love. Can you recreate that feeling?

- Bring your awareness to edges of your peripheral vision on both sides.
- Hold your attention there until you feel a shift in your emotional state.
- Project the feeling of the younger/healthier you into your body, marinate every cell in this feeling.
- Yawn to release any suppression/resistance that comes up when you do this.
- Repeat it often enough that it becomes a habit.
- Let me know how you go.

Loving Your Pet

Imagine your body is your pet and you want to make it feel loved and cared for. What would you do?

What are a few things that help bring a smile to your face and make you feel relaxed?
Some suggestions:
- Walking in nature or on the beach.
- Taking a bath or hot shower.
- Getting a relaxing massage or Ortho-Bionomy session.
- Doing meditation, mindfulness practice.
- Doing Pilates or yoga.
- Socialising.

Making your body feel safe and loved will reduce your stress levels and improve your health.

You can either invest time and some money in your health, or you can wait until your health breaks down and spend your money when you can't go to work. This often costs more, involves more suffering and includes money pressure at the same time you are paying for help. So, be proactive and extend the years you are healthy by finding what works for your body.

CHAPTER 9.
DIET AND THE SELF-CORRECTIVE PROCESS

by Hannah Moore

DIET AND THE SELF-CORRECTIVE PROCESS

Role of a Naturopath

One of the core philosophies of naturopathy is prevention over cure. The reason for this that supporting an already healthy body is much easier than trying to fix a broken one. This is why seeing a naturopath before you get really sick is definitely the best option. That being said if you have left it late, that's OK too, as there's still lots we can do to support your body.

Hi, my name is Hannah Moore. I've been practising as a Naturopath and Medical Herbalist for 11 years and my mission is to help people maintain and/or regain their health and wellness by delivering practical dietary, lifestyle and natural medicine guidance.

A naturopath's job is to support the body to be as naturally well as possible, using the most natural processes, products and substances available. By following these guidelines, a naturopath can assist the body to heal itself by prescribing nutrients, herbs, detoxes and the right foods to support the innate healing intelligence of the body.

My clinical health philosophy is based on educating and helping my clients to establish healthy habits, because 90% of our activities create wellness or sickness.

Therefore, there are no generic diets and no fads. My mission is to find the foods and natural medicines that work for my client's individual system. Because of this, I do not promote any particular way of eating (vegan, vegetarian or meat-eater, etc.). Instead, I teach my clients how to eat right for their body type by listening to what their body is saying. It's in this way that I empower my clients to find a diet and to create lifestyle habits that work for their system.

Please note: The information in this chapter does not constitute formal medical or public health advice, and you should consult your own health care practitioner if you experience any symptoms or wish to consult about your own individual health situation. This is general nutritional and lifestyle guidance, and should not be construed as treatment for any specific condition. This information does not replace the advice of a trained medical professional.

Prevention is far better than cure. However, human nature seems to do the opposite, and many people wait until they are really unwell before they come to see me. People tend to go to pharmaceuticals first then try natural medicine as a last resort. However, I encourage the opposite by following these simple guidelines.

1. Live a natural life using natural medicine, stress management and a healthy diet to keep yourself well.
2. If something more serious does develop, use pharmaceuticals to support your body during that time.
3. Ultimately get yourself well enough to no longer need the pharmaceuticals and convert to natural living and stress reduction techniques.
   The reason I say to get off pharmaceuticals is because of the strain they put on the system. They are not natural and have many negative effects. We don't have to go far to find proof of this — just read the pamphlet that comes with the drug. In most cases there's a long list of negative side effects. These are listed because they are proven to cause the health issues listed. Therefore, it's best to be off medications where and if possible, with the guidance of your doctor.
4. In some cases, the body has become so unwell it's not possible to get completely off prescriptions. This is due to long-term dysfunction that causes permanent damage to the tissues, glands and immune function. In this case, I advise people to utilize both pharmaceuticals and natural medicine together to manage their health problems. When they do this, they tend to have better results than using either alone. Another benefit of taking this approach is they tend to need lower doses of medications and suffer less from the side effects of pharmaceuticals. Therefore, both natural and pharmaceutical medicines have a place in restoring and maintaining health and wellness. To deny the correct use of either form of medicine is naïve.
5. Use pharmaceuticals for acute problems: they are generally best for emergencies and acute situations. An acute condition is severe, and of sudden onset. This could describe anything from a broken bone to a heart attack. Therefore, pharmaceuticals work incredibly well at saving lives and reducing symptoms. However, the problem is they are not designed to increase the body's innate ability to heal, since the body needs an increased level of nutrients (specific to the health problem) and rest to do this.
6. Use natural medicine for chronic health concerns: These are long-term conditions like irritable bowel syndrome or eczema. They aren't life threatening as such, but can cause a huge amount of distress and suffering. These sorts of health concerns are best managed with natural therapies as the underlying cause often lies in poor diet choices, organ stress, accumulation of toxins and hidden pathogenic load, e.g., parasites. This is where natural medicine excels — helping the body to gently restore its own natural corrective process and health balance.

Exceptions: There are always exceptions to the rule when making generalisations. Asthma and type two diabetes are good examples. These common conditions are both chronic and acute in nature. These long-standing conditions can quickly change into an acute life-threatening situation. It's with these types of conditions that pharmaceutical management may always be required. This being said, significant improvements of these two conditions can be made with the implementation of a comprehensive natural medicine protocol. To do this, a person needs to employ the guidance of a skilled natural health practitioner who understands how to assist the body back into balance. Just taking a few over the counter supplements will not be enough, as a systemised process needs to be followed.

It is important to understand that Naturopathic medicine is very different from conventional or pharmaceutical medicine. It works gently and slowly by giving your body the building blocks and energy it needs to heal itself. Pharmaceutical medicine is strong and fast-acting. It forces the body to shut off symptom expression. This isn't healing but symptomatic relief, which is very helpful in reducing pain and suffering. Long-term, we want to be able to regain optimal health. To do this, we need to get the body to correct the dysfunction underlying the health concerns.

Living Organisms Intrinsically Know How to be Well

There is a natural intelligence that life itself provides. All living organisms know what they need to do to stay healthy and well, and believe it or not, this includes humans! We are imbued with this knowledge. However, humans have become so separated from nature that we have forgotten how to listen to and understand our bodies. A good example of this is a woman's cycle. When I first see them, 95% of women have no idea where they are in their cycle, yet this is easy to detect when they are in-tune with their natural rhythm. The irony here is, often their partners have a much better idea! Due to their symptoms and moods LOL ;)

This disconnection from ourselves, our bodies and nature are part of the same story, and is one of the main causes of poor health. When I teach my clients how to understand their body, to spend more time listening to what it's saying, and more time destressing, their health starts to improve. Every day in my clinic I see how this disconnection from self and the rules of nature contributes to why we are now suffering with so many lifestyle and dietary based health concerns (diabetes, heart disease, obesity, etc).

To be clear, I'm not saying, go live in a cave, but to eat clean and natural. Learn to listen to your body and understand what it's saying. Plus enjoy the benefits of modern life, but don't make yourself sick with stress, junk foods and the overuse of prescription drugs.

But Wait, What About Genetics?

This is a common question I get asked, e.g., This (health problem) is in my family so this is why I'm sick isn't it? The answer to this is Yes and No.

Yes, our genetics do predispose us to certain health problems, but that's as far as it goes. Just because something is in our family it doesn't mean you have to "get it."

In fact, Bruce Lipton did some amazing research on this, showing that cells respond to the environment they are in, and that they are NOT controlled by genes. He says our genes are just a blueprint but it's the environment that our cells (50 trillion of them) are in that makes us healthy or sick, and it's this environment that can also catalyse a healing response within a body.

So, What Makes Up the Environment?

A cell's environment is what you expose your body to. It includes the quality of the foods and drinks you consume, the toxins you ingest, breathe in or apply to your body, the amount of exercise you do, plus your thoughts and beliefs.

Naturopathic medicine works on this underlying principle: If you create a healthy environment for the cells, the body will experience good health. However, the contrary applies. If you create an unhealthy environment for the cells, the body will experience poor health.

Therefore, if you're experiencing poor health it's because you have immersed your cells in a poor environment. It's unhealthy to some degree or another. This is why a diet focused on increasing nutrients such as a wholefoods diet (unprocessed fruit and vegetables, quality proteins and fats), plus living a clean life that includes low alcohol and stress, regular exercise, and addressing emotional concerns can significantly improve your health.

Start With Listening to Your Body

Your body's signs and symptoms are its way of talking to you. The question though is, are you listening? Do you recognise when your body is not happy? Once you do realise something is not right, do you do anything about it?

You wouldn't believe the number of people I've heard say, "Oooooh so you're saying (their symptom) is not normal?! I just thought this is what everyone's digestive system was like or I just thought PMS and period pain was part of life or oh I thought poor health was just part of getting old."

My answer is "No, absolutely not." We are designed to have good health. It's our lifestyle, diet, stressors and traumas that create these health imbalances. We can help the body to correct these problems by supplying the ingredients it needs to heal itself.

So, what are the signs and symptoms that you might be overlooking and thinking are normal, just being a part of life or the aging process?

- Lethargy and fatigue before, after or between meals
- Food cravings and not feeling satisfied after a meal
- Always hungry
- Food intolerances and sensitivities
- Headaches and migraines
- Digestive complaints such as constipation, loose stools, gas, bloating, nausea, IBS, pain on bowel motions
- Seasonal or environmental allergies that affect the skin, eyes, mouth or sinuses
- Poor sleep quality and or insomnia
- Blood sugar issues: hypoglycaemia, hyperglycaemia, insulin resistance
- High blood pressure
- Thrush and fungal conditions
- Mood problems such as depression, anxiety and overall moodiness
- Immune problems such as inflammation, frequent colds and flu, or sore throats.

These symptoms are all your body's way of saying HEY BUDDY, SOMETHING'S NOT RIGHT, PLEASE PAY ATTENTION TO ME! They aren't life threatening, but in time if ignored are likely to worsen and possibly develop into something more sinister or much harder to resolve. This is why I'm always saying, "A health problem is like a stain, the faster you get on to it the faster you will get better." The longer you leave it, the harder it is to regain your health.

Let's take a deeper look at some of the above symptoms.

Gut Problems

There are five main culprits that cause gut problems.

1. A diet high in processed foods. This is the first thing to change and correct. Cut out as much processed foods, bad fats, and sugar as possible and feed your body with whole, unprocessed foods. Refer to the diet section below for more information.

2. Low hydrochloric acid (HCL) production. This is a key player. Many food intolerance symptoms also match the symptoms of low HCL: gas bloating, reflux, undigested food particles in the stool, digestive pains, microflora imbalances, diarrhoea and constipation. All of these may be due to low stomach acid. Stomach acid production requires adequate levels of Chloride, Zinc and B6. Many gut symptoms, including problems with dairy and wheat, may be minimised by correcting HCL production. Stress directly impacts HCL production, so stress reduction is also key.

3. Food intolerances, sensitivities and allergies. My clients often think they are reacting to the foods they eat, and in many cases they are correct. However, they tend to think it's a specific food such as a vegetable, fruit, or legume. But the truth is it is usually not a healthy food such as a vegetable that's causing the problem. Rather, gut problems or sensitivities tend to be due to a combination of poor food quality, an imbalance of gut flora, stress, poor liver function, and too much dairy and/or wheat in the diet.

Before I go any further, let's distinguish food intolerance or sensitivity from an allergy. Allergies are full-blown immune responses where your immune system identifies certain proteins as harmful, triggering the production of immunoglobulin E (IgE) antibodies to neutralise the protein (allergen). A true allergy causes a reaction by your body to the food that you've eaten or been exposed to, causing symptoms like hives, itchiness, or swelling of some body part.

Unlike a true allergy, an intolerance or sensitivity doesn't directly trigger an immune response. Even so, symptoms can still be very pronounced. They may develop when the body has had an ongoing level of stress in the gut. This is where the gut gets inflamed due to common gut irritants such as gluten and dairy, toxins, junk food, and imbalances in gut flora. Symptoms can be varied, including bloating gas, diarrhoea, constipation and digestive pain.

Dairy and Wheat:
The most common food intolerances are to wheat and dairy.

Wheat contains gluten, which is a plant protein also found in barley, rye and oats. All gluten proteins share the same grass family ancestral origin. Gluten and its counterpart gliadin play a significant role in gut inflammation, sensitivities, and allergies. This is because they are hard to digest and break down in the human gastrointestinal tract. Gliadin is the main component of gluten that celiac disease patients react to. Celiac disease is an inflammatory condition of the gut that's caused by gluten in genetically susceptible individuals.

Adding to this, today's wheat has been bred to contain an incredibly high percentage of gluten compared to the ancient grass-based grains. Therefore, our digestive systems are subjected to much higher levels of gluten than ever before. This is one theory to why there is such an increase in celiac disease and other gluten-related health problems.

Gluten intolerance is used to describe three types of gut disorders: celiac disease, wheat allergy, and non-celiac gluten sensitivity (NCGS). These all create similar symptoms, of varying severity, which include bloating, nausea, fatigue, vomiting and diarrhoea among others. People with gluten sensitivity have also been shown to have an increased likelihood of nutritional deficiencies, autoimmunity, and decreased bone mineral density compared with the general population. This is due to the inflammatory process that occurs in the gut when gluten-containing foods are digested. This impairs nutrient absorption, and causes immune stress. This is why many people are advised to go off or at least significantly reduce their intake of gluten and to follow a professionally prescribed gut healing protocol. The best way to correct a gluten sensitivity is to reduce gluten intake. Doing this may aid the body's natural healing response and may also help prevent other conditions from developing later on.

Gluten is also attributed to causing leaky gut syndrome. This is a naturopathic term used to describe a weakened gut lining. Gluten consumption increases the production of a peptide in the gut, called zonulin. This plays a part in regulating tight junctions of the gastrointestinal cell walls. Zonulin appears to be partly responsible for the increased permeability of the gut (leaky gut). When leaky gut is present, proteins from your food may go straight into the bloodstream without being broken down properly. This may trigger an immune response at the gut wall and contribute to an inflammatory response throughout the body.

Dairy: Milk-based products have two main components that cause issues, these being lactose and casein.

Lactose intolerance: Many people do not produce enough lactase. This is the enzyme required to digest the lactose (the sugar contained within milk). Lactose intolerance is known to cause inflammation in the gut and give gastrointestinal symptoms such as bloating, gas, diarrhoea and abdominal discomfort.

Casein intolerance: Milk also contains casein and whey. Thirty-eight percent of the solid matter in milk is made of protein. Of that total protein, 80 percent is casein and 20 percent is whey. This is where it starts to get interesting: There are two types of casein, in fact you may have heard of A2 milk, which refers to the second type of casein. A1 beta-casein is the most common. A2 beta-casein is only found in certain breeds, commonly Guernsey and Jersey cows.

This is important because, when digested, A1-containing milk has been shown to release much higher levels of beta-casomorphin[7]

(BCM-7) than A2. Casomorphins have been shown to act like opiates in the body, causing the addictive effects of dairy consumption. If you've ever wondered why you crave dairy so much, this is why! Also, if you suffer from constipation, dairy may be contributing as opiates cause a slowing down of the bowel transition time (the rate in which faecal matter moves through the digestive tract).

The problem is that casomorphins have been shown to directly raise histamine and to cause gut inflammation, bloating, digestive pains and loose stools, all of which contribute to an inflammatory response within the body and can contribute to the development of actual allergies.

The symptoms of casein sensitivity will usually vary depending on the amount of dairy consumed, and symptoms may be delayed due to the rate of digestion. However, symptoms can range from diarrhoea, constipation, bloating, cramps, skin rashes, joint discomfort and fatigue through to behavioural alterations such as problems with attention or attention deficit, increased impulsivity, and sleeping disorders.

Sensitivities to wheat and dairy cause inflammation and damage to the gut lining for many people. In time, this process can predispose a person to an increased likelihood of developing actual allergies due to the development of leaky gut. This is why so many people find that not only their gut symptoms, but their other health problems improve when they go dairy and wheat free.

Gut pathogens: parasites, bacterial and fungal overgrowths or imbalances. Good health, or poor health for that matter, begins in the gut. This is another naturopathic philosophy that more recently has been scientifically proven with all the research done on the microbiome. This research has shown that poor gut health negatively affects many other body systems, and therefore when wanting to improve one's health, addressing the microbiome is a key player in reactivating the self-corrective process.
"Poor gut health" refers to imbalances in the microbiome, such as parasites, yeast overgrowths and bacterial imbalance. These imbalances have been connected not only to gut disorders but to mood, immune, and other serious inflammatory diseases.

Naturopathically we use herbs, diet, probiotics and specific cleansing protocols to balance gut flora, in order to aid the self-corrective process of the body.

Some of the key tips for balancing gut health are:
- Quitting processed foods, sugar, and avoiding alcohol.
- Reducing dairy and wheat for people who have problems digesting it or who have sensitivities.
- Eating a diet that's high in fibre (fruit and veggies) and lower in meats
- Improving HCL production

What about probiotics? Here's what my 11 years of working with people with gut problems have taught me. You aren't going to fix all your problems with just one little pill.

Correcting gut health has many steps. Probiotics is one of the last steps. What I find works best is for people do the above (clean up their diet) and do a professionally guided antimicrobial protocol. Just throwing any old herb won't work, it needs to be correct for your body, and health concerns.

You also need to address your stress levels and unresolved trauma as these both significantly affect gut health due to the stress response's effect on digestive function. Once you have all of this in place, then yes, start adding in some probiotics, but they have to be the correct ones. When you have these components all correct, probiotics may be of great use in helping to rebalance gut health.

What about kombucha and other fermented foods? First, the bacteria in fermented foods are a mixture of who knows what, which may or may not be good. Scientists have concluded that fermented foods do not have the same health benefits as probiotics. Furthermore, fermented foods have unidentified microbial content and can easily become contaminated with mould, fungus and bacteria when made at home. Essentially, there needs to be further research in this area to make any real beneficial claims here.

In clinical practice, I find many people with gut problems actually do better to remove these fermented foods. It is necessary to first correct the microbe imbalances with herbs and diet as explained above, then to add in probiotics and maybe some fermented foods afterward.

Liver/gallbladder dysfunction The health of the liver also plays a major role in gut health and the overall health of the body. The liver is a large organ located in the right upper abdomen. One of its main jobs is to convert the nutrients we eat into substances our body can use. It also stores vitamins and other useful substances for when our cells need them. The other amazing thing it does is to sequester toxins from the blood, and converts them into forms that can be excreted from the body through our stool and urine. This is a process known as detoxification .

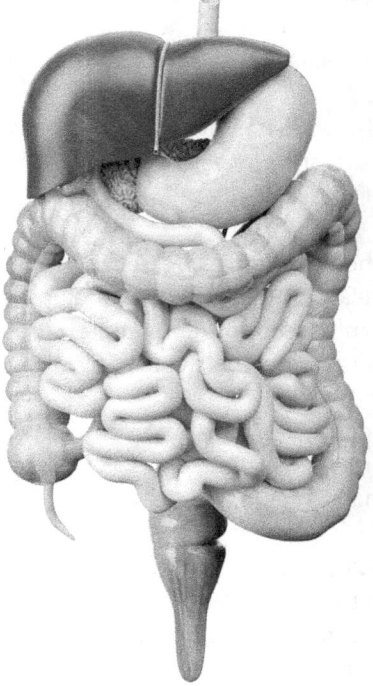

The gallbladder is the liver's counterpart. Its job is to store and concentrate the bile made by the liver and to release bile when fats are eaten. Bile is an essential part of fat absorption, breaking down large globs of fat into small droplets. This aids the second step in fat absorption, where digestive enzymes are released from the pancreas. The enzymes break the fat down into even smaller particles so that they can be absorbed.

Gut symptoms will start to appear when the liver/gallbladder aren't working properly. This is commonly due to nutritional deficiencies, infections and a build-up of toxins. Common gut symptoms associated with liver and gallbladder dysfunction are: Nausea, diarrhoea, constipation, clay coloured stool, nausea and or diarrhoea after eating fatty meals, gallbladder pain, reflux, gas and bloating.

Naturopathically I use diet, herbs, certain vitamins and minerals such as B complex, and Selenium, plus specific detoxification agents and liver/gallbladder cleanses to help the body restore liver health.

Inflammation, Pain and Emotions

As we saw in the chapter on stress, inflammation is an important part of how your body heals damaged tissue. There is however an interaction between inflammation and the intensity of pain. When you have an injury, it makes sense that the area needs to be protected from further damage. The chemicals released that create inflammation also increase the feedback from the nociceptors, which increases the pain from the area and makes the body reduce the movement, thus allowing the damaged area to heal. In chronic inflammation, the irritation of the nociceptors can lead to greater sensitisation of the area. This then increases the amount of feedback from the area and is part of the chronic pain pattern.

As well as the relationship with stress, there is some evidence that how we think influences our levels of inflammation. Hostile attitudes were found to increase inflammation and be associated with depression .

One of the common areas of inflammation is the digestive system. This can be due to eating foods you are intolerant to on a regular basis. With the huge increase of gluten intolerance, IBS, Crohn's disease and other bowel issues, it is interesting to ask what has changed in our diets in the last 10-20 years that is creating this ill health.

Many things have changed, but one of the standout chemicals that has increased massively in the food chain is glyphosate, the active ingredient of Roundup. As you may have heard, Monsanto (now Bayer) has lost two large court cases for Roundup causing lymphoma, and there is a large class action in process at the moment.

In pigs, GMO soy in the feed increased the inflammation of the gut compared to non-GMO soy. The key here is that GMO foods are designed to withstand Roundup, so they are sprayed more often, as weeds are becoming resistant to glyphosate.

Unfortunately, most grains/legumes including wheat, lentils, chickpeas, rye, buckwheat are sprayed with Roundup just before harvest, in order to desiccate the crop (dry it out so there is less likelihood of mould or sprouting when the crop is stored).

So, you are exposed to glyphosate in a diet with non-organic foods. The glyphosate kills off the microbes in your gut, changing how your digestive system works, and since our gut microbes make our Vitamin B, serotonin (80% of our happy hormone is made in the gut) and some dopamine (a majority of our reward hormone is also made in the gut), is it a wonder that the general population feels more depressed and less fulfilled by life?

Once the gut is inflamed, the gut lining is less able to absorb nutrients and is more likely to become sensitised to other chemicals. Bloating, gut pain, diarrhoea, constipation, a constant need to eat can all be signs of inflammation of the gut.

Inflammation is an essential part of our immune response. It's the body's way of repairing itself after a trauma: injury, an operation, or sickness, and it's how it defends itself against infections. Therefore, the inflammation process is key for good health.

However, there are two types of inflammation: short-term (acute) and long-term (chronic). This is the type that naturopaths are constantly dealing with. In fact, this is one of the areas that we are most specialised at helping people with. Chronic inflammation is very different from acute inflammation in that acute inflammation is fast to come and go, isolated to the affected area, and intense. It lasts a few days to a week, or two at the most. Symptoms associated are heat, pain, redness and swelling.

Chronic inflammation is long-term, spread throughout the body, and lasts from months to years or even a lifetime. It is the underlying cause of most long-term health concerns. It affects all organs, glands, tissues and systems of the body. Therefore, it can cause a wide range of symptoms such as mood and fatigue issues, poor gut health, reproductive problems, skin issues and sleeping problems. It underlies all the common chronic lifestyle-induced conditions (non-alcoholic fatty liver disease, type 2 diabetes, heart disease, and metabolic syndrome). It is also the underlying cause of immune challenges such as autoimmune diseases all the way up to cancer and dementia.

So, what causes inflammation?
There is no one cause, but the main factor is free radical damage, or what we call oxidative stress. Therefore, the actual question we need to ask is, what causes free radicals, and what are they?

Free radicals are unstable molecules that can cause damage to cells and therefore contribute to illness, the disease process, and aging. To put it very simply, they are the opposite of antioxidants (protective molecules that improve health through their protective ability).

Here's what's happening on an atomic level when you have free radical damage:
An atom is surrounded by electrons that orbit the atom in layers called electron shells. For an atom to be stable, each shell needs to be full. If the outer shell isn't full then it's considered unstable and it will try to fill its shell by bonding with other atoms. It uses another atom's electrons to complete its own outer shell. This is what a free radical is. When there are too many free radicals compared to antioxidants, you end up with oxidative stress. Correcting free radical damage is all about restoring balance of antioxidants to free radicals within the body.

When an atom is in a free radical state, it reacts with the substances it comes into contact with, thus creating oxidative damage. This causes damage to the DNA, lipids (fats) and proteins of the body's tissues and cells, which in turn causes inflammation.

Another thing to consider is that whenever you have a lot of oxidative stress occurring, the mitochondria can become damaged, resulting in reduced mitochondrial function.

Mitochondria are the powerhouses of your cells. They are located within each of your cells and are responsible for producing cellular energy or ATP (Adenosine triphosphate).

In chronic inflammatory states, the oxidative stress is so great that it can cause cell death or apoptosis (breaking up the mitochondria into lots of little pieces). This is known as DAMP's (Damage-Associated Molecular Patterns).

These little pieces of mitochondria then float around within the cells. It's the immune system's job to clean this up, and the way the immune system works is to trigger an inflammatory process. Therefore, it's a vicious cycle as oxidative stress causes inflammation and inflammation causes oxidative stress.

What you eat and subject your body to directly affects the production of free radicals. Here is a list of things that increase free radicals within the body.

Main causes of free radicals:
1. A diet that's high in sugar, processed foods, bad fats and meat and that's low in fruit veggies, good fats and fibre.
2. Toxins including environmental (chemicals and heavy metals) as well as by products of medications, and metabolism.
3. Chemical-based personal care products.
4. Pathogens: bacteria, viruses, parasites, mould, fungus, stealth infections.
5. Certain medications.
6. Nutritional deficiencies.
7. Pesticides, such as glyphosate and many others.
8. Chronic stress, a lack of sleep, and working night shifts.
9. Health conditions such as blood sugar imbalances, leaky gut syndrome.

The way to reduce these is to eat a clean, non-refined diet that's free from man-made chemicals and products .

How can we reduce inflammation.
When it comes to reducing inflammation there are a few things to consider such as where is the inflammation stemming from and what is the trigger? Answering these questions are essential to enable you to find something that's going to be effective, as if the wrong herb or substance is given it will not be that effective.

Inflammation tends to come from these places: Gut, diet, infections, toxins, allergies, injury and stress. These are the things that cause the immune system to fire up and go on an inflammatory rampage. Remember the body doesn't do things for no reason. If you have inflammation in your body there is a reason. Our job is to work out WHY? Then take steps to help the body find its own balance.

1st address your diet. Clean it up by getting off processed foods etc and address underlying nutritional deficiencies.

2nd Heal your gut and clear microflora imbalances and infections in the body.

3rd Detox your body of heavy metals, and chemicals from foods and the environment. Do this through liver cleansing prescribed detox products specific to your problems and fasting if appropriate.

4th Reduce stress. Stop coffee and do meditation + adjust your lifestyle to reduce inflammation.
Note: The first 3 are best done with the guidance of a practitioner.

If you have had an injury then supply the body with ample rest, and nutrients to heal. Zinc, vitamin C and Ionic trace minerals are a good start. If bone related then a good bone formula + glucosamine and conjointin for bones and joints + MSM can also be useful. Acupuncture and hands on energy healing may assist the healing process too.

Once you have done these steps then you can add in some additional anti inflammatory support such as a Bioavailable form of turmeric.
Good quality clean cod liver or fish oils.
Nigella black seed oil and bromelain enzymes for more allergy related things.

There are lots of other natural anti-inflammatories.
Many herbs are anti-inflammatory but again it's very hard to list off the ones that are best as it really is dependent on where the inflammation is located as they all have special affinity for different parts of the body.

The Importance of a Healthy Diet

Symptoms of poor health originate from many places, although one of the major and most common causes of poor health is a bad diet. The great news though is, there's one thing you can do for all of the above-mentioned problems and this is to change the things you put in your mouth. It really is this simple! You can literally kick-start your body's self-corrective processes by simply moving away from processed foods and choosing healthy wholefoods. From there you can get further assistance from a skilled naturopath for fine tuning, herbal medicine, supplemental support and detoxification guidance. Specific protocols and cleanses are recommended for each health problem, but that is a whole other book. So, if you want more information, please reach out and I can personally guide you through a cleanse. As a special offer, I am offering a free 30-minute online consult for people who read this book. You can contact me through my website www.hmnaturopath.com.au or through the Exploring your intelligent body Facebook page.

How to Help Yourself Get Better Using Diet

Diet is the first place we need to start when wanting to improve our health, since what we eat either feeds our body and keeps it strong and healthy or it slowly makes it sick.

I need to acknowledge that our body doesn't just go from vibrant, healthy and well to sick, overweight and depressed. Getting unwell takes time, often years. The great thing though is it can be reversed by simply doing the opposite of what got you unwell, e.g., instead of eating processed, junk foods choose to eat healthy whole and unprocessed foods.

We've all heard it's important to eat a balanced diet for good health. However, what does this actually mean and why do we say this?

The simplest answer is that the nutrients you get from the food you eat feeds your body and its 37.2 trillion cells. Yes, humans need to eat to stay alive, be healthy and well. However, there is one component that we don't hear talked about that often and it's the quality of the food you are eating. This is the next most important aspect of eating for wellness.

Food Quality

Food quality is king, or queen for that matter.

How our food is grown, the environment it's grown in, what it's fed, plus how it's harvested, packaged, processed, and how refined it is all impacts health. These factors affect how many nutrients are available to you when you consume it. It makes sense that if the nutrients aren't present in the food, then your body cannot absorb nor utilise them. In many cases today we are eating empty foods that are low in nutrients and high in chemicals and toxins.

Genetically engineered foods such as corn, soy and sugar beets have been made to be resistant to roundup which means the levels of roundup being consumed by people is higher than ever before. The problem here is the roundup is a known endocrine disruptor that has been shown to inhibit the natural detoxification pathways of the body, and thus are likely to contribute to many more health issues.[14]

One thing you can do if you can't afford organic is to wash your fruits and vegetables in tap water. This was shown to reduce the 9 of the 12 pesticides used in a study.[15]

Table 1. Results of tap water rinsing in reducing residues across all commodities

Pesticides	Pairs of Data	Significantly Reduced	Water Solubility
INSECTICIDES			
Endosulfan	60	Yes	0.32
Permethrin	37	Yes	0.2
Diazinon	22	Yes	40
DDE	21	Yes	<1
Chlorpyrifos	13	No	2
Methoxychlor	12	Yes	0.1
Malathion	7	Yes	130
Bifenthrin	7	No	0.1
FUNGICIDES			
Captan	34	Yes	3.3
Vinclozolin	23	No	3.4
Iprodione	13	Yes	13
Chlorothalonil	9	Yes	0.6

This lack of nutrients and increased levels of toxins in our foods starts at the farm and ends in the factory. The "bottom line" is what the majority of companies focus on. Therefore, little care is taken in retaining nutritional value, and keeping toxins out of our food. Today's commercial farming techniques cause soil depletion as they tend to focus on fertilising with N, P, K (nitrogen, phosphorus and potassium), which creates a good looking, big plant that is low in essential trace minerals .

Next is the processing and refining step. It's in this phase that fibre, skins, husks and hulls are removed, and with these go the nutrients. This means that the more processed and refined a food is, the lower in nutrients it is. Here's a nutrient profile of white flour compared to whole wheat flour. You will see, many nutrients have a significant reduction.

The Kernal of Wheat

Sometimes called the wheat berry, the kernal of wheat is the seed from which the wheat plant grows. Each tiny seed contains three distinct parts that are separated during the milling process to produce flour. The kernal of wheat is a storehouse of nutrients needed and used by man.

Fresh-Ground Whole Wheat vs. White Flour

Nutrient	Whole Wheat	White Flour*	Nutrient	Whole Wheat	White Flour*
Total Dietary Fibre	12.2g	2.7g	Selenium	70.7mg	33.9mg
Calcium	25mg	15mg	Thiamin	0.5mg	0.1mg
Iron	3.6mg	1.2mg	Riboflavin	0.1mg	0.04mg
Magnesium	124mg	22mg	Niacin	5.7mg	1.3mg
Phosphorus	332mg	108mg	Pantithenic Acid	0.9mg	0.4mg
Potassium	340mg	107mg	Vitamin B6	0.3mg	0.04mg
Zinc	2.8mg	0.7mg	Foliate	43mcg	26mcg
Copper	0.4mg	0.1mg	Vitamin E	1mg	0.06mg
Manganese	4.1mg	0.7mg	Total Fats	1.9g	0.98mg

Per 100 grams (approx 3 ounces)

* = unenriched

Source: USDA National Nutrient Database (2004)

Therefore, one of the most important keys for eating healthy is to eat a wholefood-based diet. This consists of whole, non-processed fruits, nuts, legumes, grains, fats and proteins. The Mediterranean diet is essentially this. "A large body of research data suggests that traditional dietary habits and a lifestyle unique to the Mediterranean region (Mediterranean diet, MD) lowers the incidence of chronic diseases and improves longevity."

A note on this pyramid: I put this image here, as it simply shows us to eat wholefoods, to limit sugar, alcohol, dairy and meat. Included in this pyramid are dairy, and gluten containing grains, which you need to assess for your personal circumstances. They may or may not be affecting your health adversely. If you think they are, it may be best to remove gluten containing grains and dairy from the diet.

There's a note on fish, too. Fish used to be considered a very healthy option for humans due to being a good source of minerals, protein and essential fatty acids. However, sadly today, eating fish can actually be bad for our health.

This is due to bioaccumulation of toxic metals such as mercury (Hg), and xeno-estrogens from plastics and chemicals such as DDT. These toxins do not break down, but stay in the food chain as invisible toxic chemicals.

Therefore, when eating fish, it's important to choose wisely. The habitat of the fish and where it lies on the food chain are the most important factors, not the size of the fish. A baby shark will still have a huge load of Hg, as it's a predator species.[18]

Questions you need to ask when choosing fish are:
Habitat
Was it caught in an estuary or near a mine? (Bad choice.)
Was it farmed or wild? If it was farmed, what was it fed? It's hard to know this without asking the manufacturer of a fish-based product.

Food chain
Is it a predatory fish? (If so, it's a bad choice.)
Is it a small fish that eats phytoplankton and the small creatures of the ocean? (Good choice.)

Xenoestrogens is a group of chemicals commonly found in today's fish. They disrupt endocrine function in animals and humans; they have estrogen-like effects in the body, increasing the total amount of estrogen resulting in a phenomenon called, estrogen dominance. Xenoestrogens are not biodegradable, so they are stored in our cells. A build up of xenoestrogens is known to cause fatigue, headaches, muscle aches and pains.

Xenoestrogen toxicity can affect your hormonal system, immune and nervous system:
Hormone toxicity affects reproduction, menstruation, libido, metabolic rate, stress tolerance glucose tolerance.
Immune toxicity can play a role in asthma, allergies, skin disorders, chronic infections and cancer.
Nervous system toxicity may also affect cognition, mood, and over all neurological function .

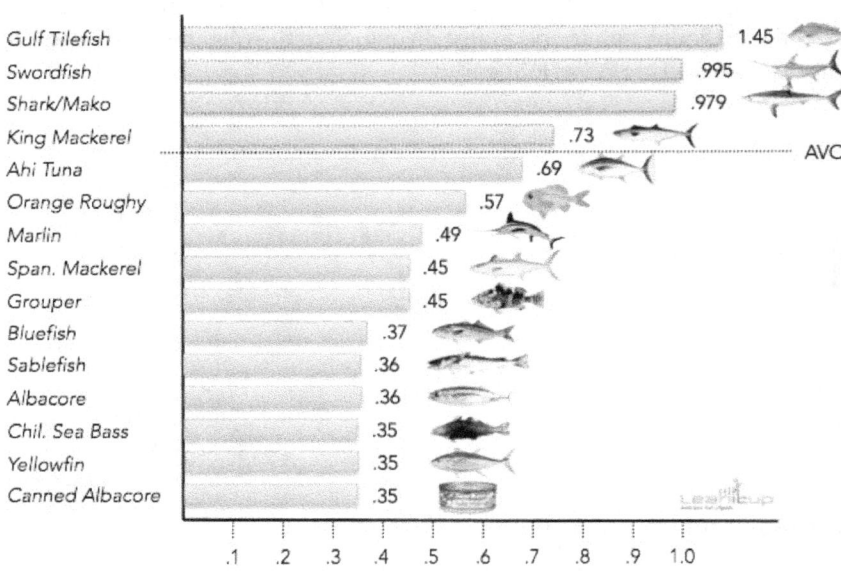

The simplest way to think of xenoestrogens is that they are man-made chemicals. So, if it's not naturally made it's likely a xenoestrogen. Below is a small list of some of the common xenoestrogens.

Skincare:
- 4-Methylbenzylidene camphor (4-MBC) (sunscreen lotions)
- Parabens (methylparaben, ethylparaben, propylparaben and butylparaben commonly used as a preservative)
- Benzophenone (sunscreen lotions)

Industrial Products and Plastics:
- Bisphenol A (monomer for polycarbonate plastic and epoxy resin; antioxidant in plasticizers)
- Phthalates (plasticizers)
- DEHP (plasticizer for PVC)
- Polybrominated biphenyl ethers (PBDEs) (flame retardants used in plastics, foams, building materials, electronics, furnishings, motor vehicles).
- Polychlorinated biphenyls (PCBs)

Food:
- Erythrosine / FD&C Red No. 3
- Phenosulfothiazine (a red dye)
- Butylated hydroxyanisole / BHA (food preservative)

Building Supplies:
- Pentachlorophenol (general biocide and wood preservative)
- Polychlorinated biphenyls / PCBs (in electrical oils, lubricants, adhesives, paints)

Insecticides:
- Atrazine (weed killer)
- DDT (insecticide, banned)
- Dichlorodiphenyldichloroethylene (one of the breakdown products of DDT)
- Dieldrin (insecticide)
- Endosulfan (insecticide)
- Heptachlor (insecticide)
- Lindane / hexachlorocyclohexane (insecticide, used to treat lice and scabies)
- Methoxychlor (insecticide)
- Fenthion
- Nonylphenol and derivatives (industrial surfactants; emulsifiers for emulsion polymerization; laboratory detergents; pesticides)

Other:
- Propyl gallate
- Chlorine and chlorine by-products
- Ethinylestradiol (combined oral contraceptive pill)
- Metalloestrogens (a class of inorganic xenoestrogens)
- Alkylphenol (surfactant used in cleaning detergents

The thing I love about the Mediterranean diet is that it's holistic in that it encompasses habits and lifestyle such as exercise, and socialising. Interestingly, loneliness has been shown to be more detrimental to health than smoking or even a poor diet! This was shown in what's known as The Dunedin Study, in which they studied 535 males and 503 females from birth to age 32.[21] This study indicates how essential it is to treat the whole person when wanting to maintain or improve health.

Prevention has to be a full holistic approach, not just looking at one aspect of health such as diet alone. We have to be happy in our hearts, feel supported and loved, eat well, rest sufficiently and exercise regularly. When we are consistently able to do these things, good health usually prevails. When we don't (for an extended period of time), poor health is almost guaranteed.

How Much Food Do We Need to Eat?
The answer to this very much depends on your body, your genetics, how much exercise you do, and any current health conditions you have.

Different theories advocate different guidelines. I tend to follow the ayurvedic guidelines, which are:
- To not eat within three hours of your previous meal or snack, and to not go without food for more than six hours.
- Have a warm drink before breakfast, such as herbal tea or lemon water. This allows your digestion to wake up, and creates a natural hunger.
- Eat breakfast at 8:00 am, lunch between 12-2 pm (this is when your digestive power is the strongest), and dinner before 8:00 pm.
- Meals after 7:00 pm interfere with sleep, as the body is meant to be cleansing toxins from the system. If it's still digesting, it has trouble doing this and you can wake up feeling groggy and tired.
- Breakfast should be modest. Have a larger and satisfying lunch, and a lighter dinner, which may even be skipped, depending on how hungry you are.
- You can use this ancient technique to help: Cup your two hands together in a bowl shape and limit your portion to this size. This is said to be approximately two-thirds the size of your stomach.
- Overeating leaves you feeling sleepy, and puts on weight. In contrast, a healthy portion improves your energy — as long as you're eating healthy food of course!

Different body types, also known as constitutions in traditional medicine, have different hunger and food requirements, so it's really about learning to eat right for your body type. This is something I specialise in and teach to all my clients. I discuss this more below, but before I go into that, you need to understand the basics of food.

Food Facts: Protein, Carbs and Fats
Proteins, fats and carbs are called macronutrients; these are required in large amounts in the diet.
Ensuring the quality of these nutrients is key and, in this section, I discuss what this looks like.

Protein:
Getting enough protein in your diet is essential for balanced mood, energy, weight regulation, immune function, healing, cell repair, and growth. Therefore, every meal should have protein in it. The amount you need varies according to your metabolic type. In general, most people require 1 to 1.5g of protein/kg of bodyweight. This can be met from all food sources including plants.

Amino acids are the small parts that make up a protein. There are nine essential amino acids. This means that you have to get them from your diet. Meat is one of the best sources of amino acids. However, a vegetarian/vegan lifestyle is also possible for many people (however, not for all). This requires you to combine your grains and legumes for optimal protein supply.

Grains contain two or three essential amino acids, and legumes contain the rest. You will notice that traditional vegetarian diets always do this, e.g., Indian dhal and rice or dhal and roti are served together.

Non-essential amino acids are produced in the human body, so it is not necessary to obtain from our diets, but this can still be beneficial if you have specific health goals such as weight loss or muscle gain.

In exercise/muscle building: Branched-Chain Amino Acids account for 35% of the essential amino acids in our muscles and may assist in building muscle and reducing muscle fatigue post workout. These three essential amino acids are leucine, isoleucine, and valine. They have aliphatic side-chains with a branch in their atomic structure. Hence the name.

Amino acids that can be made by the body from essential amino acids
- Alanine
- Arginine
- Asparagine
- Aspartate
- Cystine
- Glutamic
- Glycine
- Ornithine
- Proline
- Serine
- Tyrosine

Essential amino acids that must be sourced from the diet
- Histidine
- Isoleucine
- Leucine
- Lysine
- Methionine
- Phenylalanine
- Threonine
- Tryptophan
- Valine

Carbohydrates

Carbohydrates are the sugars, starches and fibres found in fruits, grains and vegetables. Most people today tend to avoid carbs to reduce weight. However, carbs are one of the basic food groups and are very important in a healthy, balanced diet.

The next thing to know is what I simply refer to as good carbs, not so good carbs and bad carbs. You want to mostly eat the good ones and avoid all the bad ones as much as possible.

Sources of Carbohydrates listed good to bad
Good: aim to get most of your carbs from these sources.
Vegetables and herbs
Root veggies
Whole grains: rice, millet, whole rye, whole barley
Fruit (2-3 pieces per day)

Fine in moderation: limit your intake
Processed flours: rye, rice, barley, millet
Raw, natural desserts made with maple syrup, etc.
Wheat flour: breads etc (sourdough best) — should be avoided if you have inflammation in the body, hormone problems, a gut issue, or allergies

Bad: eliminate completely and avoid as much as possible
Processed packaged foods: cakes, biscuits, chips
Takeaways
Soda drinks
Sweets, desserts, sugar, etc.

People don't like it when I say this, but this is the truth.

Everyone is best to avoid all processed, sugary foods long-term. This is not a short-term diet, it's a lifestyle change that needs to happen and stay in place forever, if you are going to maintain healthy blood sugar levels, hormones, moods and weight.

The idea is to replace sugar and refined products with wholefoods, whole grains and stoneground flour products. Use stevia combined with xylitol, 100%, maple syrup, or a little coconut sugar as sweeteners instead of sugar. Avoid all artificial sweeteners (e.g., Equal, NutraSweet) as they are made from aspartame (aspartic acid and phenylalanine), which can be toxic to the nervous system in certain people and cause side effects such as: headaches, depression, asthma, fatigue, hyperactivity, insomnia, dizziness, twitches, spasms .

Fats - The Good Vs The Bad

The first thing you need to know is, fats and oils are essential for good health (hormone production, nervous system and brain function, skin, mood and gut health and much more). The cell wall of every single cell in your body is made of fat. Therefore, your body needs fat every day to remain healthy and well.

Sadly, with today's food manufacturing techniques and profit-focused industries, it means that many of the foods you buy from the supermarket and restaurants are full of the cheapest, bad quality fats.

Bad fats (trans-fatty acids) are inflammatory, and increase oxidative stress. Because of this, bad fat can contribute to most if not all health problems, since inflammation and oxidative stress are main causes of poor health.

The great news is that good fats are the opposite: they are anti-inflammatory and contribute to good health. This is why it's important to learn the difference between good and bad fats and make a real effort to eat as little bad fat as possible. This is also why making your own meals is essential, because most restaurant and store-bought foods contain bad fats.

I find you only really need three good quality fats for standard home cooking — anything else is an optional extra:
- Organic, grass-fed butter and or ghee used sparingly (New Zealand dairy is renowned for this).
- Cold pressed, extra virgin olive oil (ensure it's in a dark glass, bottle or tin).
- Organic, non-refined coconut oil, used sparingly.

The Difference Between Saturated and Unsaturated Fats

This is important to know, because saturated fats are stable, meaning they don't get damaged by heat, light or air. Saturated fats are coconut, lard or meat fats, (excluding fish oils), butter, ghee and cocoa butter.

Unsaturated fats are all oils (including fish oils) and are liquid at room temperature (excluding coconut). They are easily damaged, and when this occurs, they increase free radical or oxidative damage throughout the body. This is a known contributing factor to heart disease . Oils are damaged by light, heat and air. So, when you are buying or storing oils, you need to ensure the following:
- It's in a dark, glass jar or tin — no clear glass or white plastic bottles.
- It's been stored somewhere cool — not beside the oven or in the sunlight.
- It's stored in the dark — not on the bench.
- It's stored with the lid tightly sealed so air cannot oxidise the fats.

TIPS

- Stay away from cheap fish oils. These are possibly doing more damage than good as quality is always an issue when heavily promoted supplements like fish oils are cheap.
- If an oil or any food that's high in oils such as nuts, seeds, crackers, whole grains, etc. tastes bad do not eat it — it's likely rancid and very bad for you (pro-inflammatory causes oxidative stress throughout the body; refer to the inflammation section).
- A "neutral flavour" in an oil is also generally bad: Some of the most toxic fats have no flavour at all, and in these cases, we can't rely on taste to warn us that an oil contains bad, oxidized, trans fatty acids.
- Eating out: canola, soy and other vegetable oils are the preferred oils used in restaurants due to the neutral flavour and low cost. Restaurants like a neutral flavour so that it's easier to make dressings and mayo's that consistently taste the same. A non-refined oil should have a strong flavour profile. If it doesn't, don't use it. Light olive oil is in this category; it's not a good fat as it's been refined and likely damaged in the processing.

For a more detailed list on good and bad fats, please refer to the picture on the next page It outlines things nicely. Cate is an American doctor who has done lots of studies on the effects of good and bad fats.

Good Fats		OK But Not Great	Bad Fats	
Traditionally used Fats and Oils		Refined Traditional Fats	Polyunsaturated	Trans
Not highly processed, and not refined		Label says "Refined"	Refined Bleached Deodorized	Label says "Hydrogenated"
All Purpose	**Caution w/ Heat**	**Limited Use**	**Don't Eat**	
Olive oil	Walnut oil	Refined Peanut	Soy oil	Fake whip cream
Avocado oil	Flax oil	Refined Avocado	Sunflower oil	Fake butter spreads
Peanut oil	Sesame	Refined Coconut	Safflower oil	Store-bought pastries
Butter/Ghee	Walnuts		Canola oil	Chicken nuggets
Tallow&Lard	Seeds		Corn oil	Margarine
Cocoa Butter	Fatty Fish		Cottonseed oil	Shortening
Mac Nut oil	Artisanal grapeseed		Hydrogenated oil	Restaurant fried foods
Coconut oil			Refined Palm	Most chips & crackers
Almond oil				Most protein bars
Unrefined Palm			Mostly in Restaurants:	Most salad dressings
Palm Kernel oil	DrCate.com Version Jan 2019		Grapeseed oil	Most mayo brands
			Ricebran oil	Most granola & cereal

"Nature does not make bad fats, factories do."

Avoid:

- Refined Palm oil. It's highly refined = trans fatty acids = bad fat
- All hydrogenated oils: Anything that says hydrogenated, because it's going to be a vegetable fat that's been over-refined and damaged more trans fatty acids
- Vegetable oils: When you see the words "vegetable oil," it almost always means it contains one of the cheap, refined, seed oils listed above therefore avoid using them.
- Store bought/restaurant made mayonnaise and salad dressings: These are almost always made with bad quality fats. The best thing to do is to ask for the dressing on the side when out. When at home, make your own mayo and salad dressings from extra virgin olive oil. It will have a stronger flavour so may take a few times for you to get it right.
- Avoid all margarines: they are all made from hydrogenated fats. This includes a certain brand of vegan butter that I won't name that is incredibly popular amongst vegans in Australia and the like. If you're vegan you know what I'm talking about. Avoid it.

There are a few things to know when cooking with fats:

- Stir frying: The higher the heat, the more you need to be stirring (unless you're going for a specific effect, like char flavour or crispy skin). This reduces damaging the fats.
- Health oil combinations:
  - Butter + Olive oil: Add a pat of butter to olive oil when cooking at high heat (baking and frying). The saturated fat in the butter protects the olive oil and the antioxidants in the olive oil protect the protein in the butter that might otherwise burn.
  - Sesame + peanut: Add sesame to peanut oil for Asian dishes. The ratio should be roughly 4-8:1 Peanut: Sesame. Sesame is high in Polyunsaturated Fatty Acids (PUFA), but it has powerful antioxidants that, when added to low PUFA peanut oil, protect all the PUFAs.

Micronutrients: Vitamins and Minerals

Your body needs nutrients to heal, grow and thrive. The food we eat is meant to provide us with all these nutrients to maintain a healthy body. However, this is often not the case in today's world due to reasons discussed above in the food quality section.

Minerals are the base layer and provide the foundation for good health. Just think about how minerals make up the periodic table — they are the elements that make everything in this world into "something." It's the same with your health. Once you have enough minerals then the rest of the nutrients you eat or supplement with will be able to work better. Minerals are inorganic and hold on to their chemical structure (are not broken down by heat, air, light or acid). They are supplied to our body through the plants, animals, and fluids you consume.

The dictionary states that "a vitamin is any of group of organic compounds which are essential for normal growth and nutrition and are required in small quantities in the diet because they cannot be synthesized by the body." Unlike minerals, vitamins are broken down by light, heat, air and acid, and we get them through our diet.

A note on supplements: Creating wellness is not just about supplements. It's mostly about diet, stress reduction, sleep, hydration, exercise, emotions etc. Think of vitamins and minerals as "supplements." They are designed to supplement your diet and to speed the healing process. I am always saying to my clients, "It's what you do outside of the clinic in conjunction with supplements that creates the change and maintains good health, not the supplements alone." This is a key concept to understand and get right when correcting a health problem.

OK, so now you have the basics to understand how to eat right for your body type.

One Diet Does Not Fit All — Individualising Your Diet to Your Body Type Is a Must!

With today's abundance of information and health gurus all over social media spouting their latest weight loss programs, the average person has no idea what to eat. Does this sound like you? "Should I eat a no carb diet? Are fruits OK? Is paleo healthy for me or is there too much meat? Does eating fat really not make you fat? Are grains really all bad? What's a wholefood diet and how do I do that? Ahhhhh!"

I'm going to simplify everything for you as eating healthy shouldn't be and doesn't have to be hard.

1. Each person is unique. We all have different body types, so no one way of eating will be right for everyone. The first thing is to forget the one size fits all model, since it does NOT work.
2. There are four important factors to remember when working out what foods are best for you.
   - Eat a diet that focuses on quality, nutrient dense, fresh foods. Eat foods as they come from nature (paddock direct to plate). Avoid processed, refined, packaged or canned foods.
   - Avoid all processed and refined sugars. Enjoy a couple of pieces of fruit per day.
   - Avoid bad quality fats (margarines, vegetable oil, canola oil, deep fried foods).
   - Enjoy good quality fats (organic grass-fed butter, non-refined coconut oil, extra virgin olive oil).
   - Each meal should be made up of at least 30-50% veggies (a mix of cooked and raw).
3. Work out your metabolic type. Once you do this, you can really start eating right for YOUR body type.

There are three general metabolic body types:

1. Protein types: They feel satisfied and full, and will have good energy that lasts over three hours after eating a meal that focuses on lots of veggies and is higher in protein and fat.
2. Carb types: They feel satisfied and full, and will have good energy that lasts over three hours after eating a meal that focuses on lots of veggies and is higher in non-refined carbohydrates and lower in fat.
3. Mixed types: They feel satisfied and full, and will have good energy that lasts over three hours after eating a meal that focuses on lots of veggies and is a mix of both protein, non-refined carbohydrates and fats.

When working out your metabolic type, it's best to think of it as a scale. Everybody requires a mix of carb, fat and protein in each meal. The key is working out which end of the scale you sit. When you eat the right ratio, your energy and mood may stabilise, you're less likely to be hungry between meals or need to snack, and less likely to overeat. This means your weight may start to naturally reduce and/or stabilise, if diet is the main cause for your weight issue.

Metabolic Typing to Work This Out

Metabolic typing is a simple way of eating right for your body type. It takes all the guesswork out of eating by simply putting the focus on how you feel after you eat a meal.

One of the best things about knowing your metabolic type and eating to suit it is: you never feel hungry, you have consistent energy without peaks and troughs, you're never on a diet and you always feel satisfied. This is because you are eating the right foods for your body type.

Let's face it, most diets are BS and don't work; they are often too complicated and make you feel like you're starving. The number one concern I hear from my clients is "I just don't know what to eat." So right now, I invite you to forget every dieting tip you have heard, learnt and tried and start eating the right way for you. The following pages outline how to do this.

Your metabolic type determines what sort of foods your body thrives on and what foods you don't feel good on. The simple rule with metabolic typing is to firstly get educated around the basics of food, and nutrition to eat a whole foods diet (explained above). Once you know what foods to eat, all you have to focus on is eating foods that keep you full for the longest and give you the most energy.

Protein type	Dark fatty meats High fats and oils Low carbs	40% protein: meats, nuts legumes, mushrooms 30% fats: fatty meats, nuts seeds, oils and butter 30% carbs: grains, fruit and veggies (eat most veggies, least grains, medium fruit)
Carb type	Lower protein Light-coloured low-fat meats Low fats and oils High carbs	25% protein: low-fat light-coloured meats, fowl, seafood's, low fat dairy, some legumes and nuts 15% fats: limited olive oil and butter 60% fruits, vegetables and grains
Mixed type	Mixture of high protein, dark & light meats Mixture of high and low fats and oils Mixture of high and low carbs	30% proteins: red meats, fowl, seafood, dairy, legumes and nuts 20% fats: animal fats, dairy, nuts, seeds, oil, butter 50% carbs: fruits, grains and vegetables

Please note: metabolic typing was developed by someone who is meat focused. This doesn't mean you can't be a vegetarian or vegan; the exact same rules apply. However, what I have witnessed is that vegans and vegetarians tend to do OK on lower protein if they are a carb type, but they tend to struggle and get unwell if they are a protein type. In saying this, if you are vegan it can be done, it's just a lot harder and you will need to have a very high focus on eating plant-based proteins with every single meal — absolutely no fail.

You can work out what Metabolic type you are is by doing these three things after eating each meal:

1. Notice how long you felt full for after eating the meal. Four or more hours is great. This meal was likely well balanced for your body type. Less than four hours is not so great, and indicates the wrong balance of carbs/protein/fat/fibre in your meal. You will need to play around with the ratios of each to get it right after eating a meal. Good or bad?
   Good: this meal was likely well balanced for your body type containing the right balance of carbs/protein/fat/fibre.
   Bad: likely not right balance of carbs/protein/fat/fibre in your meal and you will need to play around with the ratios of each to get it right.
2. Did you feel satisfied after your meal and did not need a snack between main meals?
   If so, this meal was balanced.
   If not, it's not the right balance of carbs/protein/fat/fibre in the meal and you will need to play around with the ratios of each to get it right .

Trial and error is the way you work metabolic typing out. So, don't just do one meal and give up. I generally recommend people do a protein breakfast such as eggs and bacon one day, and compare how they felt to eating a carb-based breakfast of oats with a few nuts and fruit with yogurt the following day. Note how you felt after each meal (energy, mood, satisfaction and how long you stayed full for) then repeat it a few times making changes, tweaking the ratios of carb, protein and fats and vegetable at each meal until you find the right balance.

The above information is an introduction to metabolic typing. If you want more information on this please feel welcome to contact me for an appointment or refer to the book by Trish Fahey and William L. Wolcott, The Metabolic Typing Diet.

Fasting and Detoxing - Let's Just Call It Cleansing for Ease

Another very popular tool that seems to come and go is fasting. At the time of writing, intermittent fasting and times restricted eating are popular, and yes, these ways of restricting calories and food intake can be beneficial, but in many cases they are not. I find many people have got the concept backward. They think fasting and cleansing will fix their problems if they do it enough. However, what people need to understand is that if you a healthy diet, you won't need to do as many fasts. The other concept is that fasting and detoxing don't make up for a crap diet, nor does taking copious amounts of supplements.

I'd like to remind people that we are designed to eat, not to starve ourselves. And yes, periodically our ancestors would have gone without food, but not often out of choice. We need food and nutrients for a healthy body. Contradictory to the above statement is overeating. Today, it is a big problem and it's likely why fasting and detoxing has become so popular. But just fasting and detoxing alone will not fix the underlying issue, which is too much food of a poor quality, and the wrong ratios of foods. So, the main concept to take away here is balance. Don't overeat, eat clean, healthy foods, and don't over-fast or detox yourself in excess.

Cleansing can be helpful once we have established healthy habits of eating well, sleeping well, and exercising well. When we do this, the body will start to self-correct. Then we can use supplements and herbs, and if we still have a few issues, fasting and detoxing can be of use.

Cleansing is always the last step in a health program, not the first, unless the person is already proficient in the above practices.

Cleansing is great when it's done well, but can actually make you very sick if the wrong kind is done, and if the body is not strong enough to do it. I say this because nine out of ten people who come to see me are in a fatigued and nutritionally depleted state. This is a sign of the times we live in (stressful and busy). It's also due to our modern-day food manufacturing techniques.

In most long-term health conditions, there's a combination of toxin accumulation, low energy and low life force, hidden pathogens (infections) and reduced organ function. To address chronic conditions effectively and with the fewest side effects, we have to build you up before we can get stuck in doing the heavy-duty work (detoxing, fasting, and killing off pathogens). This is because the body isn't strong enough to kill off bugs, fast or to detox effectively, because both require large amounts of nutrients and good energy levels to do it well. This building phase is very important and can take a few weeks to a few months. Think of it like laying a strong foundation for building a house.

We have to follow a sequence to getting better.

> Step 1: Build up nutritionally starting with minerals, clean up the diet, reduce toxin exposure, implement lifestyle and daily habits that encourage good health.
>
> Step 2: Increase energy levels with herbs, diet, exercise, and supplements.
>
> Step 3: Improve immune function and kill off pathogens (viruses, bacteria, parasites, mould, fungus).
>
> Step 4: Repair gut, adrenal, kidney and liver function, plus any other affected organs.
>
> Step 5: Detox/fast and continue to improve immune function.
>
> Step 6: Repeat the repair and detox phases again as there's only so much self-correcting your body can do until more repairing and detoxing has to be carried out.

So, there are 4 Key Steps to Wellness:
1. Clean up your diet, and eat a whole food-based diet.
2. Eat right for your body type by tuning it to what your body needs (take out and add in foods in the right ratios).
3. Establish and maintain healthy routines, such as low alcohol and coffee, quit smoking, do regular exercise, focus on stress reduction, meditation and improving sleep.
4. Cleanse and aid the body to heal itself with herbs, vitamins and minerals.

The above steps are what I guide my clients through when they come and work with me. Therefore, if after reading this section you feel you want some additional support, please do get in touch. I would love to help you activate your body's natural corrective process. So, you can feel vibrant, healthy and alive once again!

Please contact me on +61 4747 287 23, or thought my website, www.hmnaturopath.com.au I offer a free 30 minute consultation for people who are keen to work with me.

References

1. Lipton, B. (2009) The Biology of Belief. Hay House
2. Balakireva, A and Zamyatnin, A. (2016) Properties of gluten intolerance: Gluten structure, evolution, pathogenicity and detoxification capabilities. Nutrients, 8, 644
3. Kamiński, S., Cieślińska, A., & Kostyra, E. (2007). Polymorphism of bovine beta-casein and its potential effect on human health. Journal of applied genetics, 48(3), 189-198
4. Boutrou, R., Gaudichon, C., Dupont, D., Jardin, J., Airinei, G., Marsset-Baglieri, A. and Leonil, J. (2013). Sequential release of milk protein—derived bioactive peptides in the jejunum in healthy humans. The American Journal of Clinical Nutrition, 97(6), 1314-1323
5. Kurek, M., Przybilla, B., Hermann, K., & Ring, I. (1992). A naturally occurring opioid peptide from cow's milk, beta-casomorphine-7, is a direct histamine releaser in man. International Archives of Allergy and Immunology, 97(2), 115-120
6. Lindau-Emmert, D, Emmert, V, Fusz, K., Prémusz, V. and Tóth, G. (2019) P319 The unexpected 'troublemaker' – Behavioural changes in children with cow's milk protein allergy Archives of Disease in Childhood 104:A285
7. Alam. R, Abdolmaleky, H. M, Zhou, J. R. (2017) Microbiome, inflammation, epigenetic alterations, and mental diseases. Am J Med Genet B Neuropsychiatr Genet. 174(6):651-660 Maranduba, C. M., De Castro, S. B., de Souza, G. T, Rossato, C., da Guia, F. C. and Valente, M.A. (2015). Intestinal microbiota as modulators of the immune system and neuroimmune system: impact on the host health and homeostasis. J Immunol Res 931574
8. InformedHealth.org (2009) [Internet]. Cologne, Germany: Institute for Quality and Efficiency in Health Care (IQWiG); 2006-. How does the liver work? [Updated 2016 Aug 22]. Available from: https://www.ncbi.nlm.nih.gov/books/NBK279393
9. Brummett, B. H., Boyle, S. H., Ortel, T. L., Becker, R. C., Siegler, I. C. $ Williams, R. B. (2010) Associations of depressive symptoms, trait hostility, and gender with C-reactive protein and interleukin-6 response after emotional recall. Psychosom Med 72(4), 333-9 Jong, S. R. & Dong, H.S. (2018) Damage-Associated molecular patterns in inflammatory diseases. Immune network 18(4)
10. Crinnion, W. J. 2010, Organic Foods Contain Higher Levels of Certain Nutrients, Lower Levels of Pesticides, and May Provide Health Benefits for the Consumer, Alternative Medicine Review, vol. 15, no. 1, pp. 4–12
11. Richard, S., Moslemi, S., Sipahutar, H., Benachour, N. & Seralini, G. E. (2005) Differential Effects of Glyphosate and Roundup on Human Placental Cells and Aromatase, Environmental Health Perspectives, vol. 113, no. 6, 716–720
12. https://portal.ct.gov/CAES/Fact-Sheets/Analytical-Chemistry/Removal-of-Trace-Pesticide-Residues-from-Produce
13. Davies, D. R., Epp, M.D. & Riordan, H.D. (2004). Changes in USDA food composition data for 43 garden crops, 1950 to 1999. Journal of the American college of nutrition 23(6):669-82
14. Romagnolo, D.F. & Selmin, O.I. (2017). Mediterranean diet and prevention of chronic disease, Nutrition Today, 52:(5) https://www.ncbi.nlm.nih.gov/pubmed/29051674
15. Wartian-Smith, P. (2010), Woman's Hormones, MPH, p12
16. https://www.zmescience.com/ecology/pollution-ecology/mercury-levels-tuna-18022015/
17. Poulton, R., Moffitt, T. E. & Silva, P. A. (2015). The Dunedin Multidisciplinary Health and Development Study: overview of the first 40 years, with an eye to the future. Soc Psychiatry Psychiatr Epidemiol 50:679–693.
18. Stratham B., (2006). Chemical Maze, Summersdale Publishers
19. Ascherio, A., Stampfer, M. J. & Willett, C. W. (1999). Trans fatty acids and coronary heart disease. The New England Journal of Medicine, 340(25):1994-1998
20. https://drcate.com/list-of-good-fats-and-oils-versus-bad/
21. https://www.lexico.com/en/definition/vitamin
22. Fahey., T. & Wolcott, W.L. (2002). The Metabolic Typing Diet. Penguin

Fine Tuning Your Diet to Meet Your Genetics

The more information you can get about your body, the more accurately you can meet it and optimise your entire system. So ideally if we could look at your epigenetic expression (the complex interaction between our genetic make-up and mental, emotional and environment you live in) then we would be a lot closer to fine tuning your diet to meet your body.

There is a company that has created a computer-based algorithm that enables a more precise way to meet your body's epigenetic expression and suggest what foods are likely to work for you as well as how to maximise your productivity in a number of other fields.

ph360 (personalised health 360) includes information from 15 different layers of research which together give you an overall picture of your epigenetic type.

As you can imagine this is a highly complex set of interrelating fields that requires an algorithm to make sense of all the possible interactions. You can access the basic information from this process for free through a 3 minute health quiz. Once you have done this you can get detailed report on your health type.

You will probably recognise things you know about yourself already as well as get insights into things you do. In order to fully unlock the dietary and individualised aspects of the personalised health program you need to get accurate measurements of your body as well as complete a questionnaire which gives the algorithm much more information about what genes you are expressing. The algorithm then uses the information to give you recommendations in 6 categories, these include;

Food – dietary recommendations based on your epigenetic expression

Lifestyle – ways to fine tune your day to maximise productivity

Mind – ways to use your mind to maximise your health and productivity

Place – environmental factors that affect your health.

Social – the need for social engagement varies depending on epigenetic expression these recommendations may improve how well you deal with other people and the demands they make on you.

Genius – you have talents that will come naturally to you due to your genetic expression, these recommendations give insights as to what might optimise your success.

As you can see this goes well beyond a simple diet plan which are often generic.
Once you're logged in the information is extensive, fully personalised to you and can help you to prevent health risks later in life. To get the most out of the information specific for your body and mind, you may want a coach to work with you, at least in the beginning.

Access to the full individualised program is via paid subscription and you can find coaching options with individuals or groups in online options or you might be lucky and find a coach in your area.
For more information about ph360 go to their website www.ph360.me

> ph360 is a publicly available preventative & precision health tool, for purchase via their website and affiliated websites, www.ph360.me
>
> Please note, ph360 and their associated products and services are third parties to this e-book. Should you have any questions about their products and services please contact them directly on support@ph360.me

CHAPTER 10.
BRINGING IT ALL TOGETHER

BRINGING IT ALL TOGETHER

With a book like this it can be easy to get lost in the different techniques and not know what to use, particularly when you are stressed.
So, this chapter gives you a structure to follow to find the necessary tools. The key piece with most things is do you feel safe. The feeling of safety is one of the most important aspects of health. If you want to review the exercise on safety just click the page number at the end of the sentence and the bookmark will take you to the right page.50

Emotional Crisis
If you are having an emotional crisis the first step is to shift out of your stress response or maintain your ability to stay out of your stress response. You will find the techniques in chapter 2 help with this.

When you are not stressed making time to release resisted emotions and creating the internal sense of safety will help you be more resilient during stressful situations.
In chapter 2.

Chapter 2 – Working with the stress response
- Exercises for shifting out of fight, flee and freeze (page 32)
- Exercise for exploring your physical response to stress (page 43)
- Breathing to stabilise during an emotional crisis (page 45)

Once you can shift out of your stress response it might be useful to increase your sense of feeling safe and get good quality sleep. Techniques to assist improving your sleep you will find in chapter 3.

Chapter 3 - The importance of sleep
Tips for improving your sleep (page 53)
- Creating safety- techniques for stimulating an oxytocin release (page 54)
- Feeling safe exercises (page 55)
- Pineal gland meditation (page 58)

Once you have created this foundation where you are emotionally more stable then exploring how you can change the situation is the next step.

Is the cause an external event (eg death of a loved one)? In which case allowing yourself to grieve and feel the loss is what needs to happen in order to process the event. Getting whatever support you need during this time is a good idea.

Is the crisis due to a build-up of stress or being triggered by someone else, which maybe due to resisted emotional content that you need to handle in order to free yourself from reoccurring incidents like the one you are experiencing.

Looking at the tools in chapter 5, 6 and 7 can help you find an efficient way to approach this side of things.

Chapter 5 – Working with the mind
- Scale of importance (page 81)
- Creating a broader perspective (page 81)
- Still point in the heart (page 84)
- Gratitude & forgiveness (page 85)
- Creating happiness (page 86)
- Creating contentment (page 87)
- Creating a sense of wellbeing (page 87)

Chapter 6 working with emotions
- Working with resisted emotions in the body (page 98)
- Releasing stress from the psoas, digestive system & upper back (page 99)

- Recognising emotions exercise (page 101)
- Reprogramming the default mode network (page 104)

Chapter 7
- Traveling (page 110)
- Clearing the heart (page 116)
- Traveling tones when pain is present (page 124)
- Creating high tones in yourself (page 125)

Chronic Pain

If your stress originates from chronic pain you may want to work slightly different way.

Start with experimenting with the periaqueductal grey exercise in chapter 4

Chapter 4 – How pain works
- Exercise to stimulate the PAG to reduce chronic pain, anxiety & fear (page 63)

If you can get some relief from the pain then start working with the resisted emotions by using the tools in chapters 6 & 7.

- If you cannot get any relief then use minding the edges (page 35) to shift out of it that way.
- Also, try yawning (page 38). The key is to bring your awareness into the pain this shifts you out from the output of the limbic system in the brain to the stimulus from the body. The stimulus is not pain (see chapter 4 if this doesn't make much sense).

You may also find that the some of the tools in chapter 8 might be useful for some painful conditions.

Chapter 8 Exploring your ability to self-correct
- Increasing awareness of your patterns (page 128)
- Lower back pain (page 129)
- Self-care for breathing (page 136)
- Self-care exercises for neck pain (page 139)
- Increasing movement in the neck (page 140)
- Releasing pins & needles in the hands (page 141)
- Working with the virtual body (page 142)

Tackling inflammation can also be really important for chronic pain. As what you put in your mouth 3 times + per day is important for systemic inflammation fine-tuning your diet can be useful to help with this. Taking the time to become aware of how different foods affect you is a worthwhile investment in your future health. Check out chapter 9 for Hannah's suggestions about how to do this.

You may also choose to use a turmeric based anti-inflammatory as a short-term measure. But finding what is creating the inflammatory conditions is an important step.

Finally, with both emotional and chronic pain the next step is to prioritise internal work. This shift from healing what hurts to developing as a person is what is covered in the next chapter.

Digestive Complaints

There are 4 areas to look at with digestive issues – stress, what you put in your mouth, dysfunctions such as parasites and resisted emotions. Start with stress, diet and resisted emotions and reach out for help if you need it.

So, notice if you are in your stress response and use the tools in chapter 2 to shift out of it (page 32).

- Then use the relaxation technique for the digestive system (page 99)
- If you do this daily it will help you become more aware of what is happening you will then be able to track if particular food creates an adverse response for example bloating.

Working with a Naturopath to deal with the underlying causes such as parasites can also be useful. You can contact Hannah Moore through her website, www.hmnaturopath.com.au if you would like her support with this (page 166).

- The digestive system is also an area where we hide our resisted emotional stuff so yawning (page 38) can be very useful as well as working with the tools in chapter 7 (page 109) will be helpful. For further support to explore traveling contact Lisa Tyree by email on latyree@gmail.com

Sleeping Issues

Problems with sleeping may include not being able to get to sleep, light sleeping, jolting awake and not being able to go back to sleep.

- In all these cases working with your sense of safety will help (page 54)
- Shifting out of your stress response (page 34)
- Reprogramming your default mode network will also be useful (page 103)
- Releasing resisted emotions is also vital in order to be able to switch off and feel safe enough to drop into a deep sleep (page 98)
- Also preparing for sleep with the tips in chapter 3 (page 55)
- When you are lying down ready for sleep play with the pineal gland meditation (page 54) while doing hand on sacrum, hand on sternum exercise (page 59)
- If you do wake up just return to the sacrum/sternum release and yawn extending the exhalation (page 38)

Breathing Issues

With breathing issues, first you want to shift out of your stress response (page 34)

- Release any tension in your psoas (page 129), ribcage (page 137) and diaphragm (page 136)
- If you have had an asthma attack there will be fear locked in your system as not being able to breath is life threatening. You may benefit with working with someone to help keep you grounded while you release this fear.
- Working with resisted emotions will also be beneficial (page 116)

Quietening the Mind

Sometimes even when we aren't more stressed than normal your mind may be always on.
To help create stillness there are a few things to do.

- Notice if there are any foods that may make this worse – for me wheat products do this.
- Work on reprogramming the default mode (page 104)
- Release resisted emotions using tools from chapter 6 & 7 (page 116)
- Practice dropping into your heart space (page 84)

If you need a hand with physical painful conditions finding an Ortho-Bionomy practitioner near you will be a great addition to your self-care toolkit.

Losing Weight

Finding the important parts for your body is the key to losing weight.

- If you have done everything (change your diet, increase exercise) and still don't lose weight then you may need to work on your internal sense of safety (page 54)
- Getting 8 hours of sleep/night is also really important (page 53)
- If you comfort eat this is a sign you need to do work on the emotional level (page 114)
- You may also need to get assistance from a naturopath to ensure your digestive system is working properly (page 163)
- There is also a lot of value in checking out what PH360 has to offer, whether you do the free 3-minute biotype quiz online or sign up to work with a coach (page 167)

CHAPTER 11.
PERSONAL DEVELOPMENT

PERSONAL DEVELOPMENT

*Between stimulus and response there is a space. In that space is our power to choose our response.
In our response lies our growth and our freedom.*
Viktor Frankl

In Chapters 6 and 7, we looked at working with emotions from an emotional self-care perspective, which is healing what hurts and freeing up some attention. However, there is a much broader application for the tools presented. Whenever you are with another person, you get an opportunity to explore how you are interacting, which is a mirror for you to recognise previously unnoticed patterns that run in the background.

Because we focus on sensory data that confirms our pre-existing beliefs, we are often blind to how we select the information we are receiving. This is what subconscious means. When a pattern becomes conscious, that is, we realise our part in creating the interaction, then we can explore the pattern and unwind it. Often it will integrate without further effort once we become aware of it.

For example, a while ago, a friend and I were having a conversation about whether you can feel someone else's emotions, or do you feel your own interpretation of their emotions?

Whenever I talked about what I had learnt from reading about mirror neurons, my friend got a bit triggered and responded in a harsher tone.

I realised that I was using what I "know" to take a dominating position in the conversation, which was really suggesting that my point of view was more credible because I had done some research into how the brain works in processing emotions (this is my theory of why my friend became reactive, but he may see things quite differently).

So, it wasn't the content but how I expressed it that was triggering my friend.

The next step was to feel into how I dominate people with knowledge rather than connect with them and be curious about how they see reality. There is also the underlying pattern of why would I feel the need to dominate to start with, and so from an observation of someone else's reaction, I got to discover a number of things about how I operate in some situations. Having observed these patterns, I then felt through the different patterns and observed them integrate. The test is always when you come back in contact with the other party and see if there has been a change in how you interact with them. In this case, the next time I had a conversation with him he was much less reactive and I felt I could contribute information in a softer way that moved the conversation along, rather than trying to dominate it.

Becoming aware is a continuous process, and recognising a pattern should be celebrated, as it is an opportunity to integrate it.

One of the challenges when you start with this way of personal growth is that there are so many overlapping, interacting patterns that you bounce around so quickly, it's hard to slow down enough to identify one pattern. If you have a racing mind, rapidly changing moods, or really hit it around certain people, then this is part of what is going on.

If you need a holiday, feel fatigued by the life you have created, have ongoing conflict or are feeling stuck, then creating some time to invest in your self-development is very worthwhile.

The great thing is that this isn't about needing to sit by yourself for extended periods of time. Although Vipassana-style meditation (10 day silent retreat) is one way to push through and become more aware, it isn't the only way. The tools in this book can enable you to increase your level of responsibility and awareness while still being productive and functioning in your day to day life you can use in your day to day life.

Spending five minutes feeling through what just happened in an uncomfortable interaction and unpicking your part of it can sometimes completely change the future direction of that relationship.

Using awareness and taking responsibility for yourself and your own actions are the core of this practice. Seeing how others are acting toward you as a mirror of something in yourself allows a constant feed of material. As you change your patterns, the people in your life will start changing how they treat you. Alternatively, as you change your limiting patterns, your sense of what you deserve/ how you deserve to be treated changes and you will no longer be willing to put up with how you are being treated by others, and leave the situation, and this opens the door for a more fulfilling reality.

The only thing you need is the decision to review your interactions with others in a neutral way, looking for signs of emotional charge. So, after you have had an interaction with someone, recall what you were feeling and notice changes in your emotional state.

This can be a change in motivation, wanting to change something about them, wanting them to do something in particular. The phrase "you should" is a giveaway for this pattern.

This could be an attempt to manipulate, trying to get something, or force a particular outcome. Underneath the desire to manipulate is the belief that you can't create the intended outcome, so you need to force or coerce someone else to do it for you. This narrows down your ability to create the desired outcome to only one possibility. Integrating the willingness to manipulate others frees you from the game of struggle and the idea that there is not enough to go around.

There are many other common patterns. The real challenge is to find your own and integrate them to free yourself from slipping into your automatic reactive patterns.

The first step in finding your patterns is to become aware when the emotional content changes during the flow of a conversation. You can then contemplate that moment of the interaction by feeling into what was happening in your space right then. This is the first time when you will have to decide to not blame the other person for how you feel, otherwise you will head off into excuses for why it is all their fault.

If you feel into changes in your emotional state, you can then find the "edge" of the pattern. This is the first hint of how you are acting through the automatic program. Imagine you have a roll of transparent sticky tape. To find where it starts you need to look or feel for the edge. This is what we are doing with the emotional patterns. When you find a pattern, it will almost certainly make you feel uncomfortable. If you aren't feeling uncomfortable, you are probably hiding from what you have been doing or why you are doing it.

The greater your ability to be honest with yourself about having motivations that may not feel so nice, the faster you will notice the underlying patterns. Whenever you have a conflict, notice how you are being. How does it feel?

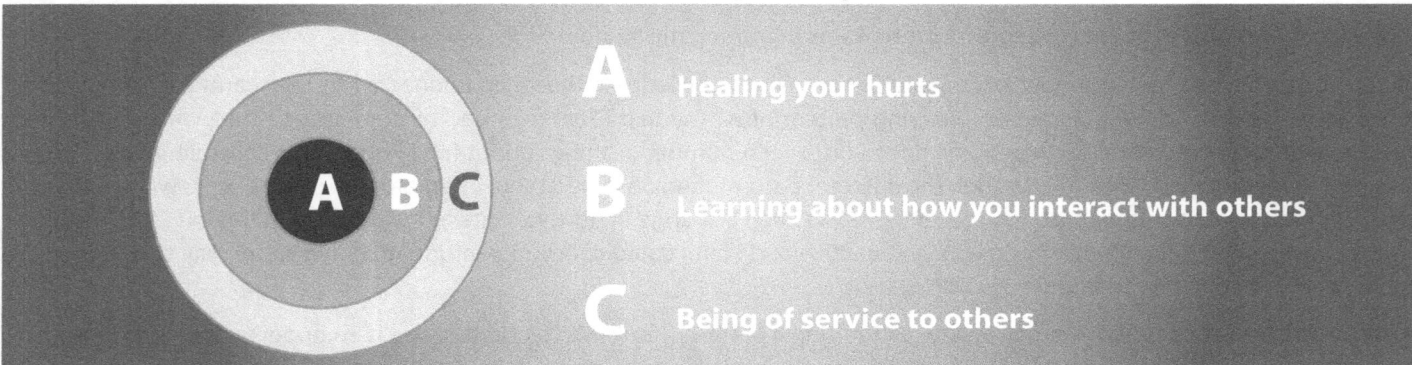

What Is The Payoff for Running This Pattern?

We have these patterns of manipulation because there is some advantage to doing so. It may make you feel better than the other person, and social hierarchy is an important driver for your subconscious: it creates the expectation that the others will do as you ask/demand. This creates the illusion of safety and predictability in an unpredictable world.

To start with, you will notice these patterns after they have been activated — looking backward at the interaction. Once you clear some space, you will start to notice when you feel the emotional change happening. The challenge then is to observe the emotional change in present time rather than reacting to it.

We all have areas we are blind to. When our patterns take over, we are on automatic pilot, and blaming others is a clear indication that this is where we are.

This process is one of learning in small steps with occasional epiphanies that shift you quickly. So, persistence and honesty with yourself are the main determinants of success.

There are also different domains you can work in.

To free up your attention, you need to initially clear up your internal pain. Heartbreak, grief, trauma, fear, stress, etc. will limit your ability to be aware of anything outside of yourself.

The next step is to notice your interactions with others and learn from that domain about your subconscious patterns.

This can also include exploring patterns from your past. Make some time and think of an area of your life that isn't as productive as you would like it to be. Think about what would be a stretch for you. Your limitations will surface when you put your attention on this area. You can then feel into them and either yawn, or become really curious and travel the tone as Lisa discussed in chapter 7. The aim is to explore it till it integrates.

Revisit your original thought to see if your space feels clear, or if there is something else to integrate.

Third is to come into service to others. This doesn't mean quitting your job and working for a charity, although you may do that if you feel it's what you want to do. It is more about your internal focus. Shifting from being in service to self — "what's in it for me" to being in service to others — How can I assist the person in front of me to become more?

Or taking on responsibility in a bigger domain, how can we shift our society in a direction of more awareness and to reduce the suffering of other beings, and the planet we live on?

What part can you play in this?

One advantage about being in service to others is that you have no attention on yourself. It is like a holiday from your emotional "stuff."

There are no value judgments about where you are working at present. We all go from one level to another and back again as we go through life. Sometimes we change level on a daily or hourly basis.

The key is to spend more time in service to others than resisting what is happening in our own lives. You can be in service to others in any job or career or if you are retired. Focusing on improving the world around you has many benefits including the time you spend not ruminating about what isn't working in your life.

A Model Of Consciousness and How We Can Operate It Differently

A model is like a map. It is a reflection of the terrain but it isn't the terrain.

The reason for this disclaimer is that I'm going to connect structures of the brain with particular functions. Neurons are about 100th of a millimetre wide, are highly branched. Some estimates have each neuron having 1000 different connections, and everyone has grown their brain to have unique connections. Because of this, there is a massive level of complexity, and therefore the scale I'm using to discuss the functions makes it unreliable. However, there is great value for doing this as you will see, as the model explains many things about how we process information as well as leads us to efficient ways to change where we are operating from.

The following model of brain function comes from Jill Bolte-Taylor, a neuroscientist. Her TED talk about what she learnt from having a stroke is in the reference section and is worth watching if you haven't seen it already.

The brain is split into two very different hemispheres connected by the corpus callosum This is made up of a small number (approx. 300 million) neurons.

The right hemisphere (RH) takes the huge volume of sensory data that constantly flows into the brain from receptors throughout the body, and is mainly concerned with experiencing the present moment: feeling connected to others, being embodied, feeling energy flowing, having a quiet mind are all aspects of the RH. The output from the RH of the brain is either in images or in the felt sense. So, images in your mind's-eye are generated by the RH of the brain.

The left hemisphere (LH) includes areas for processing language. So, the ability to read and interpret this book means you will be using regions in the LH of your brain. From the huge volume of data available from the senses that is coordinated by the RH, the LH narrows down what to pay attention to. This is in relationship to what has happened in the past and what the consequences may be for the future, so, what you believe has a big impact on what the LH focuses on. Any sense of threat will increase the vigilance of this process. Therefore, a fear-based reality (for instance the belief that the world is dangerous or you are unsafe) or warning signals from your body (such as anxiety) will create a greater focus on information that will confirm these beliefs.

Many of the positive outcomes from things like yoga and meditation are the outcomes from operating from RH of the brain. In effect, getting out of the LH dominant processes brings much-needed relief.

As the RH is focused on making sense of the present moment, there is the possibility that this non-verbal part of the brain is more efficient at assessing risk in the present moment than the LH. Intuition is probably the prioritised flow of information from the RH to the LH. This has a quite different feel to what happens when the LH selects the information from the RH to focus on.

Interestingly, women often have larger numbers of neurons connecting the two hemispheres of the brain (corpus callosum), which may lend credibility to the idea that women are more intuitive than men.

You can explore how this works in your life, if you feel into a situation and get a sense of what feels "right" for you. This is a quite different process from thinking about the situation and working out what is best for you.

There is increasing information that we decide on things at a much deeper level, using our less rational, part of our consciousness, then create reasons why we have made that decision.

So, if we come into the present moment and are more embodied, we are healthier, less stressed and are more likely to enjoy life.

Are there simple ways to actively shift where we are operating from?

Yes, and we already have covered tools for this.
Gratitude, acceptance and appreciation all shift where you operate from.
So, if you stop and focus on being grateful for something in your life and track how that changes your emotional state, also notice if there is a location where you feel the sensation of gratitude.
By becoming aware of where and how you can focus to create the feeling, you can then use that as a tool to deliberately shift states when you need to.

Balancing Where You Operate From

You probably know people who operate very differently from you. Some people are very analytic, want to work things out, others are much more into feeling what is happening.
The ideal would be to be able to use both hemispheres as tools and use the appropriate tool for the job it's designed for.
The first step is to recognise where you operate from now and then play with the other side, challenging yourself.
So, LH dominant people may use gratitude to shift across and activate the RH of the brain.
RH dominant people may choose the take the time and analyse a situation, exploring all the possible outcomes from a possible course of action. Taking up chess could be a good way to strengthen this aspect.

A great outcome would be to have the capacity to flick between the functions of left and right hemispheres to create balance, which reduces stress and fear and improves productivity.

As most people will probably have a tendency to be LH dominant, because we use language a lot, cultivating a way of being that enables you to spend time in your RH gives you the ability to be more present in the moment. It's like finding another gear, which steps around the reactiveness of the LH.
One way to cultivate this is to deliberately bring your awareness to your hands. Imagine you are listening with your hands. This of course makes no sense right up till you get the sensation, then it fits. This state helps you stay embodied. Feeling textured surfaces or touching someone else encourages you to stay in this mode.
This is one of the states people develop through Ortho-Bionomy training.

When you deliberately create the feeling of compassion, gratitude or acceptance, you will shift into the RH way of operating. The more regularly you reinforce this neurological pathway, the more stable the behaviour becomes.
Other ways to interact with your RH include drawing, playing with your intuition, and art therapy type techniques. A lot of alternative type things such as using a pendulum, divining, using tarot cards are probably just ways to give the RH of the brain a different way to communicate. Exploring what works for you and repeating the process is an investment in being more in the present moment.

The Relationship Between Your Internal World and External World
How we talk to ourselves, how we talk/treat others and how we perceive that they talk/treat us is all related.
For instance, if we are highly judgemental with others, we will often be harsh with our own internal self-judgment and feel that we are judged harshly by others. The key piece is that one pattern we are blind to will have an impact through multiple different areas of our life.

It is easy to notice if for instance you feel that you are the victim of others. In addition, feel for how you interact with the same pattern of victimhood in yourself. Do you use being a victim as an excuse for not doing something? Or use it to justify your own negative behaviour? And do you either make other people out to be abusers (you being the victim of their negative intention) or do you dominate them in order to get control?
If you are not feeling uncomfortable when exploring these sorts of patterns, you aren't alone. Feeling how we manipulate others is not an area of comfort for most people.

Exploring these patterns in feel is the way to have them integrate, but one form of denial that is easy to fall into is to intellectualise when things feel uncomfortable. The statement to watch for is "I know I do that, but…"
This is where being honest with yourself comes in. Feeling how you treat others and take yourself out with the same pattern requires you to deeply feel the emotional pattern. The great news is that once you feel through it and the connections between the parts, you will integrate the pattern and you will no longer have it show up in your life or when it does you will recognise it and be able to integrate another layer of it.

The Best Friends
One of the greatest allies you can have when working on becoming aware of your unperceived patterns is people who are honest with you about what they notice. This is different to telling you what you are doing/being.
What a person notices is closer to their sensory data, although it will still be viewed through their beliefs. If that person is in a compassionate space, the feedback is likely to be in the form of a question: "What did you notice when this happened?"
This creates the opportunity for you to explore your reality and find an edge, which can lead to greater understanding of yourself. With someone skilled, you can quickly find the relationship between the three parts mentioned above, and integrate the whole pattern.

The other option is more likely to be a statement: "You are being…"
Or, "Do you realise you are doing…"
These statements have the sensory data at their core and therefore hold some truth, but also have a level of interpretation, which is a by-product of the other person's beliefs.
If these statements are delivered with great certainty, they are a form of indoctrination.
When someone tries to land their view of reality on you with great certainty — "you are being…" it creates a duality: either you can accept their view of you, which has been perceived through their beliefs etc., or you reject their view. Neither option leads you to integrate the underlying pattern.

The third option, which takes a bit of space to use, is to ignore the story and charge of the other person and see it as a strong reflection of a pattern you have running. Then you can feel through and integrate your part of the interaction.

Indoctrination
Our brains like certainty. Putting things in automatic helps to keep your attention free to focus on other things. One of the ways of creating certainty is to use our social hierarchy to indoctrinate people around us on how they should see the world, behave and believe. Making others predictable helps the people in power stay there, or pass on that power to their children.

The Catholic church is a perfect example of the power of indoctrination. The fear-based reality they created, with God and the devil fighting for the soul of each person, kept people predictable and created enormous wealth for the church.
One of the maxims of Catholics, which has fortunately been found to be false is, "Give me a child to the age of 5 and I'll give you a Catholic for life." With a mix of fear and guilt, the Catholic church has controlled minds for generations.

Fortunately, fear-based religions are losing followers as people start to question how we create our own reality, and thanks to improved communication outside of religions they are finding different answers.

The new version of this seems to be "give god your money and you will be showered with blessings." This is the Hillsong version of Christianity.

With individuals, indoctrination is often used in subtle ways. If you can create the narrative (the story), you can dictate who is right/wrong. A person who is accustomed to being in a higher position socially, for instance a professor/teacher/judge etc., will often expect to dictate how reality is outside of their field of expertise.
Just because you have a degree doesn't make you more qualified in what reality is and how it works for someone else. Accepting indoctrination leads you to be less in control of yourself, and therefore less able to be aware of how you are creating your reality. This is a great disservice, as you are not able to change something from this place.

As our nervous system is set up to notice threat as a priority, one of the easiest ways of controlling someone else is to create a fear; the stress response. If you combine a belief system with a threat of punishment, you have a very effective form of indoctrination. Now that people in general aren't "God-fearing," the threat of economic collapse, gangs of youths from a particular ethnic background, etc. can be used to create predictable behaviour. This sometimes works better as people get older, but regardless of age if you have a fear based reality, then this form of manipulation will work well on you.

The funny thing is, we often support the belief that the world is a dangerous place by what we choose to watch online or on TV/movies. For things to keep our attention, they need to create a neurological effect. Threat or excitement are biochemically the same: the stress response is triggered. The content creators, whether it is the news or movies, need to create this response or you will focus on something else. How often have you turned off a boring movie?

Being deliberate about what you feed your mind is the first step in challenging indoctrination. Noticing when someone attempts to force an idea on you is also useful.
A good question is, what motivates the indoctrination — is it that the other person has just dropped into a pattern they are blind to?
Phrases like "You should..." are signs of this, although it usually isn't meant in a harmful way.

Another possibility is that a person undermines you, or finds something wrong with what you are doing so they can then offer a solution. This is a more detrimental pattern, for both parties involved. It will be a great gift for you to notice and give feedback about this pattern. It won't often be well received, since the pattern creates the space for the person to be right and an authority, but once they recognise and integrate that the pattern is there, they will have the opportunity for creating better relationships.

One of my friends introduced me to the acronym FGO, which stands for Fucking Growth Opportunities. Having people around you who will make you aware of how you are interacting with them is so valuable. The truth is, we all slip into patterns we are blind to and having aware people around is a great gift, even when they make you feel uncomfortable by showing you your unconscious patterns. Therefore, talk to your friends about FGOs and if/when there is a wobble in your relationship, you can discuss the content as something to learn from. This builds trust, and enables better communication after the FGO is processed.

FGOs within the Family
Some of the best mirrors for finding your resisted patterns are your family, and usually there is so much going on that it quickly becomes confusing. The value of doing internal work is that you will free up your attention from patterns with your parents and allow your children to be free of similar patterns. Taking a gradient approach is useful. Select a relative you get along with most of the time and free up any attention you have locked up in arguments from the past. Then move onto the tougher people to forgive. Using the compassion exercise can also be useful (see next page).

The other important thing is to recognise that this is a process. Finding yourself in a reactive, contracted space will happen from time to time and it is more important to be real than resist it and pretend. Pretending that you are perfect or have all your shit sorted locks you into a very narrow place where you cannot be real. It takes courage to be real, the cost of hiding who you really are because you want to pretend your perfect is just too high. The idea with tools is to use them. So, when you hit your shit, work with it, learn from it, integrate the underlying pattern and move on.

Compassion Exercise

Honesty with yourself leads to compassion for others.

Objective: To increase the amount of compassion in the world.

Expected results: A personal sense of peace.

Instructions: Run through each step with your attention on the person you are hoping to help shift out of their stress response.

Step 1: With attention on the person, repeat to yourself:
"Just like me, this person is seeking some happiness for his/her life."

Step 2: With attention on the person, repeat to yourself:
"Just like me, this person is trying to avoid suffering in his/her life."

Step 3: With attention on the person, repeat to yourself:
"Just like me, this person has known sadness, loneliness and despair."

Step 4: With attention on the person, repeat to yourself:
"Just like me, this person is seeking to fulfil his/her needs."

Step 5: With attention on the person, repeat to yourself:
"Just like me, this person is learning about life."

Adapted from Resurfacing: Techniques for exploring Consciousness by Harry Palmer[76]

How Your Beliefs Create Your Reality.

There are two different concepts here – how you create your perspective of external events, which is easy to accept as our beliefs focus our attention on what information from our senses to prioritise. For instance, if you expect a person not to like you, you are likely to find that their mannerisms/body language/tone of voice/words they use confirm that belief.

The second is in a much broader sense how we create the events in our lives. That relationship between our thoughts and what happens to us. This maybe more challenging for some people to accept so play with the idea. The key is that you have different levels of consciousness that function at the same time. The person you are when you are stressed is different to the person you are during a holiday or after a week-long meditation retreat.
The higher levels of consciousness are more cooperation based and playful as well as having a more clarity and creative power. The more you can still you mind, and balance the left/right hemispheres of your brain by being in the present moment. The more you can start to intentionally create.

As well as what we resist, our conditioned beliefs play a big part in influencing what you notice and what you create in your life. What you believe is often conditioned or taught to you before you have any recognition that you have a choice what you believe. This of course happens mostly in childhood but can also be connected to a traumatic event or abuse.
The level of certainty which you hold a belief effects the amount you empower that belief to control your reality.
Some people are very good at creating absolute certainty in their beliefs, these people are also often convinced that they are right and will generally become leaders because certainty is an admired quality in leaders. Unfortunately, they also create limitations and often miss a broader range of options due to this narrow perspective and when reality demonstrates that their beliefs were a narrow view of what was happening they often feel crushed that they got it so wrong. Unfortunately certainty in poor policies that change our society means their narrow mindedness has implications for many other people too.

The pattern is once you have a belief you will automatically search for evidence that that belief is true this selects the information from all the possible data to create what you notice.
When there isn't sufficient evidence then your default mode network can work with what you have and create whole new experiences that confirm your belief. You may have had the experience that you have been dwelling on an interaction overnight or

for a few days and when you next see the other person it turns out none of the stuff you were thinking was real.

One technique I use is to intentionally look for information that disproves the belief. If there isn't any or it is doubtful, then the belief is probably true.

Religion has used this relationship between beliefs and reality for thousands of years. Large buildings and an important position in the community and acting as the voice of god increase the certainty that religious leaders have so any beliefs they espouse carry greater weight than what an individual might think. In really controlling religions any questioning of the doctrine leads to social isolation as punishment and this is then used as an example to control the other members. When there isn't any evidence to support a belief that is when faith is required. Faith is not a bad thing if you originate the belief yourself, so for instance I believe I will succeed is a great belief to have faith in. But when someone else originates the belief and you are required to have faith in it, then that is indoctrination.

Intentionally creating beliefs that lead to realities that you would prefer to experience is the optimal way to create your reality. The way to do this is to state what you would prefer and feel what comes up instead of the stated belief/experience.
For instance, if you would like to experience being open hearted and you state "I am open hearted" but you feel restriction in the chest. Then you have are able to feel one of your obstacles to being open hearted. So, feel deeply into that restriction without resistance and that feeling will disperse. Then repeat. With each layer you go through the original statement will feel more certain and create more of the experience.
This is the part that is missing from positive affirmations. If you do not fully experience what you have already created with your beliefs, then you are trying create over the old beliefs this leads to pretending rather than creating. Integrating the old beliefs by experiencing them fully creates the space for the new beliefs to create something new for you to experience.

Treat the idea that you create your reality as an exploration, release everything that comes up that doesn't feel like what you want to create. Then shift your attention to the outside world and see what happens. If you are creating an emotional state this of course will create within you when you integrate what is in the way.

The same process can be used to create things in the external world. Play with this decide on something with unique characteristics, so that you will recognise it when it shows up. Use your intuition to feel what is right for you rather than try and plan and analyse things. Then create a statement that represents that for you and integrate everything that comes up when you say it.
If you are creating something external to yourself then it may take longer to materialise so give it time.

Practice at modifying reality by changing beliefs will strengthen your faith in the process of doing so. Knowing you can change your reality is one of the beliefs you can use to improve your life. There is of course whole books and multiple courses that are all about how you create your reality with your beliefs. Exploring this can lead you to discover a lot about your conditioning and limitations within your mind. Enjoy the journey.

Playing with the Placebo Effect

One of the biggest hurdles for a new drug is proving that it is more effective than one already on the market, but also that the effect is actually due to the drug not just the placebo effect.

It is well documented that if a person is administered a sugar pill when expecting a drug, a certain percentage will get better.

In some antidepressant trials, the rate of improvement in the placebo group was between 50 – 75%, and 79% of those who responded well to a placebo treatment remained well 12 weeks after end of the trial.[61,62] So, the placebo effect can make up the bulk of the effectiveness of some treatments.

In fact, two sugar pills are more effective than one sugar pill, and a saline injection is more effective than two sugar pills.

The colour and size of the pills also affects the size of the response. Red, yellow and orange pills were associated with a stimulating effect, blue and green pills had a tranquilising effect.[63]

The placebo effect has more impact in conditions like chronic pain, blood pressure, depression, anxiety and irritable bowel syndrome, where the brain is generating the symptom or increasing the sensitivity to the pain.[64,65]

In the science literature, this is seen as a fake treatment, which is interesting, since this 'fake' treatment is sometimes more powerful than the effect of some drugs.

Even things like surgery for knee pain can be challenged when sham surgery experiments are done. A research project compared real surgery with sham surgery and found no significant difference in level of pain between the two groups.66 One possible reason for this result is that the sham surgery triggers the body to heal the physical tissue in the area.

Sham acupuncture has also been shown to have a similar effect for some conditions as real acupuncture.67
The obvious conclusion is that 'real' drugs and treatments depend on the body's ability to heal itself, just as much as the work of faith healers. There is an increased focus on how to work with this and it is becoming better researched. However, there is a modality that has been working with sugar pills since the late 1700s. This is homeopathy.

In general, when we find techniques/treatments that work, we then go looking for why they work. This theory is a best guess with the limited amount of information and as time and research progresses this often shows that the initial idea about how things worked was wrong. Science gives us the ability to be less wrong more often, rather than to be right.

This is the same for western medicine as for alternative health, and really irritates our need to create certainty. A quick look at dietary advice and chronic disease over the last decade is a great example of this and despite all the research and new approaches we still have more people having chronic disease than ever before.

Back to sugar pills – if homeopathy shifted to embrace the research on the placebo effect, they could fit beautifully within the western medical model. The use of sugar pills with no side-effects would make a great first point of treatment under the supervision of a GP, rather than outside the system. This would protect the patient from delayed diagnosis for a serious condition that may need surgery or some other intervention. Of course, that would require patient health to be more important than big pharma profits, which maybe a pipe dream at present.

One note on homeopathy – it works well on animals. I'm not sure that animals have the equivalent of a placebo effect, but it would be interesting to see a well-designed animal trial on this.

I recently had a beautiful rescue dog called Andy come and live with me.
Andy had been beaten with a stick at some point and was traumatised. I picked up a stick to throw for him and he dropped to the ground, shaking. He was also really scared of leaving the yard on a lead, tail between his legs and scared of other dogs.

I gave him a few drops of homeopathic rescue remedy one night, the next morning he had jumped the fence and took off for an explore of the neighbourhood by himself. Since then he has been a completely different dog. This is of course a tiny sample size (of 1) and anecdotal evidence of an effect, but there was a marked change.

The research suggests that a number of components improve the placebo effect.

1. Expectation and conditioning — if you believe that the person giving you the sugar pills is an authority, trustworthy and caring, the pills will create more of an impact.
2. The belief in the action —if you have had success with the approach/medicines before, you are more likely to trigger a placebo response.

It seems the more seriously you take the story around the action, the stronger the placebo effect will be. This is possibly why some people find that faith-healing, laying on of hands and prayer create massive change.

In repeated studies all over the world, it is apparent that GPs use placebos on a regular basis as well. For instance, this could be prescribing antibiotics for a viral infection. The percentage of doctors who responded to online surveys who had used either a pure placebo (supplement) or impure placebo (other drug or remedy) within the last year ranged from 48% (UK, US & Germany), 77% (Australia), to 90% (Switzerland).[68–71]

As there is a real risk that antibiotic resistant bacteria are becoming more widespread thanks mostly to the use in animal industries producing pork, chicken, fish, and cattle in feedlots and dairies, unnecessary use of antibiotics should be minimised. Therefore, the use of antibiotics for anything other than a bacterial infection is a breach of medical guidelines.

> It is fairly evident that the placebo effect is one aspect* of the body's ability to heal itself, and the better we become at stimulating the body's innate ability to self-correct, the faster we can assist the body in becoming more functional. It is a great outcome if this can be done with no adverse side effects.
>
> - With new clients they often have no idea what Ortho-Bionomy entails, they don't often see the practitioner as an authority, or at least much less than they might see a doctor and are sometimes sceptical that this way of working will get different results from everything else they have tried, so any changes are not just due to the placebo effect.
>
> There is some evidence that the greater the effort you make to access the treatment, the more investment you have in a positive outcome. This is probably why people felt going on a pilgrimage changed their lives. It is also why a shamanic ritual in a foreign country will be far more powerful than the one run by a guy who lives down the road.
>
> The placebo effect actually changes the biochemical state of the body as if a drug had been administered.[63] The fact that a "sham" treatment can do this suggests we can do this without the treatment if we create the right conditions. This is really the core of positive psychology, and creating a positive forward-leaning belief.
>
> The exercise of creating a younger, healthier version of yourself is another way of utilising this effect.

Creating Something as Sacred

What do flags, plant medicine, crystals, books, statues, cheesy toast, bones from other people all have in common? Someone has considered them sacred. There is a psychological benefit to having something that you consider to be sacred. Being in the presence of such an object generates a unique feeling. It puts your ego in its place, and creates a connection to a greater whole with great reverence. This is another way to use the underlying principles behind the placebo effect. It is expectation, conditioned response and belief in the action.

The greater the investment in time and resources, the bigger the effect. This of course isn't a new idea, look at the size and investment involved in a cathedral in order to create awe of god and the old blokes dressed in dresses with funny hats who were the experts on gods will. Spending a few hundred years to build a spectacular building is a real investment in creating a sacred space.

The downside with creating something considered as sacred is that when someone with a different belief system treats your sacred widget with contempt, you are likely to be offended and that's oneway wars begin. So, creating something as sacred should be done deliberately, not through indoctrination. Choose something and create that connection, it is helpful if you have an intuitive attraction to the object. So, if you like crystals creating a sacred connection is easy, if you think they are rocks, then you need to integrate that before you will feel any deeper connection.
Revisit the state often, but stay flexible about what others must believe, and if someone offers you a super-sacred widget for heaps of money because it's twice as sacred than the one you have already, then you will get to see how effective the sense of sacredness is as a sales pitch.

Success is a great source of dopamine
but failure is a better source of learning.
Fail often in small ways and learn all you can from these failures.
Really the only time you truly fail is when you don't explore and learn from what happened.

Grit — The Attribute That Creates Success

Perseverance is really the only attribute you need if you can learn from your failures.
And conversely, if you can see your failures as steps to learn from on the pathway to success, then you have the key ingredients for perseverance.

The idea presented earlier that perfection is dynamic and inbuilt in that is a lot of failure is another perspective on this.

So, whatever your goal, stay curious, look for what you can learn from your failures (even though the only real failure is doing nothing/not learning), use that information to fine tune what you are doing and go again. The idea is to fail small and often till you build your skill base, then deepen your understanding by teaching someone else.

There is a great ted talk by Angela-Lee Duckworth on perseverance in the section below that is worth a look.

Emotional Courage
The willingness to feel the acute discomfort of shame or the deep ache of heartbreak or grief or the like takes courage. But it is the only way through the swamp of resisted emotions. It is the price you pay in order to clean up your space so you can be present in the moment and fully experience what is in your life now.
Turning and facing what you have resisted for years or decades is the real path of the warrior. It is not about defeating anything but fully experiencing whatever is there and allowing it to move through you. It is not an easy thing to do but the rewards are a life with more internal peace, less stress and being more present in the moment.

Susan David does a great TED talk on this subject. The link is in the references below.

A Technique to Help with Allowing Things to Flow Through You
As this is a more energetic technique, words are a bit clumsy, but see if you can get a sense of what I mean.

If you have been working with the tools in this book, you may have noticed your thought processes have slowed down and you are able to hold a thought in place.
Notice that when you have a thought or emotion, it occupies a space within you.
Notice this space has edges.
Bring your awareness to the outside of the space occupied by the thought/emotion
When you are exploring resisted emotions or emotionally changed events, just try and keep 20-50% of your attention in the space outside your thoughts/emotions.
This creates a calm space to help you remain stable while the resisted emotion flows through you.

This is similar to the idea that if you shift how you talk about emotions it can help create space. For instance, "I am sad" puts you right in the middle of the emotion.
"I notice I feel sad" puts you outside of the emotion but still experiencing it.
Play with this when you are exploring emotions that don't trigger a big response in you, then you can hold that space when you are triggered in a bigger way.

Being Yourself
The aim of internal work is to free you from being in your stress response, bouncing from desire to resistance and back again. When you find yourself, you can drop into a space that feels calm even when there is a storm happening around you. In this space you can learn more efficiently and be more productive. Being you is an exercise in practice, noticing when you react, feeling what happened, integrating the underlying emotional/mental patterns, then shifting out of your stress response and finding your internal sense of balance. This is of course a big topic. There is a great TED talk by Caroline McHugh on the art of being yourself, so check it out the link is below.

In this book, I have focused on exploring the body and its ability to self-correct. One area I haven't discussed is looking at the self-corrective process from a spiritual perspective, although Lisa Tyree does touch on this in her chapter.

There is a growing body of evidence that some of what has been described as spiritual experiences are corelated with changes in brain chemistry — a surge in neurotransmitters or activation in a particular area of the brain. What triggers these surges in neurotransmitters or activation of different combinations of areas of the brain is an interesting question.

For example, when brain surgeons do awake craniotomy surgery and stimulate the temporo-parietal junction with electrodes, there have been repeated incidents of patients having out of body experiences (OBE), where they felt like they were looking down at their body from above.[72-74]
The TPJ is involved in many functions, including incorporating information from the thalamus, limbic system, visual, auditory and somatosensory systems (information from the body). So, the TPJ mixes information from the external world with created information from your internal world. When there is a dysfunction in the combining of this information, an OBE may occur.

Interestingly, damage to the TPJ has also been found to inhibit moral decision making.
This suggests that although the TPJ has a normal role in the functioning of the body/mind, when stimulated in a different way it can create an experience that has been associated with near-death experiences.

The way the brain/body/mind functions is fascinating in the level of complexity and how everything seamlessly integrates to give us the experience of our reality. We are one system with the amazing capacity deal with the dynamic world within us and around us.

The potential for using awareness to change what is happening within our body as well as what is happening in our external world is massive and is far beyond what has been discussed in this book. The key piece is to approach life with curiosity so you get more information about the dysfunction and increase awareness. Allowing any resistance to integrate and exploring the underlying issues this then allows change to occur. Once things have shifted, switch to focusing on something you would prefer to create.

To summarise, the body is an intelligent system. When there is a dysfunction, it needs more information rather than needing to be fixed. When we find the level of dysfunction, and add the relevant information to the nervous system so that the body can recognise and learn about the dysfunction, the body will then respond by self-correcting.

If you would like to try Ortho-Bionomy you can (hopefully) find a practitioner on the following websites.
www.ortho-bionomy.org.au (Australia).
www.ortho-bionomy.org (US).

or search Ortho-Bionomy for the relevant association website in your country

If you are interested in learning Ortho-Bionomy, there are courses run in different places around the world. If no one is teaching close to you and there is a group interested in learning, send me a message via the Facebook page below and we might be able to organise a class.

If you have any questions, you can get in contact with the authors through the Facebook page "Exploring Your Intelligent Body."
https://www.facebook.com/yourselfcorrectiveresponse

Recommended Talks
Stress and resilience
https://www.ted.com/talks/kelly_mcgonigal_how_to_make_stress_your_friend?utm_campaign=tedspread&utm_medium=referral&utm_source=tedcomshare

Dr Zach Bush on glyphosate and gut health
https://youtu.be/X3aOQ0N74PI

Seth Porges on the polyvagal theory safety & trauma
https://youtu.be/br8-qebjIgs

Dr Sue Carter on oxytocin
https://www.youtube.com/watch?v=YA_ZCCsJVvc&list=PL8K5X2jaEwaw0PWFrt8QW_tPp0x-nZbLf

Dr Matt Walker on sleep
https://binged.it/31r7JuV

Jill Bolte-Taylor difference in perception of left & right hemispheres of the brain
https://www.ted.com/talks/jill_bolte_taylor_my_stroke_of_insight?utm_campaign=tedspread&utm_medium=referral&utm_source=tedcomshare

Dr Ben Goldacre – Battling bad science
https://www.ted.com/talks/ben_goldacre_battling_bad_science?utm_campaign=tedspread&utm_medium=referral&utm_source=tedcomshare

Sara Lazar reviews some of the evidence of the effects of meditation on brain structure.
https://youtu.be/m8rRzTtP7Tc
Sandeep Jauhar looks at the physical changes to the shape of the heart during grief

https://www.ted.com/talks/sandeep_jauhar_how_your_emotions_change_the_shape_of_your_heart

Brene Brown TED Talks on Vulnerability and shame
https://www.ted.com/talks/brene_brown_on_vulnerability?utm_campaign=tedspread&utm_medium=referral&utm_source=tedcomshare

https://www.ted.com/talks/brene_brown_listening_to_shame?utm_campaign=tedspread&utm_medium=referral&utm_source=tedcomshare

Angela-Lee Duckworth on perseverance.
https://www.ted.com/talks/angela_lee_duckworth_grit_the_power_of_passion_and_perseverance

Susan David the gift of emotional courage
https://www.ted.com/talks/susan_david_the_gift_and_power_of_emotional_courage

Caroline Mchugh : The art of being yourself
https://youtu.be/veEQQ-N9xWU

References

1. Refinetti, R. (2010). The circadian rhythm of body temperature. Front Biosci. doi:10.2741/3634
2. Marieb, E. N. & Hoehn K. (2007). Human Anatomy and Physiology, Pearson Australia
3. Chen, E. & Miller, G. E. (2007). Stress and inflammation in exacerbations of asthma. Brain Behav Immun. doi:10.1016/j.bbi.2007.03.009
4. Reiche, E. M. V., Nunes, S. O. V. & Morimoto, H. K. (2004). Stress, depression, the immune system, and cancer. Lancet Oncol. doi:10.1016/S1470-2045(04)01597-9
5. Thompson, S. B. N. (2014). Yawning, fatigue, and cortisol: Expanding the Thompson Cortisol Hypothesis, Med Hypotheses. doi:10.1016/j.mehy.2014.08.009
6. Argiolas, A. & Melis, M. R. (1998). The neuropharmacology of yawning. Eur J Pharmacol. doi:10.1016/S0014-2999(97)01538-0
7. Neumann, I. D., Wigger, A., Torner, L., Holsboer, F. & Landgraf, R. (2000). Brain oxytocin inhibits basal and stress-induced activity of the hypothalamo-pituitary-adrenal axis in male and female rats: Partial action within the paraventricular nucleus, J Neuroendocrinol. doi:10.1046/j.1365-2826.2000.00442.x
8. Porges, S. W. (2011). The polyvagal theory. Natl Inst Clin Appl Behav Med. 1-28.
9. Porges, S. W. (2004). Neuroception: A Subconscious System for Detecting Threats and Safety. Zero Three 24(5) p19-24
10. Chandola, T., Britton, A., Brunner, E., Hemingway, H., Malik, M., Kumari, M., Badrick, E., Kivimak, M. & Marmot, M. (2008). Work stress and coronary heart disease: What are the mechanisms? Eur Heart J. doi:10.1093/eurheartj/ehm584
11. Berk M., Williams, L. J., Jacka, F. N., O'Neil, A., Pasco, J. A., Moylan, S., Allen, N. B., Stuart, A. L., Hayley, A. C., Byrne, M. L. & Maes, M. (2013). So depression is an inflammatory disease, but where does the inflammation come from? BMC Med. 2013. doi:10.1186/1741-7015-11-200
12. Monteiro, R. & Azevedo, I. (2010). Chronic inflammation in obesity and the metabolic syndrome. Mediators Inflamm. doi:10.1155/2010/289645
13. Luyster, F. S., Strollo, P. J., Zee, P. C. & Walsh, J. K. (2012) Sleep: A Health Imperative. Sleep. doi:10.5665/sleep.1846
14. Lima, S. L., Rattenborg, N. C., Lesku, J. A. & Amlaner, C. J. (2005). Sleeping under the risk of predation. Anim Behav. doi:10.1016/j.anbehav.2005.01.008
15. Campbell, S. S. & Tobler, I. (1984). Animal sleep: A review of sleep duration across phylogeny. Neurosci Biobehav Rev. doi:10.1016/0149-7634(84)90054-X
16. Tononi, G. & Cirelli, C. (2003). Sleep and synaptic homeostasis: A hypothesis. Brain Res Bull. doi:10.1016/j.brainresbull.2003.09.004
17. Keogh, R. & Pearson, J. (2018). The blind mind: No sensory visual imagery in aphantasia. Cortex. doi:10.1016/j.cortex.2017.10.012
18. Besedovsky, L., Lange, T. & Born, J. (2012). Sleep and immune function. Pflugers Arch Eur J Physiol. doi:10.1007/s00424-011-1044-0
19. Imeri, L. & Opp, M.R. (2009). How (and why) the immune system makes us sleep. Nat Rev Neurosci. doi:10.1038/nrn2576
20. Irwin, M., Mcclintick, J., Costlow, C., Fortner, M., White, J. & Gillin, C. J. (1996). Partial night sleep deprivation reduces natural killer and cellular immune responses in humans. FASEB J. doi:10.1096/fasebj.10.5.8621064
21. Cote, K. A., McCormick, C. M., Geniole, S. N., Renn, R. P. & MacAulay, S. D. (2013). Sleep deprivation lowers reactive aggression and testosterone in men. Biol Psychol. doi:10.1016/j.biopsycho.2012.09.011
22. Walker, M. P. & Stickgold, R. (2004). Sleep-dependent learning and memory consolidation. Neuron. doi:10.1016/j.neuron.2004.08.031
23. Baglioni, C., Nanovska, S., Regen, W., Spiegelhalder, K., Feige, B., Nissen, C., Reynolds, C. F. & Riemann, D. (2016). Sleep and mental disorders: A meta-analysis of polysomnographic research. Psychol Bull. doi:10.1037/bul0000053
24. Mattis, J. & Sehgal, A. (2016). Circadian Rhythms, Sleep, and Disorders of Aging. Trends Endocrinol Metab. doi:10.1016/j.tem.2016.02.003

25. Neumann, I. D. & Landgraf, R. (2012). Balance of brain oxytocin and vasopressin: Implications for anxiety, depression, and social behaviors. Trends Neurosci. doi:10.1016/j.tins.2012.08.004
26. Satpute, A. B., Wager, T. D., Cohen-Adad, J., Bianciardi, M., Choi, J., Buhle, J. T., Wald, L. L. & Barrett, L. F. (2013). Identification of discrete functional subregions of the human periaqueductal gray. Proc Natl Acad Sci USA. doi:10.1073/pnas.1306095110
27. Behbehani, M. M. (1995). Functional characteristics of the midbrain periaqueductal gray. Prog Neurobiol. doi:10.1016/0301-0082(95)00009-K
28. Graham, J. E., Robles, T. F., Kiecolt-Glaser, J. K., Malarkey, W. B., Bissell, M. G. & Glaser, R. (2006). Hostility and pain are related to inflammation in older adults. Brain Behav Immun. doi:10.1016/j.bbi.2005.11.002
29. Brydon, L., Strike, P. C., Bhattacharyya, M. R., Whitehead, D. L., McEwan, J., Zachary, I. & Steptoe, A. (2010). Hostility and physiological responses to laboratory stress in acute coronary syndrome patients. J Psychosom Res. doi:10.1016/j.jpsychores.2009.06.007
30. Thongprakaisang, S., Thiantanawat, A., Rangkadilok, N., Suriyo, T. & Satayavivad, J. (2013). Glyphosate induces human breast cancer cells growth via estrogen receptors. Food Chem Toxicol. doi:10.1016/j.fct.2013.05.057
31. Samsel, A. &, Seneff, S. (2013). Glyphosate, pathways to modern diseases II: Celiac sprue and gluten intolerance. Interdiscip Toxicol. doi:10.2478/intox-2013-0026
32. Moseley, G. L. & Butler, D. S. (2015). Fifteen Years of Explaining Pain: The Past, Present, and Future. J Pain. doi:10.1016/j.jpain.2015.05.005
33. Kosfeld, M., Heinrichs, M., Zak, P. J., Fischbacher, U. & Fehr, E. (2005). Oxytocin increases trust in humans. Nature. 435(7042):673-676. doi:10.1038/nature03701
34. Shamay-Tsoory, S. G., Fischer, M., Dvash, J., Harari, H., Perach-Bloom, N. & Levkovitz, Y. (2009). Intranasal Administration of Oxytocin Increases Envy and Schadenfreude (Gloating). Biol Psychiatry. doi:10.1016/j.biopsych.2009.06.009
35. Frijling, J. L. (2017). Preventing PTSD with oxytocin: Effects of oxytocin administration on fear neurocircuitry and PTSD symptom development in recently trauma-exposed individuals. Eur J Psychotraumatol. doi:10.1080/20008198.2017.1302652
36. Liljencrantz, J. & Olausson, H. (2014). Tactile C fibers and their contributions to pleasant sensations and to tactile allodynia. Front Behav Neurosci. doi:10.3389/fnbeh.2014.00037
37. Lumley, M. A., Cohen, J. L., Borszcz, G. S., Cano, A., Radcliffe, A. M., Porter, L. S., Schubiner, H & Keefe, F. J. (2011). Pain and emotion: A biopsychosocial review of recent research. J Clin Psychol. doi:10.1002/jclp.20816
38. Cacioppo, J. T., Hawkley, L. C., Crawford, L. E., Ernst, J. M., Burleson, M. H., Kowalewski, R. B., Malarkey, W. B., Van Cauter, E. & Berntson, G. G. (2002). Loneliness and health: Potential mechanisms. Psychosom Med. doi:10.1097/00006842-200205000-00005
39. Loder, E., Tovey, D. & Godlee, F. (2014). The Tamiflu trials. BMJ. doi:10.1136/bmj.g2630
40. Gupta, Y. K., Meenu, M. & Mohan, P. (2015). The Tamiflu fiasco and lessons learnt. Indian J Pharmacol. doi:10.4103/0253-7613.150308
41. Borrell-carrió, F. Suchman, A. L. & Epstein, R.M., (2004). The Biopsychosocial Model 25 Years Later : Ann Fam Med. doi:10.1370/afm.245.Relationship
42. Wirtz, P. H., Elsenbruch, S., Emini, L., Rüdisüli, K., Groessbauer, S. & Ehlert, U. (2007). Perfectionism and the cortisol response to psychosocial stress in men. Psychosom Med. doi:10.1097/PSY.0b013e318042589e
43. Kyeong, S., Kim, J., Kim, D. J., Kim, H. E. & Kim J. J. (2017).Effects of gratitude meditation on neural network functional connectivity and brain-heart coupling. Sci Rep. doi:10.1038/s41598-017-05520-9
44. Freedman, S. & Enright, R. D. (2017). The Use of Forgiveness Therapy with Female Survivors of Abuse. J Womens Heal Care. doi:10.4172/2167-0420.1000369
45. Lee, Y. R. & Enright, R. D. (2014). A forgiveness intervention for women with fibromyalgia who were abused in childhood: A pilot study. Spiritual Clin Pract. doi:10.1037/scp0000025
46. Ford, B. Q., Mauss, I. B. & Gruber, J. (2015). Valuing happiness is associated with bipolar disorder. Emotion. doi:10.1037/emo0000048
47. Brewer, J. A., Worhunsky, P. D., Gray, J. R., Tang, Y. Y., Weber, J. & Kober, H. (2011). Meditation experience is associated with differences in default mode network activity and connectivity. Proc Natl Acad Sci USA. doi:10.1073/pnas.1112029108
48. Pokorski, M. & Suchorzynska, A. (2018). Psychobehavioral effects of meditation. In: Advances in Experimental Medicine and Biology. ; doi:10.1007/5584_2017_52
49. Nef, H. M., Möllmann, H., Akashi, Y. J. & Hamm, C. W. (2010). Mechanisms of stress (Takotsubo) cardiomyopathy. Nat Rev Cardiol. doi:10.1038/nrcardio.2010.16
50. Kenney, M. J. & Ganta, C. K. (2014). Autonomic nervous system and immune system interactions. Compr Physiol. doi:10.1002/cphy.c130051
51. Shin, L. M., Whalen, P. J., Pitman, R. K., Bush, G., Macklin, M. L., Lasko, N. B., Orr, S. P., McInerney, S. C. & Rauch, S. L. (2001). An fMRI study of anterior cingulate function in posttraumatic stress disorder. Biol Psychiatry. doi:10.1016/S0006-3223(01)01215-X
52. New, A. S., Fan, J., Murrough, J. W., Liu, X., Liebman, R. E., Guise, K. G., Tang, C. . & Charney, D. S. (2009). A Functional Magnetic Resonance Imaging Study of Deliberate Emotion Regulation in Resilience and Posttraumatic Stress Disorder. Biol Psychiatry. doi:10.1016/j.biopsych.2009.05.020
53. Pert, C. B., Ruff, M. R., Weber, R. J. & Herkenham, M. (1985). Neuropeptides and their receptors: a psychosomatic network. J Immunol. 135(2 Suppl):820s-826s.
54. Pert, C. B., Dreher, H. E. & Ruff, M. R. (1998). The psychosomatic network: Foundations of mind-body medicine. Altern Ther Health Med. 4(4):30-41
55. Raichle, M. E. (2015). The Brain's Default Mode Network. Annu Rev Neurosci. 38: pp 433-447 doi:10.1146/annurev-neuro-071013-014030

56. Broyd, S. J., Demanuele, C., Debener, S., Helps, S. K., James, C. J. & Sonuga-Barke, E. J. S. (2009). Default-mode brain dysfunction in mental disorders: A systematic review. Neurosci Biobehav Rev. doi:10.1016/j.neubiorev.2008.09.002
57. Gallese, V., Eagle, M. N. & Migone, P. (2007). Intentional attunement: Mirror neurons and the neural underpinnings of interpersonal relations. J Am Psychoanal Assoc. doi:10.1177/00030651070550010601
58. Geller, S. M., & Porges, S.W. (2014). Therapeutic presence: Neurophysiological mechanisms mediating feeling safe in therapeutic relationships. J Psychother Integr. doi:10.1037/a0037511
59. Gori, A., Giannini, M., Craparo, G., Caretti, V., Nannini, I., Madathi, R. & Schuldberg, D. (2014). Assessment of the Relationship Between the Use of Birth Control Pill and the Characteristics of Mate Selection. J Sex Med. doi:10.1111/jsm.12566
60. Rizzolatti, G. & Craighero, L. (2004). The mirror-neuron system. Ann Rev Neurosci. doi:10.1146/annurev.neuro.27.070203.144230
61. Rief, W., Nestoriuc, Y., Weiss, S., Welzel, E., Barsky, A.J. & Hofmann, S.G. (2009). Meta-analysis of the placebo response in antidepressant trials. J Affect Disord. doi:10.1016/j.jad.2009.01.029
62. Khan, A., Redding, N. & Brown, W. A. (2008). The persistence of the placebo response in antidepressant clinical trials. J Psychiatr Res. doi:10.1016/j.jpsychires.2007.10.004
63. Colloca, L. & Benedetti, F. (2005). Placebos and painkillers: Is mind as real as matter? Nat Rev Neurosci. doi:10.1038/nrn1705
64. Price, D.D., Finniss, D. G. & Benedetti, F. (2008). A Comprehensive Review of the Placebo Effect: Recent Advances and Current Thought. Annu Rev Psychol. doi:10.1146/annurev.psych.59.113006.095941
65. Tracey, I. (2010). Getting the pain you expect: Mechanisms of placebo, nocebo and reappraisal effects in humans. Nat Med. doi:10.1038/nm.2229
66. Sihvonen, R., Paavola, M., Malmivaara, A., Itälä, A., Joukainen, A., Nurmi, H., Kalske, J. & Järvinen, T. L. (2013). Arthroscopic partial meniscectomy versus sham surgery for a degenerative meniscal tear. N Engl J Med. doi:10.1056/NEJMoa1305189
67. Moffet, H. H. (2009). Sham acupuncture may be as efficacious as true acupuncture: A systematic review of clinical trials. J Altern Complement Med. doi:10.1089/acm.2008.0356
68. Howick, J., Bishop, F. L., Heneghan, C., Wolstenholme, J., Stevens, S., Hobbs, F. D. R. & Lewith, G. (2013). Placebo Use in the United Kingdom: Results from a National Survey of Primary Care Practitioners. PLoS One. doi:10.1371/journal.pone.0058247
69. Meissner, K., Höfner, L., Fässler, M. & Linde, K. (2012). Widespread use of pure and impure placebo interventions by GPs in Germany. Fam Pract. doi:10.1093/fampra/cmr045
70. Braga-Simõs, J., Costa, P. S. & Yaphe, J. (2017). Placebo prescription and empathy of the physician: A cross-sectional study. Eur J Gen Pract. doi:10.1080/13814788.2017.1291625
71. Sherman, R. & Hickner, J. (2008). Academic physicians use placebos in clinical practice and believe in the mind-body connection. J Gen Intern Med. doi:10.1007/s11606-007-0332-z
72. Bos, E. M., Spoor, J. K. H., Smits, M., Schouten, J. W. & Vincent, A. J. P. E. Out-of-Body Experience During Awake Craniotomy. World Neurosurg. doi:10.1016/j.wneu.2016.05.002
73. Blanke, O., Landis, T., Spinelli, L. & Seeck, M. (2004). Out-of-body experience and autoscopy of neurological origin. Brain. 2004. doi:10.1093/brain/awh040
74. Blanke, O. & Arzy, S. (2005). The out-of-body experience: Disturbed self-processing at the temporo-parietal junction. Neuroscientist. doi:10.1177/1073858404270885
75. Traber, M., Buettner, G. & Bruno, R. (2019). The relationship between vitamin C status, the gut-liver axis, and metabolic syndrome. Redox Biology. doi: 10.1016/j.redox.2018.101091
76. Palmer, H. (1994). Resurfacing: Techniques for exploring consciousness. Star's Edge Creations
77. Wagner, E. N., Aidacic-Gross, V., Strippoli, M. F., Gholam-Rezaee, M., Glaus, J., Vandeleur, C., Castelao, E., Vollenweider, P., Preisig, M. & Von Kanel, R. (2019). Associations of personality traits with chronic low-grade inflammation in a Swiss community sample. Front Psychiatry doi 10.3389/fpsyt.2019.00819
78. Kim, H. J., Im, H. K., Kim, J., Han, J. Y., de Leon, M., Deshpande, A &, Moon, W.J. (2016). Brain atrophy of secondary REM-sleep behaviour disorder in neurodegenerative disease. J Alzheimers Dis 53(3):1101-9
79. Sandhu, A., Seth, M. & Gurm, H. S. (2014). Daylight savings time and myocardial infarction. Open Heart doi: 10.1136/openhrt-2013-000019
80. Porges, S. W. (2003). Social engagement and attachment: a phylogenetic perspective. Ann N Y Acad Sci 1008:31-47
81. Stages of sleep, after Rasch, B. & Born, J. (2013). About Sleep's Role in Memory. Phys Rev, 93(2): 681-766. doi: 10.1152/physrev.00032.2012
82. Perro, M. & Adams, V. (2017). What's Making our Children SICK? Chelsea Green Publishing
83. Kharrazian, D. (2013). Why Isn't My Brain Working? Elephant Press
84. van der Kolk, B. (2015). The Body Keeps the Score. Penguin
85. Keysers, C. (2011). The Emotional Brain. Social Brain Press

www.ingramcontent.com/pod-product-compliance
Lightning Source LLC
Chambersburg PA
CBHW081436300426
44108CB00016BA/2380